Literature in Vienna at the Turn of the Centuries

Studies in German Literature, Linguistics, and Culture

Edited by James Hardin
(*South Carolina*)

Literature in Vienna at the Turn of the Centuries

Continuities and Discontinuities around 1900 and 2000

Edited by
Ernst Grabovszki
and
James Hardin

CAMDEN HOUSE

First published 2003
by Camden House

Camden House is an imprint of Boydell & Brewer Inc.
668 Mount Hope Ave., Rochester, NY 14620-2731 USA
and of Boydell & Brewer Limited
PO Box 9, Woodbridge, Suffolk IP12 3DF, UK

ISBN: 1–57113–233–3

Library of Congress Cataloging-in-Publication Data

Literature in Vienna at the turn of the centuries: continuities and disconti-
nuities around 1900 and 2000 / edited by Ernst Grabovszki and James
Hardin
    p. cm. — (Studies in German literature, linguistics, and culture)
Includes bibliographical references and index.
ISBN 1–57113–233–3 (Hardcover: alk. paper)
    1. Austrian literature — 19th century — History and criticism.
2. Austrian literature — 20th century — History and criticism.   3. Vi-
enna (Austria) — Intellectual life.   4. Vienna (Austria) — Civilization.
I. Grabovszki, Ernst, 1970–   II. Hardin, James N.   III. Studies in
German literature, linguistics, and culture (Unnumbered)

PT3817 .L59 2003
830.9'943613—dc21
                                                                2002010591

A catalogue record for this title is available from the British Library.

This publication is printed on acid-free paper.
Printed in the United States of America.

Contents

II. Arts and Culture

Illustrations

Vienna, Graben, view of the Stephansdom around 1900.
Photograph courtesy of Bildarchiv,
Austrian National Library, Vienna.

Vienna, Graben, view of the Stephansdom in 2001.
Photograph by Ernst Grabovszki.

Introduction: Notes on Literature in Vienna at the Turn of the Centuries

Ernst Grabovszki

ONE WHO DEALS WITH *fin-de-siècle* Vienna is often confronted with clichés. Elisabeth Leinfellner-Rupertsberger sums it up:

> Das Wien und mit ihm das Österreich der Jahrhundertwende sind zu einer Utopie im ursprünglichen Sinne des Wortes geworden, zu einem raum- und zeitlosen Mythos, einem Pandämonium mit mythischen Versatzstücken: dem guten alten Kaiser, der täglich seinen Tafelspitz ißt — so schon bei Josef Roth; dem weisen Ratgeber, Freud; der dämonischen Verführerin, Alma Mahler-Werfel; dem hauslosen Kaffeehausliteraten, Peter Altenberg; dem leutseligen Bürgermeister, der nur ein kleines bisserl antisemitisch ist, Lueger; und dem exilierten und in Österreich erst nach seinem Tod langsam bekanntgewordenen und schließlich in einer Apotheose verklärten Denker, Ludwig Wittgenstein.[1]

Leinfellner-Rupertsberger presents the Austrian turn of the century in an ironic way as a patchwork of true but incomplete impressions, as a time that had to cope with a variety of political and social changes such as the collapse of the Habsburgian monarchy, the breaking apart of the "Vielvölkerstaat," and the rise of nationalism.

The articles in this book aim to explore the contrasts and similarities of both turns of the centuries around 1900 and 2000 and to show how the aesthetics of literature and its historical background have influenced each other and how they have changed during a century. They seek to sound the continuities and discontinuities in Austrian literature, especially of literature in Vienna by highlighting the city's role in the development of Austrian culture now and then. The contributors show how typical characteristics of the *fin de siècle* around 1900 are still observable in contemporary literature but also concentrate on the contrasts of the two time spans.

There is evidence that *fin-de-siècle* literature and culture in Austria enjoy popularity not only among scientists of literature but also among readers for at least two reasons: first, the *fin de siècle* nowadays is frequently portrayed in transfigured, nostalgic form as a realm detached from historical fact, as an idyll of a seemingly prosperous time in all spheres of life. This is the reason, among others, why the German and Austrian publishing industry successfully publishes one book after the other on the Habsburg family.[2] It is characteristic of our time that Michael Kunze's and Sylvester Levay's musical *Elisabeth,* which sketches the life of the Austrian empress, became a major success at the Theater an der Wien from 1992 until 1998.[3] TV-specials, exhibitions, and books were a direct result of this new popularity of the Habsburg empress and of Habsburg nostalgia in general. But this nostalgic image of Austria and of Vienna in particular is shattered when it is seen from another point of view in history: from 1907 to 1913 Adolf Hitler has been living in Vienna and it was there that he brooded on race and the "deutsche Weltherrschaft."[4]

Second, Austrian literature around 1900 represents a climax, an unprecedented efflorescence in the country's literary history. Hermann Broch (1886–1951), Robert Musil (1880–1942), and Franz Kafka (1883–1924) are important not just in Austrian but in world literature. In the field of poetry Rainer Maria Rilke (1875–1926) broadened forms of poetic expression by an unconventional application of traditional forms of verse and symbolism and by his comprehensive knowledge of foreign languages and literatures. Hugo von Hofmannsthal (1874–1929) cultivated verse perfect in form and rich in imagery. After the turn of the century he devoted himself to drama and co-founded the Salzburg Festival. The most successful playwright around 1900 in Austria, Arthur Schnitzler (1862–1931), digested elements of Sigmund Freud's psychoanalysis and exposed his figures to a tissue of reality and lie. Besides Hermann Bahr (1863–1934), Richard Beer-Hofmann (1866–1954), Peter Altenberg (1862–1919), and Hofmannsthal, Schnitzler belonged to a group of writers, "das Junge Wien," who represented a counterpart to German naturalism. Their works focused typical characteristics of *fin-de-siècle* literature, such as an atmosphere of downfall, decay, and melancholy.

Austrian literature around 1900 centers on the role of the individual within a rapidly changing society. Science, especially psychoanalysis, likewise focuses on the individual. The term "psychoanalysis" was used for the first time in 1896 by Sigmund Freud (1856–1939) when he was already forty years old.[5] It is noteworthy that the publication date of Freud's *Traumdeutung* (translated as *The Interpretation of Dreams*) was indicated with 1900 although the book actually appeared in November 1899.[6] Therefore, 1900 became a symbolic year as the beginning of the age of increasing knowledge about man's psyche. It is typical of Freud's proceeding that he often referred to literature when he tried to explain his findings. Psychoanalysis and literature are closely linked to one another at this early stage of psychoanalytic research. Freud's probing of the human psyche, of spheres of life that had not been accessible up to that time finds a remarkable analogy in contemporary literature: in 1991 the novelist Gerhard Roth (b. 1942) took a *Reise in das Innere von Wien* (A Trip into the Interior of Vienna). In nine essays the author directs his attention to extraordinary, almost uncanny Viennese locations such as the "Narrenturm"[7] (a lunatic asylum from 1853 until 1869) or the "k. k. privilegierte Hetztheater"[8] (an arena in which animals were set on each other). He intends to take a look behind the metropolitan scenes as Freud did on a medical level when the latter brought his readers down to earth by claiming that every human being is not a rational entity but driven by subconscious forces. It is small wonder therefore that reviews of Roth's book often referred to Freud and that it was promptly stamped as "ein Reiseführer durch die Abgründe der österreichischen Seele."[9] Roth's approach is almost archaeological: he describes parts of Vienna unknown even to native Viennese. In contrast to Freud, Roth's object of study is not the human being but the metropolis and its "subconscious" topography which allows the reader to unveil the connecting places between collective consciousness and individual fates and biographies of Jewish families, homeless people, or artists living in a mental hospital.

Austrian art around 1900 was referred to by several terms: "Wiener Moderne," "Neuromantik," "Symbolismus," "Impressionismus," and — most popular — "*fin de siècle.*" The last term, coined in France during the 1880s, is ambivalent: it describes not only a general sentiment of decay but also of revolt which, according to Arndt Brendecke, derives from the tradition of "décadence" in France in the 1830s, "die die Sensibilitäten für die Zwischentöne der eigenen, auch seelischen Wirklichkeiten bis ins Äußerste zu schärfen suchte."[10] The mentioned terms should make us aware of the fact that the turn of the century cannot be characterized as "ein einheitliches und homogenes Phänomen in der Geistes- und Kulturgeschichte,"[11] although certain tendencies toward uniting the arts become perceptible. The novelist, playwright, and essayist Hermann Bahr, one of the key figures of Viennese cultural life around 1900, stated that art, science, and religion fundamentally would be the same, a point of view that derives from Richard Wagner's and Friedrich Nietzsche's conception of an artist striving for the unity of nature, culture, society, and the individual.

If we further focus in on the most important characteristics of Viennese literature around 1900 we note the following:[12] it was first deeply influenced by the literatures of other European nations and thus must be studied in the context of western literature in general. A massive import of German, French, Italian, Scandinavian, and American influences preceded the "Wiener Moderne."[13] Nietzsche and Wagner influenced Austrian music and literature, Hermann Bahr tried to establish Vienna as a center of the "Moderne" by transferring central ideas and terms of the time into German such as the French "états d'âme" (Seelenzustände),[14] and Ludwig Wittgenstein (1889–1950) owed a lot to the analytic and linguistic philosophy of the Cambridge School, just to mention a few examples.[15] Second, literature was closely linked with other arts such as music and graphic arts. The painter Oskar Kokoschka (1886–1980), for instance, became also known as a playwright (*Mörder, Hoffnung der Frauen* [1909, translated as *Murderer, Hope of Women*])[16] although his plays have never been staged successfully. Beyond that, Vienna had become a center of modern architecture (Adolf Loos), painting (Gustav Klimt, Egon Schiele, Oskar Kokoschka), psychoanalysis (Sigmund Freud), twelve-tone music (Arnold Schoenberg), medicine, philosophy (Ludwig Wittgenstein, "Wiener Kreis"),[17] and national economy (Hans Kelsen). In the preface to the first volume of the *Moderne Rundschau* (1891), the most important periodical of the "Wiener Moderne," the editors note programmatically:

> Die moderne Literatur ist für sich allein, abgesondert von allen übrigen Ausstrahlungen des modernen Geistes nicht zu begreifen, nur vom Standpunkt der neuesten naturwissenschaftlichen, psychologischen und soziologischen Erkenntnisse, nur vom Standpunkt der fortgeschrittensten rechts- und moralphilosophischen, technischen, volkswirtschaftlichen, sozialpolitischen Anschauungen aus sind wir imstande, die künstlerischen Dokumente des großen Lebensprozesses der Gegenwart recht zu verstehen und nach Gebühr zu würdigen.[18]

In his widely acknowledged analysis of the literature of the Habsburgian empire, *Der habsburgische Mythos in der modernen österreichischen Literatur* (1963)[19] Claudio Magris sketches a meticulously drawn picture of Austrian literature in the nineteenth and twentieth century. In the preface to the new German edition of his work Magris tried to explain "wie eine Kultur sich bemüht, die Vielheit der Wirklichkeit auf eine Einheit zurückzuführen, das Chaos der Welt auf eine Ordnung, die fragmentarische Zufälligkeit der Existenz auf die Essenz, die historisch-politischen Gegensätze auf eine Harmonie, die sie versöhnen, wenn schon nicht aufheben kann."[20] In his opinion, Austrian authors of the nineteenth and even of the twentieth century turn to the past rather than taking up topical issues. Their "quälende Bindung an die Vergangenheit,"[21] he argues, is not only a superficial frame of mind but inherent to their culture:

> Der habsburgische Mythos ist also nicht ein einfacher Prozeß der Verwandlung des Realen, wie er jede dichterische Tätigkeit charakterisiert, sondern er bedeutet, daß eine historisch-gesellschaftliche Wirklichkeit vollständig durch eine fiktive, illusorische Realität ersetzt wird, daß eine konkrete Gesellschaft zu einer malerischen, sicheren und geordneten Märchenwelt verklärt wird.[22]

Magris's notion of the mindset of the time is characterized by the authors' longing for harmony within a chaotic surrounding: the dissolving of the Habsburgian empire was compensated for in literature, although, Magris claims, the continuity of Austrian tradition lies in the incessant revolt against this tradition. The playwright Joseph Schreyvogl (1768–1832), the novelists Adalbert Stifter (1805–1868), and Heimito von Doderer (1896–1966), and, above all, Franz Grillparzer (1791–1872) are said to have fallen ill with the Habsburgian myth due to their writings which Magris presents as unpolitical and detached from historical reality. If one agrees with Magris's arguments it is small wonder, therefore, that such a characterization of Austrian literature of the nineteenth century and of the *fin de siècle* in particular leads to the aforementioned nostalgia in recent times.

Although Magris's notion of the Habsburgian myth produced opposition (it is doubtful if there is a clearly defined corpus of "Austrian" literature at all; Magris only deals with German-speaking authors; he started from an unreflected notion of "myth"[23]) it still is a major contribution to the discussion of Austrian literature of the nineteenth and twentieth century. Beyond that, Magris's work was influential for later studies such as Ulrich Greiner's *Der Tod des Nachsommers* (1979)[24] which also characterizes Austrian literature as one immune to political and topical issues. In the 1990s, the novelist and essayist Robert Menasse (b. 1954) continued to foster this image of Austrian literature as a static rather than a dynamic art due to an aesthetic of social partnership.[25] In a series of lectures he had given at the University of Sao Paolo in 1981–82 Menasse departed from the hypothesis that the content related and aesthetic specifics of Austrian literature as well as the organizational aspects of literary life in Austria derive from a societal form of organization, the so-called "Sozialpartnerschaft" (social-partnership)[26] which he characterizes by

> kräftiges Wachstum, völliges Verdrängen der Umverteilungsfrage, dabei quasi lückenloser sozialer Friede und allseitige Zufriedenheit — schlagender läßt sich wohl nicht beweisen, daß die gegenwärtige Epoche des Kapitalismus in der Sozialpartnerschaft dessen effektivste Organisationsform gefunden hat, daß also Österreich, was ihre Realisierung betrifft, innerhalb der Kapitalismen die absolute Avantgarde darstellt.[27]

The mechanism of "Sozialpartnerschaft," that is, the avoidance of conflict between employer and employee, the consolidation of power within society, the concentration of political power in order to control social developments,[28] Menasse claims, can also be traced within Austria's literary life, especially in the 1950s: this period he characterizes as lacking a generation gap between young and established writers. In contrast, the German "Gruppe 47," founded in 1947, had the goal of promoting younger writers and became so influential that many of its members soon ranked with the best known German writers, such as Heinrich Böll, Günter Grass, or Uwe Johnson. As to Austrian literature Menasse says, "wo es keine sichtbaren Zwischenräume mehr gibt, erscheint alles wie aus einem Guß, ein Block, monolitisch."[29] Beyond that, even Austrian authors who became well known in the 1960s such as Peter Handke (b. 1942), Thomas Bernhard (1931–1989), or Barbara Frischmuth (b. 1941) and who became literary celebrities, above all in Germany, were paralyzed with the affects of social-partnership which Menasse further describes as the simultaneous existence of prosperity and poverty in economic resources both in the fields of politics, economy, and literature. The number of writers increased continuously in the postwar decades but the number of publishing houses, newspapers, or radio- and TV-stations who would have given work to these writers did not. Austrian writers were forced to publish their works in Germany, Menasse continues.

Magris's, Greiner's, and Menasse's points of view meet reality only partially. There is evidence that from the mid-1970s on, Austrian writers started to develop a distanced and critical relation towards the Austrian state which derived from the writers' attempt to create a social identity for themselves within the Austrian state.[30] Although the first (and until today, the last) writers' convention in 1981 had on its agenda substantial issues such as social security for writers and further regulations of royalty payments, nothing substantive came of all the talk.[31] The discussion of the specifics of Austrian in contrast to German literature became a favorite issue within the academic community in the 1970s and 1980s. Wendelin Schmidt-Dengler concluded that "Österreichs Literatur ist in ihrer Eigenständigkeit nur in bezug auf die politische und soziale Sonderentwicklung zu begreifen, nicht aber als eine Wesenheit zu konstruieren, die von vornherein sich als eine explizit österreichische zu offenbaren imstande wäre."[32] That is to say, Austrian literature differs from German literature by characteristics that are not inherent in literary texts but to external factors, such as the publishing industry, or writers' associations.

In this connection it is useful to survey the development of the Austrian book market at both turn of the centuries in order to highlight not only the interdependence of the German and Austrian market but also to explain an important aspect of the aforementioned "soziale Sonderentwicklung." As early as 1835, Franz Gräffer, a Viennese writer and bookseller, noted that great amounts of money are running abroad because books on philosophy, history, politics, etc. find no sale in Austria.[33] A great deal of the literary production actually was sold outside the national borders, although the Austrian book trade experienced an increase both in the establishing of relevant firms and in quantity of production and sale.[34] From 1859 until 1909 the number of bookstores, publishing houses, and libraries had quintupled in Austria; in Hungary the number was even eight times as high. Books had become easily available already in the 1850s: "Während im Jahre 1859 in Österreich auf 50 Tausend Einwohner eine Buchhandlung kam, hat heute jede Buchhandlung nur mehr ein durchschnittliches Publikum von 13 Tausend Seelen,"[35] Junker states. However, numerous Austrian writers such as Peter Rosegger (1843–1918), Rudolf Hans Bartsch (1873–1952), Karl Hans Strobl (1877–1946), Arthur Schnitzler, Hugo von Hofmannsthal, or Peter Altenberg published most of their books in Germany. The S. Fischer Verlag, founded in 1886 by Samuel Fischer in Berlin, had become the most influential publishing house in the German speaking countries around 1900 and played a key role in popularizing naturalistic authors such as Henrik Ibsen. By 1918, S. Fischer had published no fewer than thirty-five Austrian writers (among them the aforementioned Schnitzler, Hofmannsthal and Altenberg).[36] The reason for this situation is twofold: on the one hand, copyright protection in Austria was modest compared to other countries. Murray G. Hall states that Austria-Hungary did not participate in international copyright regulations due to home affairs such as national controversies,[37] whereas German publishers could grant protection against pirated editions and unauthorized translations. On the other hand, the trade regulation of 1859–60 made the book trade subject to licenses and certifications of qualification. Last but not least, censorship proved to be an obstacle especially for Austrian publishers. Nowadays, censorship has been abolished and somebody intending to open a bookstore is not subject to a certification of qualification anymore. But the interdependence of the Austrian and the German book market is still of relevance: eighty percent of the books printed in Austria are exported to Germany. During the 1990s the annual turnover of book sales in Austria increased steadily.

Another institutional characteristic of Austrian literary life deserves mention, namely the formation of the "Grazer Autorenversammlung" (GAV) in 1972, a group of writers who defined themselves as a counterpart to the PEN-organization in terms of aesthetical and ideological views.[38] Austrian authors of the younger generation such as the members of the "Wiener Gruppe" (H. C. Artmann [1921–2000], Konrad Bayer [1932–1964], Friedrich Achleitner [b. 1930], Gerhard Rühm [b. 1930], Oswald Wiener [b. 1935]), or of the "Forum Stadtpark" in Graz (Peter Handke, Barbara Frischmuth, etc.) were not given access to the conservative Austrian PEN-Club although their efforts in renewing Austrian literature were undisputed. As a result, international recognition was impeded for many of these young authors. The founding of the GAV should help to increase publishing opportunities and should serve as a representation of Austrian writers' interests. Also for the PEN-organization, the year of 1972 marked a turning point: The Austrian president of which, Alexander Lernet-Holenia (1897–1976), resigned from his function protesting the bestowal of the Nobel prize of literature to Heinrich Böll (1917–1985) who then was the president of the international PEN. The poet Ernst Jandl (1925–2000), founder of the GAV, took the opportunity to attack the elitist practices of the Austrian PEN organization and unsuccessfully strove for an acceptance of the GAV as a second and autonomous PEN organization. But the GAV soon had to show authors of international reputation such as Peter Handke, the playwright Wolfgang Bauer (b. 1941), or Gerhard Roth and took its stand in politico-cultural discussions during the 1970s and 1980s. However, the importance of the GAV has declined in the 1990s and the differences between the two groups now appear to be more academic than real. The latest turn of the century is also marked by a significant break: Austria's joining the European Union, the process of European integration and, consequently, further challenges with regard to immigrants and their integration in Austrian society.[39] It is striking therefore that Austrian and Viennese literature at both turns of the century dealt and deals with political issues. This is not to say that contemporary Austrian literature is all about politics, but it is true that Magris's and Greiner's notion of an unworldly literary tradition often proves to be wrong. In his latest novel, *Das Vaterspiel* (2000, The Father Game), Josef Haslinger (b. 1955), for instance, tells the story of Rupert Kramer, son of an Austrian minister and Social Democrat, who kills time working out a computer game that aims at annihilating a virtual father. In November 1999 Kramer is called to New York to help his old flame Mimi hiding her grand-uncle, a former Nazi living in the cellar of a house at Long Island. Kramer, who hates his corrupt father, falls prey to an inner conflict of political responsibility and friendship. By depicting the fate of a Jewish, a Lithuanian, and an Austrian family Haslinger does not confine the continued existence of National Socialist thought, the problem of collective guilt and of generation gaps to the Austrian territory but makes it an international affair.

At both turns of the century authors had (and have) a special liking for discussing Austria's identity. Since identities mostly are not visible they depend on materialistic symbols in order to become perceptible. Such symbols represent significance and are able to create social communities whose members are linked to each other by means of a general idea, an ideology, language, or even by the press, for instance.[40] Such a symbol creating identity and a sense of togetherness was Emperor Franz Josef I. reigning from 1848 until 1916. He was the last living icon who could generate to some extent a feeling of solidarity within a multinational territory. After his death Austrian identity gradually disintegrated and this break actually was the beginning of the monarchy's end.[41] Karl I., the emperor's grand-nephew, became emperor in 1916 and was the last monarch of the Habsburgian empire.

If contemporary Austria is concerned with political developments which touch the composition of national identity — the most important aspect of which is the mentioned process of European integration — it is necessary to analyze the outcome of this issue. With regard to the turn of the century around 1900 it becomes obvious that language was — and still is — an integral aspect of identity: The struggles for an equality of other languages within the monarchy[42] were only the symptom of an attempt to define not only national borders but also cultural delimitations in order to create an adequate setting for political self-determination. This process of political, social, and mental disintegration was reflected in literature, too. In his trilogy *Die Schlafwandler* (1931–32, translated as *The Sleepwalkers*) Hermann Broch shows the decay of moral and values of German bourgeois society from 1888 until 1918. In his long novel fragment *Der Mann ohne Eigenschaften* (1930–43, translated as *The Man Without Qualities*) Robert Musil (1880–1942) depicts

Habsburgian Austria facing the First World War as the utopian country of "Kakanien." Musil's protagonist, Ulrich, is indeed a man without qualities, in other words, his identity is not of an undivided nature but it is split up and fissured and does not allow him a coherent view of the world. Consequently, a reality which has become a contradiction in terms — in this case: which experiences a radical change — requires a contradictory figure, someone who is not able to reach his goals in life. For him, even the work of art as an expression of purity and indestructibility has become obsolete. It is obvious that Musil's novel is highly influenced by the philosophical discourse of his time. The Wiener Kreis and the philosopher and physicist Ernst Mach (1830–1917) to whom Musil had dedicated his dissertation, serve as the philosophical background of Ulrich's split character: Mach's formula of the "unrettbares Ich" comes to life in the shape of Ulrich who represents the disintegration of an era.

In contrast to Musil's utopian country of Kakanien, contemporary authors have labeled Austria as "Quarantanien,"[43] as a country which is put (or which has put itself) under quarantine: The establishing of a new government in February 2000, that is the replacement of the coalition of the Sozialdemokratische Partei Österreichs (SPÖ) and the Österreichische Volkspartei (ÖVP) by the right-wing coalition of the ÖVP and the Freiheitliche Partei Österreichs (FPÖ) caused dissonance within the member states of the EU.[44] The governmental participation of the FPÖ became the stumbling-block for numerous Austrian artists to protest heavily against the conservative political climate.[45] It was generally noticed that the FPÖ had used negative images of foreigners living in Austria not only during the election campaign but continuously attracted attention by statements which hardly differed from Nazi vocabulary. In his contribution to the volume *Österreich: Berichte aus Quarantanien* which reflects the situation of Austria after the election, the novelist Robert Schindel (b. 1944) seeks an explanation for the result of the election sketching the characters of Vienna's inhabitants: "Der Wiener ist Zuschauer von Beruf,"[46] Schindel states, which not only means that the Viennese feel well while watching others' misfortune indifferently. His statement also implies that the Viennese inhabitant is not willing to behave adequately when danger of any kind arises. Helmut Qualtinger's (1928–1986) and Carl Merz's (1906–1979) play *Der Herr Karl* (1961, Mister Karl),[47] shows such a character. Karl is a petty bourgeois and opportunist to the bone. He has lived his life despite changing political rulers and unlucky private circumstances in order to get away as lucky as possible. Both Schindel and Qualtinger, the latter vividly remembered for his impersonation of Karl on TV and on stage, present a stereotype, of course, and in view of this it is difficult to unfold the real traits of the native Austrian and Viennese, if there are any at all. In other words, in what ways do the inhabitants of Vienna differ from those of Berlin, London, or Rome?

The statement "Es gibt ein Bild über das Wienerische, das zum Klischee verdichtet ist, ein Bild, bei dem Gemütlichkeit und Höflichkeit, Untertanengeist, Raunzer- und Querulantentum, vorauseilender Gehorsam, Titelsucht und Autoritätshörigkeit Inhalte und Konturen bestimmen,"[48] was a starting point for the psychoanalyst Harald Leupold-Löwenthal's (b. 1926) lecture on stereotypes of the Viennese. He shows historical and fictional figures who are closely connected to the city's history and whose traits are characterized as typical Viennese: "Der liebe Augustin," for instance, a homeless folksinger and bagpipe player who is said to have lived during the Thirty Years' War (1618–1648) and who escaped death despite of having spent one night in a plague-grove: "Man könnte meinen, daß ihn das Wunder des Überlebens zu einer Leitfigur der Wiener machte, die auch stolz auf ihre Überlebenskunst sind."[49] Leupold-Löwenthal further shows that the image of the Viennese as a do-nothing which is nothing but another cliché stems from German travel literature and that even Friedrich Schiller has coined this stereotype. With regard to Gerhard Roth's methodological approach to lay bare a topography of the "subconscious" metropolis it would be necessary here to dig below the surface of clichés and stereotypes. Leupold-Löwenthal finally comes to the following conclusion:

> Was einem als Psychoanalytiker aber *auffällt,* wenn man sich mit der Wiener Realität von heute konfrontiert, ist die Tatsache, daß alles, was da so phantasiert und in der Phantasie erlebt wird, nicht existiert! Sind und waren die Wiener wirklich Wiener oder waren und sind sie *"Wiener Darsteller"?*[50]

Judging the Viennese character in such a way might arouse the suspicion that Vienna even nowadays is the capital of Kakanien instead of a real existing state. However, a discussion of both stereotypes and real images of a society touches a sphere of identity this society was given or has given to itself. Schindel's dealing with the Viennese character proves that a lot of contemporary authors bring into play the national or local character when discussing Austrian identity.

The contemporary discussion on Austrian identity was stimulated when Kurt Waldheim was elected president in 1986. Josef Haslinger's essay *Politik der Gefühle* (1987) tries to catch the mindset of Austrian politics and society at the end of the 1980s. The notion of a "Politik der Gefühle" signifies a politics being reduced to the ethics and aesthetics of publicity and sales promotion, as Haslinger puts it, a politics that purposely uses rhetorical strategies and patterns in order to address people's emotions rather than to present a logical line of reasoning. Haslinger intends to explain why Kurt Waldheim was elected president of Austria in spite of his Nazi record known prior to his election. Waldheim's election, the author claims, was the result of giving a new interpretation to his past by presenting him as the victim of defamation. The mobilization of emotions which also took advantage of the "zweite Gefühlslage, mit der die Waldheim-Wahlwerbung sich verbünden konnte," namely anti-Semitism[51] made it possible that he became a sympathetic person, although the chances of being elected president seemed to be poor at the beginning of the election campaign:

> Hier wird, mit wenigen Worten, alles umgedreht. Opfer, soviel ist inzwischen klar, ist immer Kurt Waldheim und alle, die sich mit ihm identifizieren sollen. Menschenjagd seinerzeit war Pflicht, deren Kritik heute ist Menschenjagd.[52]

Waldheim, one might add, had become president because of the intended misinterpretation of history — was he the unconscious *Herr Karl* of the 1980s?

In perusing contemporary Austrian literature one realizes that the political essay is a popular literary genre among writers. But also within theater topical issues are taken up. What started with Johann Nestroy's (1801–1862) provocative plays containing topical allusions to grievances within state and society in the nineteenth century was continued by Schnitzler who portrayed anti-Semitism in *Professor Bernhardi* (1912), or Ödön von Horváth (1901–1938) whose *Kasimir und Karoline* (1932) shows the affects of economic crises on human relations. The preoccupation with Austria's past during the Nazi period reached its climax with Thomas Bernhard's (1931–1989) staging of *Heldenplatz* in 1988, shortly before the author's death in 1989. In the play, a misanthropic professor Robert Schuster fumes and forms his views on contemporary politics after having returned from Oxford to Vienna and deplores the survival and continued existence of National Socialistic thought. Fifty years after Hitler's proclamation of Austria's annexation to Germany at the Heldenplatz, the Schuster family assembles in Vienna on the occasion of Josef Schuster's funeral, Robert's brother. Josef, chased away by the Nazis and invited back to his professorial chair in the 1950s by the mayor of Vienna, finds his last resort in committing suicide. His life had become hopeless because his fear of moving back to Oxford outweighed his confidence of finding a second home in England: "Der Vater hat sich vor Oxford gefürchtet / [...] Wien ist ihm verhaßt gewesen / aber in Oxford hätte er nichts mehr gefunden / das ihm vertraut gewesen ist / auch in Oxford hat sich alles verändert,"[53] his niece complains after the funeral. Beyond that, his wife labored under the delusion of hearing the clamor of the masses hailing Hitler's words at Heldenplatz. For her, Vienna had become a haunted place to live at, and finally she ended up at the mental hospital of Steinhof. Bernhard's play was a catalyst for the discussions on the National Socialistic past in the political field.[54] While the former chancellor Franz Vranitzky characterized Austria as a victim *and* a perpetrator during the Second World War in a parliament speech in 1991, he declared himself in favor of Austria's taking moral responsibility for the Nazi collaboration on the occasion of a state visit to Israel in 1993. The most recent sign for this sense of responsibility is the establishment of a "Beauftragten für Restitutionsfragen" by the mayor of Vienna in 2001 who is in charge of returning unlawfully acquired property and means.

In his poem *wien: heldenplatz* Ernst Jandl takes up the same motif as Bernhard and explores the language-related dimension of the Nazi assumption of power by unmasking predications devoid of substance, the inhumanity of words and deeds expressed in a language that does not seem to refer to any meaning. The poem reads as follows:

> der glanze heldenplatz zirka
> versaggerte in maschenhaftem männchenmeere
> drunter auch frauen die ans maskelknie
> zu heften heftig sich versuchten, hoffensdick.
> und brüllzten wesentlich.
>
> verwogener stirnscheitelunterschwang
> nach nöten nördlich, kechelte
> mit zu-nummernder aufs bluten feilzer stimme
> hinsensend sämmertliche eigenwäscher.
>
> pirsch!
> döppelte der gottelbock von Sa-Atz zu Sa-Atz
> mit hünig sprenkem stimmstummel.
> balzerig würmelte es im männechensee
> und den weibern ward so pfingstig ums heil
> zumahn: wenn ein knie-ender sie hirschelte.[55]

There is no need to look up this poem's vocabulary in a dictionary because most of it simply does not exist. The words have detached themselves from a reality that is not able to cope with language or, more clearly, that has misused language in order to propagate inhumanity.

These preliminary notes make obvious that literature cannot be regarded as an art form detached from everyday life, and scientific, societal and technical progress. Literature rather has become an integral part of the scientific and social life, and it has done so already at the *fin de siècle*. As a consequence, a view on literature and on history may sharpen our notion not only of literary works but of the arts as a whole.

What makes the turns of the centuries around 1900 and 2000 comparable? Some aspects have already been mentioned such as the discussion of Austrian identity at both turns of the century on diverse discursive levels. The reception of foreign authors and the dealing of Austrian writers with foreign literature is another example which not only holds for the literature around 1900 but also for contemporary literature: Peter Handke's early reading of William Faulkner (1897–1962) and Feodor Dostoyevsky (1821–1881),[56] his and Friederike Mayröcker's (b. 1924) preoccupation with the French novelist and playwright Marguerite Duras (1914–1996),[57] are just a few examples. Beyond that, many Viennese (and of course Austrian) authors take an active part in translating foreign literature into German, such as Peter Rosei (b. 1946), Barbara Frischmuth, Raoul Schrott (b. 1964), Martin Amanshauser (b. 1968) or the late H. C. Artmann and Ernst Jandl.[58]

The comparison of different turns of the century in different countries makes clear that the mentioned feeling of decay was not only typical for the Viennese mindset. It should not come as a surprise that works of French poets such as Charles Baudelaire's (1821–1867) *Fleurs du mal* (1857) which became influential because of its mixture of impressionist and symbolist elements have enriched the literature of other countries. France, and Paris in particular, was a center of attraction for the novelist and essayist Stefan Zweig (1881–1942). After having finished his studies of German and Romance philology at the universities of Vienna and Berlin he visited the French capital. The image he depicts in his reminiscences is characterized by juvenile light-heartedness and the impression that this metropolis does not know any differences between skin colors or societal classes: "Paris kannte nur ein Nebeneinander der Gegensätze, kein Oben und unten."[59] It is not for nothing that he speaks of a *Welt von Gestern* (1944, translated as *World of Yesterday*) when he wrote these *Erinnerungen eines Europäers* close to the end of his life. Recalling the years before the First World War Zweig characterizes them as "das goldene Zeitalter der Sicherheit,"[60] a time when Austrians felt the old monarchy would last a millennium. His initial feeling of living in a secure and ordered setting can certainly be understood as an exemplary symptom of the Habsburg myth. *Die Welt von Gestern* was written in exile, a state of living with which the author was, in the last analysis, not able to cope. Zweig and his wife committed suicide in 1942 in Petropolis, Brazil.

The recent turn of the century is still in progress and it remains to be seen in what ways and for which aspects in (literary) history it marks a final point or what it has set going. But the most important developments both in literature and in history can be traced even now. For this reason, the contributions of Janet Stewart ("The Written City: Vienna 1900 and 2000") and John Pizer ("Venice as Mediator between Province and Viennese Metropolis: Themes in Rilke, Hofmannsthal, Gerhard Roth, and Kolleritsch") start from a discussion on the ways Vienna is presented and characterized in *fin-de-siècle* and contemporary Austrian literature and, beyond that, highlight the relationship between province and metropolis. Rüdiger Görner's essay "Notes from the Counter World: Poetry in Vienna from Hugo von Hofmannsthal to Ernst Jandl" sketches the development of poetry. Görner claims that the language of *fin-de-siècle* poetry has not left traces in contemporary poetry and lays emphasis on the fact that genuine poetry is created independently from historical circumstances. Central to the political discussions around 1900 and 2000 were and are issues such as the role of women in society and the arts, anti-Semitism, and multiculturality. These topics are dealt with in connection with the most important artists and writers such as Karl Kraus and Robert Menasse, Theodor Herzl and Robert Schindel, Veza Canetti or the filmmaker Ruth Beckermann. Kraus around 1900 and Menasse around 2000 belong to the most outstanding figures in analyzing Austria's identity and condition. In his essay "Critical Observers of Their Times: Karl Kraus and Robert Menasse" Geoffrey C. Howes highlights the authors' roles in public discourse. In his essay "Dreams of Interpretation: Psychoanalysis and the Literature of Vienna," Thomas Paul Bonfiglio discusses the continuities of psychoanalytical elements in Viennese literature. He analyzes, among others, works of Franz Grillparzer, Arthur Schnitzler, and Hugo von Hofmannsthal in the earlier *fin de siècle* and of Elfriede Jelinek, Werner Kofler, Paulus Hochgatterer, and others in the current period. Hillary Hope Herzog and Todd Herzog reflect on how Jewish life is dealt with in (literary) works of Schnitzler, Herzl, Freud, Doron Rabinovici, Robert Menasse, and Robert Schindel. Their contribution, "'Wien bleibt Wien': Austrian-Jewish Culture at Two Fins de Siècle, depicts Vienna as the center of Austrian-Jewish life although the mentioned authors provide an often contradictory picture of the city. Dagmar C. G. Lorenz surveys the role of women writers at both turns of the century in her essay "Austrian Women and the Public: Women's Writing at the Turn of the Centuries." She concludes with a global view on feminism and states that the prerequisites for an intercultural exchange of identities, knowledge, and experience is still out of reach. The interrelation of literature and other arts is likewise an important issue in this volume, which becomes obvious not least by artists who were concerned with more than just one artistic discipline, such as literature and the graphic arts. Douglas Crow's contribution "Art and Architecture 1900 and 2000" is based on interviews with contemporary artists to highlight this mutual inspiration. As mentioned above, literature around 1900 strove for a contact to other artistic forms of expression. It may surprise even specialists in German literature that Austria had a well developed film industry in the first decades after 1900 and that many writers such as Kafka, Max Brod (1884–1968), and Schnitzler were attracted to filmmaking. Willy Riemer's "Literature and Austrian Cinema Culture at the Turn of the Centuries" analyzes the historical development of Austrian film industry.

Notes

[1] Elisabeth Leinfellner-Rupertsberger, "Die Republik der Sprachen bei Fritz Mauthner: Sprache und Nationalismus," in *Die Wiener Jahrhundertwende: Einflüsse, Umwelt, Wirkungen,* edited by Jürgen Nautz and Richard Vahrenkamp (Vienna/Cologne/Graz: Böhlau, 1996), 389.

[2] Just to mention a few: Christian Dickinger, *Ha-Ha-Habsburg: Eine wirklich wahre Familiengeschichte* (Vienna: Ueberreuter, 2001); Hans Bankl, *Die kranken Habsburger: Befunde und Befindlichkeiten einer Herrscherdynastie* (Vienna: Kremayr & Scheriau, 1998); Brigitte Hamann, ed., *Die Habsburger: Ein biographisches Lexikon* (Vienna: Amalthea, 2001); Karin Amtmann, *Elisabeth von Österreich: Die politischen Geschäfte der Kaiserin* (Regensburg: Pustet, 1998); Gerhard Bruckner/Gabriele Praschl-Bichler, *Sisis Melodien: Die Musik der Kaiserin Elisabeth* (Graz: Stocker, 1998); Brigitte Hamann, *Elisabeth: Eine Kaiserin wider Willen* (Munich: Piper, 1998).

[3] *Elisabeth* enjoyed 1279 perfomances and 1.27 million visitors and was outperformed only by Andrew Lloyd Webber's *Cats* (2040 performances, 2.2 million visitors) and *The Phantom of the Opera* (1363 performances, 1.4 million visitors).

[4] See Brigitte Hamann, *Hitlers Wien: Lehrjahre eines Diktators* (Munich: Piper, 2000).

[5] Peter Gay, *Freud: Eine Biographie für unsere Zeit,* translated by Joachim A. Frank (Frankfurt am Main: S. Fischer, 1989), 122.

[6] See Thomas P. Bonfiglio's essay in this volume.

[7] Gerhard Roth, "Der Narrenturm," in Gerhard Roth, *Eine Reise in das Innere von Wien* (Frankfurt am Main: S. Fischer, 1991), 110–31. This book is the seventh volume of Roth's series *Die Archive des Schweigens* (The Archives of Silence).

[8] Gerhard Roth, "Das k. k. privilegierte Hetztheater," in Roth, *Eine Reise in das Innere von Wien* (Frankfurt am Main: Fischer, 1991), 7–13.

[9] See the cover of the pocket edition cited above.

[10] Arndt Brendecke, *Die Jahrhundertwenden: Eine Geschichte ihrer Wahrnehmung und Wirkung* (Frankfurt am Main/New York: Campus, 2000), 213.

[11] Jürgen Nautz/Richard Vahrenkamp, "Einleitung," in *Die Wiener Jahrhundertwende: Einflüsse, Umwelt, Wirkungen,* edited by Jürgen Nautz and Richard Vahrenkamp (Vienna/Cologne/Graz: Böhlau, 1996), 27.

[12] See *Die Wiener Moderne: Literatur, Kunst und Musik zwischen 1890 und 1910,* edited by Gotthart Wunberg and Johannes J. Braakenburg (Stuttgart: Reclam, 1981), 11.

[13] For an introduction to the "Wiener Moderne" see Dagmar Lorenz, *Wiener Moderne* (Stuttgart/Weimar: Metzler, 1995).

[14] *Die Wiener Moderne,* 45.

[15] Jürgen Nautz/Richard Vahrenkamp, "Einleitung," 32–33.

[16] For an English translation of Kokoschka's literary works see Oskar Kokoschka, *Plays and Poems,* translated by Michael Mitchell (Riverside, CA: Ariadne Press, 2001).

[17] Members of the "Wiener Kreis" were Moritz Schlick (1882–1936), Otto Neurath (1882–1945), and Rudolf Carnap (1891–1968). Central to their methodology was a radical rationalism and positivism and, consequently, a radical criticism of traditional philosophy, especially metaphysics.

[18] *Die Wiener Moderne,* 23.

[19] Claudio Magris, *Der habsburgische Mythos in der modernen österreichischen Literatur* (Vienna: Zsolnay, 2000). The first German translation of this book appeared in 1966. It was republished in 2000 with an additional preface by the author.

[20] Claudio Magris, *Der habsburgische Mythos,* 10.

[21] Claudio Magris, *Der habsburgische Mythos,* 21.

[22] Claudio Magris, *Der habsburgische Mythos,* 22.

[23] See Sven Achelpohl, "Eine Welt von gestern — ein Mythos von heute? Über Claudio Magris' 'Der habsburgische Mythos in der modernen österreichischen Literatur,'" http://www.literaturkritik.de/txt/2001–06/2001–06–0001.html.

[24] Ulrich Greiner, *Der Tod des Nachsommers: Aufsätze, Porträts, Kritiken zur österreichischen Gegenwartsliteratur* (Munich/Vienna: Hanser, 1979).

²⁵ Robert Menasse, *Die sozialpartnerschaftliche Ästhetik: Essays zum österreichischen Geist* (Vienna: Sonderzahl, 1990).

²⁶ Robert Menasse, *Überbau und Underground: Die sozialpartnerschaftliche Ästhetik: Essays zum österreichischen Geist* (Frankfurt am Main: Suhrkamp, 1997), 7. This is a revised and enlarged edition of *Die sozialpartnerschaftliche Ästhetik* (1990).

²⁷ Robert Menasse, *Überbau und Underground*, 22–23. Menasse states that social-partnership "zielt auf eine konfliktminimierende Zusammenarbeit der Interessenorganisationen der Unternehmer und der Lohn- und Gehaltabhängigen, um das dem Klassencharakter der Gesellschaft innewohnende Konfliktpotential zum 'Klassenkampf am grünen Tisch' zu sublimieren und auf dem Verhandlungsweg beizulegen" (19) and refers to "die offenkundigsten und nächstliegenden Konsequenzen der Sozialpartnerschaft [. . .], um eine erste Vorstellung von ihren Auswirkungen auf den geistigen Überbau Österreichs zu bekommen: Die ökonomische und politische Konfliktregelung ist gänzlich aus der öffentlichen Parteienkonfrontation herausgenommen, die Regierung kann alle schwierigen Situationen in Übereinstimmung mit den großen Interessengruppen des Landes meistern, wodurch es innenpolitisch nie zu nennenswertem Widerstand gegen Regierungsentscheidungen kommt. Alle wesentlichen politischen Entscheidungen werden im harmonischen Gespräch einer informell sich zusammensetzenden Handvoll Männer hinter verschlossenen Türen getroffen, abseits jeglicher demokratischer Kontrolle oder öffentlicher Diskussion. Auf dieser Grundlage gelangen nur noch marginale Auffassungsunterschiede zwischen Politikern (als reduzierte Form des notwendigen Ringens um Wählerstimmen) oder Skandalisierungen von ihrem individuellen Verhalten in den öffentlichen Diskurs, der dann natürlich nicht mehr als politischer, sondern nur noch als moralisierender funktioniert. Es ist daher wohl kaum zu kurz geschlossen, wenn man daraus folgert, daß sich in den Köpfen der Menschen der Eindruck der Schicksalhaftigkeit und Naturbedingtheit der gesellschaftlichen, wirtschaftlichen und politischen Entwicklung herausbilden und immer mehr festigen muß, sowie Harmoniekonzeptionen mit im wesentlichen nichtöffentlichem und nichtdemokratischem Charakter" (25).

²⁸ Menasse, 20–21.

²⁹ Menasse, 43.

³⁰ Wendelin Schmidt-Dengler, *Bruchlinien: Vorlesungen zur österreichischen Literatur 1945 bis 1990* (Salzburg: Residenz, 1995), 330–39.

³¹ See several articles in Literaturzirkel (1985), no. 9: Thomas Pluch, "Das Absurde am Literaturberuf. Handwerker, Dilettanten und Genies auf der Suche nach einem gemeinsamen Selbstverständnis" (7–11), Herbert Eisenreich, "Freiheit in Krähwinkel. Wie frei ist der freie Beruf eines Literaten?" (6), Gerhard Ruiss und Johannes Vyoral, "Wenige Promille Hoffnung. Die 'schöne Literatur' und der Buchmarkt" (13–14).

³² Wendelin Schmidt-Dengler, *Bruchlinien*, 336.

³³ Quoted in Carl Junker, "Die Entwicklung des Buch-, Kunst- und Musikalienhandels in Österreich und Ungarn 1860–1910," in Carl Junker, *Zum Buchwesen in Österreich: Gesammelte Schriften (1896–1927)*, edited by Murray G. Hall (Vienna: Edition Praesens, 2001), 116.

[34] Junker gives exact figures: In 1835 Gräffer counted 26 bookstores in Vienna, whereas other "Provinzialhauptstäde" only had 4 on an average.

[35] Carl Junker, "Die Entwicklung des Buch-, Kunst- und Musikalienhandels in Österreich," 120.

[36] Murray G. Hall, "Publizistik 1895–1918," *Wien um 1900: Kunst und Kultur* (Vienna: Brandstätter, 1985), 447. For the history of the S. Fischer Verlag see Peter de Mendelssohn, *S. Fischer und sein Verlag* (Frankfurt am Main: S. Fischer, 1970).

[37] Murray G. Hall, "Publizistik 1895–1918," 447–48. For a history of Austrian publishing from 1918–1938 see Murray G. Hall, *Österreichische Verlagsgeschichte 1918–1938*. 2 vols. (Vienna/Cologne/Graz: Böhlau, 1985).

[38] For a history of the Grazer Autorenversammlung see Roland Innerhofer, *Die Grazer Autorenversammlung (1973–1983): Zur Organisation einer "Avantgarde"* (Vienna/Graz/Cologne: Böhlau, 1983). A survey of the group's formation can be found in Wendelin Schmidt-Dengler, *Bruchlinien*, 280–88, 382–85.

[39] See Ruth Wodak/Rudolf de Cillia/Dilek Cinar/Bernd Matouschek, "Identitätswandel Österreichs im veränderten Europa. Diskurshistorische Studie über den öffentlichen und privaten Diskurs zur 'neuen' österreichischen Identität," in *Nationale und kulturelle Identitäten Österreichs: Theorien, Methoden und Probleme der Forschung zu kollektiver Identität*, edited by the Projektteam "Identitätswandel Österreichs im veränderten Europa" (Vienna: Internationales Forschungszentrum Kulturwissenschaften, 1995), 6.

[40] In this connection Benedict Anderson speaks of an "imagined community." See Benedict Anderson, *Die Erfindung der Nation: Zur Karriere eines folgenreichen Konzepts* (Frankfurt am Main/New York: Campus, 1996).

[41] See Wolfdieter Bihl, "Der Weg zum Zusammenbruch. Österreich-Ungarn unter Karl I. (IV.)," *Österreich 1918–1938: Geschichte der Ersten Republik 1*, edited by Erika Weinzierl and Kurt Skalnik (Graz/Vienna/Cologne: Styria, 1983), 28.

[42] See Miroslav Hroch, "Sprache, Literatur und nationale Identität," *Die Wiener Jahrhundertwende: Einflüsse, Umwelt, Wirkungen*, edited by Jürgen Nautz and Richard Vahrenkamp (Vienna/Cologne/Graz: Böhlau, 1996), 377.

[43] See *Österreich: Berichte aus Quarantanien*, edited by Isolde Charim and Doron Rabinovici (Frankfurt am Main: Suhrkamp, 2000). For the reactions of the member states of the European Union against Austria see Margaretha Kopeinig and Christoph Kotanko, *Eine europäische Affäre: Der Weisen-Bericht und die Sanktionen gegen Österreich* (Vienna: Czernin, 2000).

[44] For an analysis of the recent developments in Austrian politics see Gerfried Sperl, *Der Machtwechsel: Österreichs politische Krise zu Beginn des 3. Jahrtausends* (Vienna: Molden, 2000).

[45] See Geoffrey C. Howes's and Todd and Hillary Hope Herzog's contributions to this volume.

[46] Robert Schindel, "Mein Wien," *Österreich: Berichte aus Quarantanien*, 83.

[47] Helmut Qualtinger/Carl Merz, *Der Herr Karl*, edited by Traugott Krischke (Vienna: Deuticke, 1996).

[48] Hubert Christian Ehalt in his preface to Harald Leupold-Löwenthal, *Ein Wiener zu sein: Geschichte, Geschichten, Analysen* (Vienna: Picus, 1997), 10.

[49] Harald Leupold-Löwenthal, *Ein Wiener zu sein,* 22.

[50] Harald Leupold-Löwenthal, *Ein Wiener zu sein,* 46. Italics not mine.

[51] An opinion poll of the Gallup Institute in 1995 showed the following result: "In terms of the lager [*sic*] picture, the survey results are mixed. Between 1919 and 1995 attitudes towards Jews in Austria improved, and a more positive orientation toward Holocaust remembrance developed. At the same time, approximately one in four Austrians continue to express hostility toward Jews, while a somewhat larger proportion of Austrians fail to show an interest in keeping the memory of the Holocaust alive. Finally, with regard to factual knowledge about the Holocaust, Austrians are generally well informed, but many fail to acknowledge Ausria's [*sic*] role in the Jewish catastrophe" (quoted in Ruth Wodak/Rudolf de Cillia/Dilek Cinar/Bernd Matouschek, "Identitätswandel Österreichs im veränderten Europa," 14).

[52] Josef Haslinger, *Politik der Gefühle: Ein Essay über Österreich* (Darmstadt: Luchterhand, 1989 [first edition 1987]), 29.

[53] Thomas Bernhard, *Heldenplatz* (Frankfurt am Main: Suhrkamp, 1988), 61–62.

[54] For a documentation of the arguments on this play approaching the first performance see Oliver Bentz, *Thomas Bernhard: Dichtung als Skandal* (Würzburg: Königshausen & Neumann, 2000).

[55] Ernst Jandl, "wien: heldenplatz," in Ernst Jandl, *Laut und Luise* (Stuttgart: Reclam, 1976), 37.

[56] See Adolf Haslinger, *Peter Handke: Jugend eines Schriftstellers* (Salzburg: Residenz, 1992), 43, 105.

[57] Handke has made Duras's text *Le maladie de la mort* into a movie and Mayröcker admires the French writer for her novels doing without any action.

[58] Handke, among others, translated from French (Marguerite Duras), Slovenian (Florjan Lipuš), English (Shakespeare, Walker Percy); Rosei from Italian (Anonimo Triestino); Amanshauser from Portuguese (Rui Zink); Jandl from English (John Cage); Frischmuth from oriental languages and Hungarian (Sándor Weöres); Artmann from French (François Villon), English (Daisy Ashford), Yiddish (proverbs); Schrott from Greek (Euripides), English (Derek Walcott), and from several other languages for his anthology of poetry, *Die Erfindung der Poesie* (Frankfurt am Main: Eichborn, 1997).

[59] Stefan Zweig, *Die Welt von Gestern: Erinnerungen eines Europäers* (Frankfurt am Main: S. Fischer, 1999 [first edition 1944]), 155.

[60] Stefan Zweig, *Die Welt von Gestern,* 15.

Works Cited

Achelpohl, Sven. "Eine Welt von gestern — ein Mythos von heute? Über Claudio Magris' 'Der habsburgische Mythos in der modernen österreichischen Literatur.'" http://www.literaturkritik.de/txt/2001–06/2001–06–0001.html.

Amtmann, Karin. *Elisabeth von Österreich: Die politischen Geschäfte der Kaiserin.* Regensburg: Pustet, 1998.

Anderson, Benedict. *Die Erfindung der Nation: Zur Karriere eines folgenreichen Konzepts.* Frankfurt am Main/New York: Campus, 1996.

Bankl, Hans. *Die kranken Habsburger: Befunde und Befindlichkeiten einer Herrscherdynastie.* Vienna: Kremayr & Scheriau, 1998.

Bentz, Oliver. *Thomas Bernhard: Dichtung als Skandal.* Würzburg: Königshausen & Neumann, 2000.

Bernhard, Thomas. *Heldenplatz.* Frankfurt am Main: Suhrkamp, 1988.

Bihl, Wolfdieter. "Der Weg zum Zusammenbruch. Österreich-Ungarn unter Karl I. (IV.)." In *Österreich 1918–1938: Geschichte der Ersten Republik 1,* edited by Erika Weinzierl and Kurt Skalnik. Graz/Vienna/Cologne: Styria, 1983. 27–54.

Brendecke, Arndt. *Die Jahrhundertwenden: Eine Geschichte ihrer Wahrnehmung und Wirkung.* Frankfurt am Main/New York: Campus, 2000.

Broch, Hermann. *Die Schlafwandler.* Frankfurt am Main: Suhrkamp, 1978.

Bruckner, Gerhard and Gabriele Praschl-Bichler. *Sisis Melodien: Die Musik der Kaiserin Elisabeth.* Graz: Stocker, 1998.

Charim, Isolde, and Doron Rabinovici, eds. *Österreich: Bericht aus Quarantanien.* Frankfurt am Main: Suhrkamp, 2000.

Dickinger, Christian. *Ha-Ha-Habsburg: Eine wirklich wahre Familiengeschichte.* Vienna: Ueberreuter, 2001.

Gay, Peter. *Freud: Eine Biographie für unsere Zeit.* Translated by Joachim A. Frank. Frankfurt am Main: S. Fischer, 1989.

Greiner, Ulrich. *Der Tod des Nachsommers: Aufsätze, Porträts, Kritiken zur österreichischen Gegenwartsliteratur.* Munich/Vienna: Hanser, 1979.

Hall, Murray G. *Österreichische Verlagsgeschichte 1918–1938.* 2 vols. Vienna/Cologne/Graz: Böhlau, 1985.

———. "Publizistik 1895–1918." In *Wien um 1900: Kunst und Kultur.* Vienna: Brandstätter, 1985. 447–54.

Hamann, Brigitte. *Hitlers Wien: Lehrjahre eines Diktators.* Munich: Piper, 2000 (first edition 1996).

————, ed. *Die Habsburger: Ein biographisches Lexikon.* Vienna: Amalthea, 2001.

————. *Elisabeth: Eine Kaiserin wider Willen.* Munich: Piper, 1998.

Haslinger, Adolf. *Peter Handke: Jugend eines Schriftstellers.* Salzburg: Residenz, 1992.

Haslinger, Josef. *Politik der Gefühle: Ein Essay über Österreich.* Darmstadt/ Munich: Luchterhand, 1989 (first edition 1987).

Haslinger, Josef. *Das Vaterspiel.* Frankfurt am Main: S. Fischer, 2000.

Hroch, Miroslav. "Sprache, Literatur und nationale Identität." In *Die Wiener Jahrhundertwende: Einflüsse, Umwelt, Wirkungen,* edited by Jürgen Nautz and Richard Vahrenkamp. Vienna/Cologne/Graz: Böhlau, 1996. 377–88.

Jandl, Ernst. "wien: heldenplatz." In Ernst Jandl, *Laut und Luise.* Stuttgart: Reclam, 1976. 37.

Junker, Carl. "Die Entwicklung des Buch-, Kunst- und Musikalienhandels in Österreich und Ungarn 1860–1910." In Carl Junker, *Zum Buchwesen in Österreich: Gesammelte Schriften (1896–1927),* edited by Murray G. Hall. Vienna: Edition Praesens, 2001. 116–22.

————. "Zur Lage des Buchhandels in Wien am Ende des XVIII. und zu Beginn des XIX. Jahrhunderts." In Carl Junker, *Zum Buchwesen in Österreich: Gesammelte Schriften (1896–1927),* edited by Murray G. Hall. Vienna: Edition Praesens, 2001. 127–41.

Kokoschka, Oskar. *Plays and Poems.* Translated by Michael Mitchell. Riverside, CA: Ariadne Press, 2001.

Kopeinig, Margaretha and Christoph Kotanko. *Eine europäische Affäre: Der Weisen-Bericht und die Sanktionen gegen Österreich.* Vienna: Czernin, 2000.

Lehnert, Herbert. *Geschichte der deutschen Literatur vom Jugendstil bis zum Expressionismus.* Stuttgart: Reclam, 1978.

Leinfellner-Rupertsberger, Elisabeth. "Die Republik der Sprachen bei Fritz Mauthner: Sprache und Nationalismus." In *Die Wiener Jahrhundertwende: Einflüsse — Umwelt — Wirkungen,* edited by Jürgen Nautz and Richard Vahrenkamp. Vienna/Cologne/Graz: Böhlau, 1996. 389–405.

Leupold-Löwenthal, Harald. *Wien und die Fremden.* Vienna: Picus, 1992.

————. *Ein Wiener zu sein: Geschichte, Geschichten, Analysen.* Vienna: Picus, 1997.

Lorenz, Dagmar. *Wiener Moderne.* Stuttgart/Weimar: Metzler, 1995.

Magris, Claudio. *Der habsburgische Mythos in der modernen österreichischen Literatur.* Vienna: Zsolnay, 2000 (revised edition of 1966).

Menasse, Robert. *Das Land ohne Eigenschaften: Essay zur österreichischen Identität.* Vienna: Sonderzahl, 1992.

————. *Die sozialpartnerschaftliche Ästhetik: Essays zum österreichischen Geist.* Vienna: Sonderzahl, 1990.

————. *Überbau und Underground: Die sozialpartnerschaftliche Ästhetik. Essays zum österreichischen Geist.* Frankfurt am Main: Suhrkamp, 1997.

Mendelssohn, Peter de. *S. Fischer und sein Verlag.* Frankfurt am Main: S. Fischer, 1970.

Musil, Robert. *Der Mann ohne Eigenschaften.* 2 vols. Reinbek: Rowohlt, 1988.

Nautz, Jürgen and Richard Vahrenkamp. "Einleitung." In *Die Wiener Jahrhundertwende: Einflüsse, Umwelt, Wirkungen,* edited by Jürgen Nautz and Richard Vahrenkamp. Vienna/Cologne/Graz: Böhlau, 1996. 21–48.

Qualtinger, Helmut, and Carl Merz. *Der Herr Karl.* Edited by Traugott Krischke. Vienna: Deuticke, 1996.

Riggins, Stephen Harold, ed. *The Language and Politics of Exclusion: Others in Discourse.* Thousand Oaks/London/New Delhi: Sage Publications, 1997.

Roth, Gerhard. *Eine Reise in das Innere von Wien.* Frankfurt am Main: Fischer, 1999.

Schindel, Robert. "Mein Wien." In *Österreich: Berichte aus Quarantanien,* edited by Isolde Charim and Doron Rabinovici. Frankfurt am Main: Suhrkamp, 2000. 78–88.

Schmidt-Dengler, Wendelin. *Bruchlinien: Vorlesungen zur österreichischen Literatur 1945 bis 1990.* Salzburg: Residenz, 1995.

Schrott, Raoul. *Die Erfindung der Poesie: Gedichte aus den ersten viertausend Jahren.* Frankfurt am Main: Eichborn, 1997.

Sperl, Gerfried. *Der Machtwechsel: Österreichs politische Krise zu Beginn des 3. Jahrtausends.* Vienna: Molden, 2000.

Sprengel, Peter, and Gregor Streim. *Berliner und Wiener Moderne: Vermittlungen und Abgrenzungen in Literatur, Theater, Publizistik.* Vienna/Cologne/Weimar: Böhlau, 1998.

Wodak, Ruth, Rudolf de Cillia, Dilek Cinar, and Bernd Matouschek. "Identitätswandel Österreichs im veränderten Europa. Diskurshistorische Studien über den öffentlichen und privaten Diskurs zur 'neuen' österreichischen Identität." In *Nationale und kulturelle Identität Österreichs: Theorien, Methoden und Probleme der Forschung zu kollektiver Identität,* edited by the Projekt-Team "Identitätswandel Österreichs im veränderten Europa." Vienna: Internationales Forschungszentrum Kulturwissenschaften, 1995. 6–27.

Wunberg, Gotthart, and Johannes J. Braakenburg, ed. *Die Wiener Moderne: Literatur, Kunst und Musik zwischen 1890 und 1910.* Stuttgart: Reclam, 1981.

Zweig, Stefan. *Die Welt von Gestern: Erinnerungen eines Europäers.* Frankfurt am Main: S. Fischer, 1999 (first edition 1944).

Robert Musil lived in this house in
Rasumofskygasse 20 from 1921–1938.
Photograph by Ernst Grabovszki

I. Literature

Jugendstil architecture, Linke Wienzeile.
Photograph by Ernst Grabovszki.

The Written City:
Vienna 1900 and 2000

Janet Stewart

> *Vienna remains dull for those of us who have only*
> *passed by without penetrating as far as its soul.*
>
> Le Corbusier, 1911

IN 1891, VIENNA'S BOUNDARIES were extended to include the outer suburbs (*Vororte*), adding nine further districts (*Bezirke*) to the existing ten, and bringing the total population to 1,365,170. Vienna was at this time both capital city and seat of the multi-ethnic Austro-Hungarian Empire. According to Baedeker's 1892 guide to the city, its reputation as a place of artistic importance had grown considerably over the preceding decades, especially with the construction of the Ringstrasse and its collection of impressive monumental buildings.[1] Begun in 1861 and completed in 1873,[2] the Ringstrasse provided the impetus for the development and expansion of Vienna. By the turn of the century, however, competing views on future urban planning had emerged. In *Der Städtebau nach seinen künstlerischen Grundsätzen* (1889), the architect and city planner Camillo Sitte praised the historicism of the representative buildings on the Ringstrasse, including the Parliament, built in classical Greek style, the university, in the style of the Renaissance, the Burgtheater, in baroque style, and the Gothic Rathaus. He was, however, critical of the uniform grid system of the modern city that takes the street as its basic element. His alternative, based on the idea of the "organic" mediaeval city, took the city square as its central feature. In contrast, the architect Otto Wagner launched fierce criticism of the historicist buildings that lined the Ringstrasse, and reserved his admiration for the street itself. Wagner developed the idea of the primacy of the street, as an "artery of motion" (Schorske, 100) in *Moderne Architektur* (1895). He then used this as the basis for his "modular plan for the expansible city," which he described in *Die Großstadt* (1911).

A century later, Vienna has expanded to comprise twenty-three districts and houses a population of around 1.7 million. The city, capital of the mainly German-speaking Second Austrian Republic and also a federal province in its own right, views itself as an historic imperial capital, rich in architecture, museums, and art galleries. Yet now, as at the beginning of the twentieth century, it is also a city keen to make its mark in terms of urban planning for the future, and so, in 1999, a comprehensive "Strategic Plan for Vienna" was unveiled.[3] This document aims to provide the framework that will enable Vienna to assume a strong position in competition and cooperation with other major European cities. Underlying the strategic plan is an apparent commitment to transparency, contained in the idea of the Vienna Dialogues which took place in 2000, in partnership with the Europaforum, Centre for Urban Dialogue, an urban think-tank established in 1995.[4] However, despite the rhetoric of inclusion and consultation contained in the idea of a set of "dialogues," the imagined city of the 1999 strategic plan — like Sitte's communitarian vision or Wagner's expansible city — is ultimately a prescriptive blueprint for urban planning.

According to the French theorist of everyday life, Michel de Certeau, the "Concept-city," the city inscribed by urban planners, represents only one of a number of possible ways of knowing the city (94–95). This bird's-eye perspective, defined in terms of geographical location and political function, supported by statistics, provides a way of accessing the city from the outside, of viewing it from above. This perspective of the cartographer, whose maps provide us with representations of the city as exterior, that make it appear legible and transparent. However, the promise of an overview is misleading, for it can only succeed if it ignores what de Certeau terms the "fact" of the city: the "'anthropological,'" poetic and mythic experience of space" (93), only accessible to those who actually inhabit the city. Although the purpose of a map is to enable people to locate themselves in the city and make their way through its thoroughfares, there is still a gap between the plan of the city and the city as lived-in (erlebt) interior. In the same way, argues the Italian philosopher of architecture, Massimo Cacciari, there is an essential difference between looking at a house from the outside and inhabiting that house (183).

At the beginning of the twentieth century, Adolf Loos criticized his fellow architects in Vienna for failing to engage with the city as interior. In a public lecture, "Architecture," first delivered in Berlin in 1911, he attacked those who reify the city through merely engaging with representations (*Trotzdem*, 93–94). Over a decade earlier, he had challenged these architects to leave their drawing boards behind them: "Geht ins Leben, damit ihr wißt, was verlangt wird" (*Ins Leere*, 91). On both occasions, he urged his fellow architects to approach the city from its interior rather than its exterior, reading, writing and drawing the city itself, rather than relying on already existing representations. In Loos's view, only by engaging actively with the city might one, to paraphrase Le Corbusier, go beyond the potentially dull urban plan and discover Vienna's soul.

Peter Altenberg was one writer who fully embraced the injunction of his friend and contemporary, Loos, to immerse himself in the rhythms of the city, and lived his life in the public sphere. In 1902, he moved out of an apartment shared with his brother and into a room in the Hotel London, an establishment which, although located in the center of Vienna's aristocratic First District, was scarcely better than a brothel. He remained at this address for many years, before taking up residence in the Grabenhotel in the Dorotheergasse in 1913 (Barker, 33, 264). In sketches such as "Das Hotelzimmer" (ML 115), "Zimmereinrichtung" (VI, 116), and "Die Maus" (P, 162–65), he describes the freedoms and restrictions that apply to the modern hotel dweller. If his bedroom was a hotel room, his living-room was the private-public space of the Kaffeehaus or bar (depending on the time of day), and he reflects on life in the Viennese coffeehouses in texts such as "Stammtisch" (F, 60), and "Regeln für meinen Stammtisch" (ML, 44–45). At times, his living-room even extended onto the street. In "Die Kontrolle" (ML, 67–68), Altenberg describes taking his breakfast at the "Grabenkiosk," from which vantage point he could observe his fellow city dwellers as they went about their business. His lifestyle is a perfect example of Walter Benjamin's assertion that, in the modern metropolis, "the streets are the home of the collective" (GS V, 533). Making the streets of Vienna his home, meant that Altenberg was regarded as an authority on the city by his contemporaries. As early as 1898, in a lecture on modern poetry given in Prague, Rainer Maria Rilke labeled Altenberg "de[n] erste[n] Verkünder des modernen Wiens," arguing that through him, Vienna had suddenly found its own language (388). And almost a century later, the weekly newspaper *Die Zeit* reiterated this perception of Altenberg, hailing him "die wahre Eminenz Wiens" (quoted in Barker, 12).

The title of Altenberg's first collection of prose poems, aphorisms, sketches and short essays, *Wie ich es sehe* (1896), seems to privilege his own, subjective experience. However, Altenberg later insisted that the correct emphasis is "Wie ich es *sehe*" (Simpson, 6), placing what he sees, rather than the self, at the center of his texts. This is emphasized in the title of his second collection, *Was der Tag mir zuträgt* (1901), which casts Altenberg in the role of passive observer of city life. In a written reply to a collector of manuscripts in 1901, published in the literary weekly *Die literarische Welt* in 1932, Altenberg reiterated this perspective on the city by likening himself to a camera in which, "die Ereignisse des Tages scheinen sich, mir unbewußt, in mir selbst abzuphotographieren" (3). His texts are the product of "walking in the city," which, according to de Certeau, is diametrically opposed to the planners' perspective. In de Certeau's words, Altenberg could be described as an "ordinary practitioner of the city [living] below the thresholds at which visibility begins" (93). Using a more common analogy, Altenberg's work can be understood as the product of *flânerie*.

Significantly, it is the figure of the flâneur, "the secret spectator of the spectacle of the spaces and places of the city" (Tester, 7), that still offers Viennese authors such as Peter Rosei (b. 1946) with a means of writing the city in the final decades of the twentieth century. In *Das schnelle Glück* (1980, translated as *Try your Luck!*, 1993), Rosei provides the reader with snapshots of life in his Vienna by having his protagonists walk in the city, ride the transport system and look out of windows. In his later fictional texts, he continues to demonstrate a fascination with the city, and with the figure of the *flâneur*. Initially, he departs from the concrete setting of Vienna to explore the urban consciousness more or less free of specific location, in works such as the collection of stories, *Die Milchstraße* (1981, The Milky Way) and the novel, *15000 Seelen* (1985, 15,000 Souls). However, he returns to Vienna in *Rebus* (1991).[5] With its narrative form based on *flânerie*, this novel marks the culmination of Rosei's literary exploration of the city theme, and also distinguishes Rosei as the author of the first Viennese *Großstadtroman* since Heimito von Doderer in the 1950s.[6]

In *Rebus*, Rosei reflects on different ways of seeing the metropolis. In "Straßenszene," the penultimate chapter of the novel, a man emerges from the "schmutzigem Gassengewirr" of the artists' quarter into a broad boulevard. From this vantage point, he looks up into the sky and sees an airplane which, we are told, looks like one of the technical marks with which architects and city planners decorate their plans (R, 272). The juxtaposition of the dirty winding chaos of streets occupied by the artists and the open space of the boulevard, reflected in the open expanses of sky above it, is reminiscent of the distinction de Certeau makes between the "fact" of the city and the "Concept-city." Earlier in his novel, Rosei employs the metaphor of the chessboard, the archetypal rational grid system, in an attempt to describe the form of the metropolis

(R, 14). Later in the text, however, this view of the world is rejected, as Kohn, one of the central protagonists, pokes fun at his neighbor for believing that chess, or any game, could represent the world itself (R, 65).

Rosei, like Altenberg, is most interested in exploring what people see, as they inhabit the city on a day-to-day basis. As the narrator in *Rebus* reflects: "Ja, unser Stoff ist krud. Ordinär und absurd. Aberwitzig. Der ist ja ganz gewöhnlich!" (R, 218). This common interest in the culture of everyday life underlines the affinity of Altenberg's and Rosei's literary approach to the city with the discourse of urban social theorists such as Georg Simmel (1858–1918), Walter Benjamin (1892–1940), and Siegfried Kracauer (1889–1966). In much of his work, Simmel emphasized the insights to be gained through analysis of the "mundane surface" of everyday life (Frisby 1992, 165), while Kracauer's point of departure was his conviction that, "der Ort, den eine Epoche im Geschichtsprozeß einnimmt, ist aus der Analyse ihrer unscheinbaren Oberflächenäußerungen schlagender zu bestimmen als aus den Urteilen der Epoche über sich selbst" ("Das Ornament der Masse," 57). In method, there are correspondences between these urban theorists, and Altenberg and Rosei. As David Frisby has shown, Simmel, Benjamin and Kracauer were united in their belief that the nature of modernity could only be revealed through an analysis of the "fragments of modernity" (1985, 271–72).

Like many of his contemporaries, Altenberg rejected the claims of omniscience that underpin the realist novel, concentrating instead on short literary forms such as prose sketches and poems, cabaret sketches, aphorisms and short essays. He did this, he claimed, as a direct response to the changed time consciousness in modernity: "Es gibt heutzutage viele sonst tüchtige Menschen, die keine Zeit haben, 200 Seiten zu lesen. Diesen gibt man drei Seiten im Extrakte!" (BL, 164–65). Here, Altenberg is referring to his "extract theory," which he first outlined in *Was der Tag mir zuträgt*:

> Es sind Extrakte! Extrakte des Lebens. Das Leben der Seele und des zufälligen Tages, in 2–3 Seiten eingedampft, vom Überflüssigen befreit wie das Rind im Liebigtiegel! [. . .] Ich möchte Menschen in einem Satze schildern, ein Erlebnis der Seele auf einer Seite, eine Landschaft in einem Worte! (6)

The central idea expressed here is that of reduction, which provides the direct connection between Altenberg's method and that employed by Rosei. He describes the process of producing poetry as an act of "Verdichten"; the condensation into literary form of a large amount of experiential and theoretical material (Bartens, 95).

Although *Rebus* is routinely referred to as a novel, it can be described with equal accuracy as a collection of thirty-five short tales. The book's title is programmatic: *Rebus* reflects the complex puzzle-like narrative model upon which it is constructed (Rahm, 335). Like Altenberg, Rosei views Vienna as a collection of fragments. Talking about *15000 Seelen,* Rosei explained how the impossibility of describing his world as a totality had become clear to him; something was always missing from the picture. To compensate for this, he adopted a method of examining the same material from a number of different perspectives (Schwarz, 16–17). In *Rebus,* he develops this method further, using the technique of "kaleidoscopic narration" to reflect the complexity of the city. As one of his protagonists explains:

> In der Welt, da passiert vieles gleichzeitig. Eins neben dem anderen. Eins hinter dem anderen und eins vor dem anderen — aber alles gleichzeitig — wie in einem dieser Kaleidoskope! (R, 42).

The metaphor of the kaleidoscope is revealing as it points to the constant interaction between the twin processes of collecting and sorting, which both Altenberg and Rosei utilize in writing Vienna. In "Peter Altenberg als Sammler," Altenberg identifies himself as an "einfach fanatischer Sammler" (NA, 191–92), while in a description of his method, Rosei aligns himself with individuals routinely engaged in collecting evidence, such as the detective and the ethnologist (Schwarz, 3). Neither of these persons, however, is content with merely amassing data; they also seek to make sense of the world through processes of sorting, ordering and analyzing. Similarly, Simmel, Kracauer and Benjamin set out not only to collect fragments of modernity, but also to "complete the fragment, [...] to redeem it aesthetically, politically or historically" (Frisby 1985, 271). As Benjamin, himself an inveterate collector, pointed out in his *Passagenwerk,* continually rearranging and reordering a collection means that not only are the objects which make up the collection constantly seen in a new light, but that also new correspondences between them become apparent (GS V, 274). In other words, the twin processes of collecting and sorting characterize a dynamic method of approaching and writing the city, adopted by social theorists and literary authors alike.

Altenberg and Rosei both bring a degree of self-reflexivity to the process of sorting their collections of images, scenes, conversations and experiences taken from everyday life, and placing them in new literary constellations. In "Das Erlebnis," Altenberg closes a reverie on the relationship between lived experience and story-telling with the following lines:

"Peter, was Sie immer Apartes erleben! Aber wieso grad' Sie solche Sachen, und nie ein anderer?!?"

"Ich erlebe sie, weil ich sie mir erdichte!" (NF, 60–61)

In *Rebus,* the reader is reminded that, "alles ist eine Frage des Standpunkts" (175), and this is a point which Rosei later pointedly reiterated, by claiming that he could have used the material out of which he created *Rebus* to produce a textbook on the sociology of the modern metropolis (Schwarz, 41).

Rosei's approach to writing the city has, then, been influenced by modern urban theory. This is perhaps the only significant difference between his method of writing about the city and that adopted by Altenberg. But what are their findings? In the remainder of this study, the focus shifts from the approach itself to its product, with a view to comparing the accounts of Vienna 1900 and Vienna 2000 presented by Altenberg and Rosei respectively. I will do so by collecting and reassembling fragments of their texts in new constellations, considering the role of the social type, the nature and location of socio-cultural difference, social interaction in the city, locations of consumption, the money economy, production and technology, and visions of the future in their versions of the written city.

Rebus opens with the image of a piece of crumpled-up paper blowing down the street upon which is written:

NULLEN & STARS
SIOUX
MAORI
SPIESSER/GAUNER/BÜRGER
GRÖSSE QUANTEN KNALL (NICHT VERGESSEN)
ANALIESE UND EINBILDUNG (JAWOLL!) (R, 7)

Unlike a classic detective story, the significance of this list is not explained later in the text. It does, however, provide the reader with an important clue to the ethnographic approach taken in the text. And in an interview, Rosei confirmed his interest in such methods, stating that in *Rebus,* he observed the Viennese as though they were Maori (Bartens, 150). For Rosei, then, Vienna becomes the place where he, like the figure of the flâneur in Benjamin's analysis, goes "botanisieren auf dem Asphalt" (GS I, 538), identifying and classifying the social types he meets there.

This technique, often employed in nineteenth-century fiction and social reportage, is also characteristic of Altenberg's method of writing about the city. In *Wie ich es sehe,* he uses social types such as the diligent and uncomplaining chamber maid, the vain and greedy young society woman, artists, petty officials, street sweepers, cafe owners and clientele, pimps, "süße Mädels" (young lower-class women who were the playthings of the aristocracy and the *haute bourgeoisie*), and bourgeois sons and their fathers, with both comic and critical intent. Using this technique, he provides a nuanced account of a city in which the power struggle between old and new, between the aristocracy and the bourgeoisie, is complicated by a long-standing cleft between the rich and the poor.

Altenberg's use of the social type also highlights the problematic status of individualism in the modern metropolis. Particularly when he is writing about women, he makes use of detailed descriptions of clothing to establish social types. Yet fashion is a curious signifier of social type, for it works both to display and to disguise individuality. For Altenberg, as for his contemporaries, Loos and Simmel, fashion highlights the contradiction between promoting and concealing the self, between intensified subjectivity (egocentrism) and the leveling tendency of modern society.[7] However, while Simmel and Loos emphasize the importance of maintaining a strong sense of individuality under the protection of non-conspicuous clothing which can function as a mask, Altenberg shows what happens when the mask slips. He explores the dangers of pathological individualism with reference to a familiar trope at the beginning of the twentieth century: nervous illness.[8] Diagnosed by a psychiatrist at the age of twenty-four of being incapable of conforming to middle-class norms (Barker, 32), Altenberg used his own experiences to document the social type of the neurasthenic who seeks to overcome his nervous illness with recourse to alcohol and sleeping tablets. Paradoxically, he employs the social type to explain the consequences of extreme individualism.

In his presentation of life in Vienna in the last decades of the twentieth century, Rosei also demonstrates the dialectic between social type and individual. In the first section of *Rebus,* "Strassenbild" we observe a number of social types, including "der Trenchcoatman," a detective-like figure complete with notebook, a passer-by who might be a professor, a punk, an (imagined?) large-breasted woman, a crowd, an office worker, a down-and-out, a man with a dog, and a woman with a hat and suitcase. In this scene, none of the figures have names and the only connection between them would seem to be their chance meeting on the same street at the same time. Yet a number of these figures appear at other points in the novel, where they are named and the connections between them and other figures become clear. Thus, the passer-by who may be a professor is revealed to be Professor Potoschnigg, author of a book entitled *Mythos der Moderne,* husband of the opera singer, Olga, and father of the little girl in the Mercedes automobile seen in the second chapter. Other figures are less easily identifiable, but the office worker may be Kohn, while the large-breasted woman may be his sometime girlfriend, Elsa. Using this technique of switching from social type to individual, Rosei attempts to show how stereotypes are created and destroyed in the social tapestry of the metropolis.

The spectrum of social types present in *Rebus* demonstrates the complex social structure of Rosei's Vienna. Circulating through the text, we find politicians, activists, terrorists, businessmen, the homeless, foreigners, actresses, an opera singer, a journalist, a theater director, a writer, an architect and others, each of whom allows Rosei to present a different way of experiencing the city. The architect, Baulöw, first appears in the penultimate section of the book, in a chapter entitled "Architekten." Here, we find him in conversation with Kayman, head of a multi-national electronics firm. The juxtaposition of these two figures allows Rosei to highlight the connection between building in the concrete sense and the power invested in building up a "business empire." The connection between architecture and the display of power becomes apparent in the discussion between Kayman and Baulöw about plans for Kayman Inc.'s new European Head Office. While at the end of the nineteenth century, the Ringstrasse, with its array of impressive public buildings, became a signifier of the ascendant liberal bourgeoisie, in Rosei's Vienna, it is global capitalism that is displaying its "Megalomanie, Machtanspruch" (R, 227) and its desire for hegemony. Like the Ringstrasse, the new Kayman Headquarters is to draw its symbolic effect from an eclectic range of architectural styles:

> In der Mitte, als Zentrum, der Goldene Schalter oder Stecker — ein Schrein: ganz nach der Form, wie die Inder das machen: Amritsar! Oder auch Kambodscha: Angor Wat! Karnak. Ein bißl Stonehenge habe ich auch dabei: also Zentralbau, Rotonde und Symmetrie. Rundherum habe ich dann Klassizismus zug'legt, jede Menge: Rampen, Säulenfoyers; viel Archaisches garniert — Korinthisches — Jugendstil . . . (R, 227)

Fittingly, the headquarters of the multi-national Kayman Inc. will draw inspiration from Western and non-Western architectural sources alike. As well as displaying the global power of the electronics empire, the planned building is also symbolic of cultural difference.

At the beginning and at the end of the twentieth century, cultural difference plays an important role in defining the nature of Viennese city life as documented by Altenberg and Rosei. In the summer of 1896, an "African village," peopled by the Ashanti, was erected in the zoological garden in the Viennese Prater. Altenberg was a regular and fascinated visitor at the exhibition and his experiences inspired him to publish a collection of sketches under the title *Ashantee* (1897). As a number of his contemporaries noted in their reviews of Altenberg's book, these texts set about revealing the inherent racism of late nineteenth century Viennese society, and also demonstrate the Ashanti's awareness of the role that they are required to play in Vienna (Barker, 114):

> Ganz närrisch ist es. In Afrika könnten wir so nicht sein. Alle würden lachen. Wie "men of the bush," ja, diese. In solchen Hütten wohnt niemand. Für dogs ist es bei uns, gbé. Quite foolish. (A, 14)

However, Altenberg does not reflect on the significance of the location of the "African village," ghettoized and on display in the zoological garden. Paradoxically, although for him, the Ashanti symbolize "freedom, nobility and naturalness" (Simpson, 236), they are effectively imprisoned in the center of the city.

While the Ashanti were on display in the center of the city, the foreigners in *Rebus* are less immediately visible; along with the unemployed, they occupy the unnamed outer suburbs (R, 142). In this socially and geographically stratified city, they are almost as far removed from the glamour of the city center (the location of art, culture and corporate headquarters) as the homeless people who scavenge on rubbish heaps located "vor die Stadt hinaus" (R, 37). Although not on exhibition like the Ashanti, the social type of the foreigner in Vienna is clearly marked out as different through his idiosyncratic use of the German language (R, 142–49). And the racist attitudes that Altenberg laid bare at the beginning of the twentieth century are still present at its end. Talking to Baulöw, Kayman maintains: "Die Slums gehören ausgeräuchert — mit Stumpf und Stiel. Da braucht man eine harte Hand. Wir haben viel zu viele Ausländer hier" (R, 230). In the light of such statements, it should not come as a surprise to find that Rosei's Vienna (like Thomas Bernhard's or Elfriede Jelinek's) is also a place where anti-Semitism continues to flourish (R, 108; 179).

In both Altenberg's and Rosei's texts, such attitudes take root in a socially stratified city, in which there is limited interaction between the different social types that inhabit the city. In "Geselligkeit des Abends im Kaffeehaus" (LA, 235–36), a prose sketch that ostensibly discusses the nature of sociability, Altenberg paints a bleak picture of restricted social relations in modernity, showing that sitting together around a table is no guarantee of true empathy. Revealing the influence of Edgar Allan Poe on Rosei, in *Rebus*, the lack of social interaction in the city is symbolized by the figure of the man in the crowd. This figure is presented in an ambivalent fashion; while at times, he is described as heroic in his individualism (R, 189), soon after, he is shown to be in an unhappy position of isolation (R, 193). Yet the individual figures in *Rebus* are also linked through a web of personal and social connections. This representation of a "freie Verbindung der einzelnen" (R, 107) is very similar to Simmel's diagnosis of the complexities of social identity in the metropolis, where the individual stands at the intersection of the various social circles of which he is a member (119–20). Like Rosei's figure of the man in the crowd, the individual in Simmel's analysis of metropolitan life is simultaneously presented with new freedoms, and bound by new restraints.

Logically, there is a discrepancy between the ideal of a "freie Verbindung der einzelnen" and a stratified city, and in *Rebus* this is reflected upon in the idea of "Ungleichzeitigkeiten zwischen Überbau und Volk" (R, 136). A few chapters later, the claim is made that only the free-floating elite are able to avail themselves of the flexibility of social structures based on the idea of the network (R, 170). Significantly, this strong claim is immediately juxtaposed with a different conception of the social structure. Kayman explains that the criss-cross effect often to be found in the interiors of modern trains, where it is impossible to tell which stripe crosses over and which under, symbolizes the interdependence of the elite and the masses. But there is more to this pattern, which Kayman describes as follows: "ein Strich von links, einer von rechts, einer von oben, einer von unten — alles durcheinander!" (R, 171). As such, it symbolizes the dismantling of established class and political structures in Austria which, as commentators such as Armin Thurnher argue, finally contributed to the striking rise in popularity of the FPÖ (the Austrian Freedom Party) in the 1990s.

However, even as old class structures are being dismantled (R, 65, 86), in the chapter entitled "Waldsterben," the idea of a red-green revolution takes shape, backed up in a later episode by the specter of a general strike (R, 262–63). This is another point of connection between Altenberg and Rosei, since *Wie ich es sehe* includes a cycle of sketches under the title, "Revolutionär." In "Gesellschaft," one of the sketches in this cycle, Altenberg uses the description of a stylized soiree to explore the conflict between the established (aristocratic/haute bourgeois) and the emergent (social democratic) social orders. As early as 1896, Altenberg is to be found questioning the aristocracy's mythical status and so prophesying the demise of their power and influence (Barker, 104–5). Like Rosei, Altenberg presents the city as the locus of social confrontation. And indeed, twentieth-century Vienna has seen its fair share of conflict: from the May Day parades and language riots that shook Vienna in 1890 and 1897, respectively, to the storming of the Palace of Justice in 1927, the civil war of 1934, and then the mass demonstrations against the coalition between the conservative People's Party (ÖVP) and the populist Freedom Party (FPÖ) in the winter of 2000–2001.

The focus on socio-political conflict and confrontation paints a rather different picture of Vienna from the one commonly found in guidebooks, both at the beginning and the end of the twentieth century. In these publications, the city appears as a place for consumption par excellence, resplendent with opera, theater, museums, art galleries and literary coffeehouses. Neither Altenberg nor Rosei ignore this aspect of the city. Indeed, in *Rebus,* Vienna's great attraction and unique selling point is that at a time of increasing globalization, and the ever-greater homogenization of cities world-wide, Vienna, the "Metropole der Künste" remains a place where people want to live (R, 47). Meanwhile, Altenberg's Vienna is a prime location of consumption, and the majority of his texts are set in coffeehouses, hotels, the Prater, holiday resorts, salons, parks, concert halls, cabarets and bars. Yet his is no "heile Welt," and these places of leisure are the setting for his often biting cultural criticism. He is, for example, particularly fascinated by the *demi-monde,* the shady world of prostitutes, destitutes, and their exploiters. The social conflicts and double standards dealt with in stories such as "Nachtcafé" (NA, 149–50) are, however, not peculiar to these seedy locations. As we have seen, Altenberg exposes the ingrained racism of the Viennese bourgeoisie in his sketches focusing on the Ashanti, and highlights social conflict in his texts located in the "civilized world" of the bourgeois salon. Similarly, Rosei turns the glamorous world of the Opernball into the backdrop for racist attitudes, political sleaze, and a catfight between two "respectable" women (R, 247–57). Both Altenberg and Rosei lay bare the connections between the rarefied world of high culture and the dark side of modernity.

It was in part Rosei's talent for making unsettling connections and disrupting widely-held assumptions about the nature of Vienna that led Albert von Schirnding, in his 1990 review of *Rebus,* "Per Geisterbahn in den Hades," to argue that the readers of *Rebus* find themselves simultaneously in the Vienna portrayed by Schnitzler, Horváth, Helmut Qualtinger, and Bernhard — and in Hades. Von Schirnding's evocation of the ghost train in conjunction with Vienna immediately calls to mind the amusement park in the Prater, which is another key location in Altenberg's texts, and indeed, a place which fascinated many of Altenberg's contemporaries, such as Loos, Kraus, Schnitzler and Felix Salten (1869–1945). The latter's investigation of everyday life in the "Wurstelprater" focuses on its status as a magical "other" separated from the rest of Vienna by a viaduct. It is a place where normal rules governing social interaction are suspended (Salten, 5). Similarly, in "Große-Prater Schaukel," Altenberg describes the "otherness" of the Prater by using absinthe intoxication as a metaphor (WT, 172–73). Yet both he and Salten also show how this "otherness" is integral to life in Vienna at the turn of the twentieth century. In these texts, the Prater is a prime location of modernity, a place where the re-enchantment of the modern world — which Walter Benjamin would later argue is a marker of modernity (Buck-Morss, 253–54) — becomes fully visible.

Although there is no direct reference to the Prater in *Rebus,* there is a scene where, just like Altenberg's protagonists in "Große Prater-Schaukel," Kohn and his girlfriend, the busty blonde butcher, flout convention to make love in a park. Not only that, but the scene in which the butcher leaves Kohn takes place against the backdrop of a *Volksfest,* with its roller-coaster and carousel. The carousel, signifier of the merry-go-round of social relations in Max Ophüls's film adaptation of Schnitzler's *Reigen,* is linked formally, through the idea of circulation, to another location of the consumption of entertainment which figures prominently in both Altenberg's and Rosei's Vienna: cabaret and variety theatre. Characterized by rapid turnover and a continual search for the new, cabaret and variety theatre have been characterized as archetypal sites of modernity, reflecting the continuous flux and circulation typical of the structure of the metropolis (Nenno, 148–49).

Altenberg was involved in Vienna's cabaret and variety theatre on a number of levels: as critic, writer, and as a source of inspiration for Egon Friedell's popular Altenberg anecdotes (Barker, 199). His introductory remarks on the Cabaret Nachtlicht presented him with the opportunity to reiterate his "extract theory" (BL, 164–65). And the sketch, "Maske der Frau" (PA, 384), first performed in the Cabaret Fledermaus in September 1907 (Barker, 198), is a masterly depiction of the dialectic of social type and individual that is typical of life in the modern metropolis. In *Rebus,* "Auf Hermesflügeln," the first chapter in the section entitled

"Alternativen," is set at the rehearsals for an extremely complex, extremely ambitious "Jahrmarktpawlatschen" (R, 81–87). As was the case with the Cabaret Fledermaus, there are pretensions towards the creation of a *Gesamtkunstwerk:* the huge set is being architect-designed, the Philharmonic is providing the music, Jesus, Mata Hari, Lenin and Trotsky all appear in the show, along with a horde of homeless people. The key element of this performance is the depiction of excess, suggesting that Rosei's Vienna is, in part at least, a place of excess and illusion.

Underlying the illusion, however, is the reality of the money economy. In Rosei's chapter on the "Jahrmarktpawlatsche," there are a number of references to sponsors (industry, the tabloid press) and questions about who should cover the costs. Similarly, in many of Altenberg's texts, money underpins relationships between protagonists. The most extreme example of this is the relationship between client and prostitute ("Absinth 'Schönheit'" in WS, 241–45), but it is also the case in relationships between members of a *Stammtisch* (a circle of regular drinking companions in a coffeehouse, bar, or restaurant) ("Stammtisch" in F, 60), or between the poet and his benefactor ("Pumpen" in VI, 143–44). We also find in Altenberg's work a critique of the characteristic social aspects of the money economy: for example, of the work ethic ("Pathalogisch" in N, 129), and of conspicuous consumption ("Werdet Einfach!" in F, 218–19).

Rosei works with a more self-consciously theoretical description of aspects of the money economy, which echoes Simmel's formal analysis of the metropolis as the site of the money economy (118). In *Rebus,* money is described as a fetish object and as the universal medium of exchange (R, 247), while the description of an "Automatenhalle" enables Rosei to invoke the processes of circulation typical of the money economy (R, 222). It also allows him to include hints of other theoretical works on the nature of the modern money economy. The "Automatenhalle" is called "Good Luck," suggesting a connection between money, chance and fate, similar to the constellation explored by Ulrich Beck in *Risikogesellschaft: Auf dem Weg in eine andere Moderne* (1986). The risk element of the money economy is emphasized by the "restructuring" of Kayman Inc., which leaves many of its Viennese employees suddenly redundant. Such events form part of the sustained critique in *Rebus* of "late industrial society" in which the shareholders of large corporations form the real world government (R, 207), and the elite's common interest is capital, rather than politics (R, 171).

The existence of Kayman's electronics company allows Rosei to make connections between consumption, the money economy and production.

However, his Vienna is more a site of consumption and sales, than of production. Although the headquarters of Kayman Inc. is located in Vienna, production is carried out at factories in Hannover, Malaysia, Brazil, and Seattle, and its sales offices are scattered throughout the world (R, 47). In contrast, despite his emphasis on locations of consumption, Altenberg also provides images of an industrialized Vienna, such as the following, taken from the prose sketch, "Sonnenuntergang im Prater":

> Donau, kleines Bahngeleise, große Lederfabrik, holperiges Granit-pflaster, gut genug für Schneckengang gehende breiträderige Last-wagen! [. . .] Da hatte man einen Rundblick auf bleigraue Hügel, schwarze Fabrikschornsteine und die Glut des Sonnenunterganges. [. . .] Die Lederfabrik war wie ein schwarzes Ungeheuer, und drei riesige Schornsteine sandten Rauch in die Glut [. . .]. (ML, 90–92)

Here, Altenberg is fully aware of the impact of industrialization and modernization on his Vienna. Similarly, *Wie ich es sehe* is predicated on "the coexistence of the old and new, the latest fashions and technological advances, electricity and the railways exist alongside horsedrawn car-riages" (Simpson, 9). This diagnosis of a city based on paradox bears striking similarities to the Vienna described by Loos, whose texts "ar-ticulate the experience of being torn between modernity and antiquity, modernism and traditionalism, change and stability, Neu-Wien and Alt-Wien" (Stewart, 169). In both Altenberg and Loos, we find ambivalence toward modernity and the metropolis. On the one hand, modernization offers new freedoms; but on the other it brings new forms of alienation.

A century later, ambivalence towards technology and progress is a constitutive element of Rosei's Vienna. Some voices in *Rebus* argue for the inevitability of progress: "Die Eisenbahn fahrt [sic] ja heute auch. Und was haben sie nicht aufgeführt, die Maschinenstürmer?!" (R, 62). Others, however, take a more pessimistic view: "Wir haben, dank dem Fortschritt, unsere Meere und Flüsse ruiniert, die Böden sind dabei, vollkommen vergiftet zu werden" (R, 238). It is the latter position for which Professor Potoschnigg argues in his newly-published book, *Mythos der Moderne*. His main thesis seems to be that "Wenn wir so weiter machen, gibt's bestimmt eine Katastrophe" (R, 178), which is a simplifi-cation of Benjamin's position on modernity: "daß es 'so weiter' geht, ist die Katastrophe" (GS I, 683). Earlier in *Rebus*, we find a clear echo of Marx's claim that the bourgeoisie will produce its own gravediggers (33). In "Gespräche," one of the young men discussing the state of the world voices his fear that blind faith in "progress" could lead the "so-called" developed nations to poison themselves with their own giant chemical laboratories (R, 38). This would pave the way for "Lebenskünstler" to passively assume control of the world.

Perhaps inspired by such events, in one of several science-fiction-style futuristic chapters, "Träume," Rosei offers a bleak view indeed of times to come. Were this the only possible future envisaged in the text, it would link Rosei to the hand-wringing of conservative cultural criticism, but he is (post)modern enough not to offer this as a single linear teleological future. Instead, he, like Altenberg, also uses his diagnosis of Vienna in the present to explore the possibility of a better world. In so doing, they are following up on one of the central promises of the Enlightenment, from which modernization itself draws some of its impetus. Altenberg's vision of a better world, based on true friendship rather than the false social relations of the capitalist world, is outlined in *Ashantee,* but it is in *Prodomos* (1905), the most prescriptive of his texts, that he presents his view of a better world based on hygiene and nutrition. Here, Altenberg proclaims his alliance with the diffuse *Lebensreform* movement which, as Eva Barlösius shows, began to take hold throughout Europe around the turn of the twentieth century, offering alternatives to the rapid onslaught of the rationalized and regulated capitalist world. The international Garden City Movement which, as Eve Blau demonstrates, helped to shape Red Vienna in the 1920s, developed out of *Lebensreform* ideas.

Rosei, writing well after the publication of Adorno's and Horkheimer's indictment of the Enlightenment, is less straightforwardly optimistic about the possibilities offered by "Lebensreform" as he explores the remnants of the *Mythos der Moderne*. He illuminates the search for alternatives to global capitalism throughout *Rebus* and then, in two related chapters, "Phalansterra" and "Das Umspannwerk," he finally presents two alternative, but related futures, both of which are characterized by their reliance on information and communication. In the former, it is envisaged that people will be engaged in research, learning and studying, the results of which will be fed into a communal "Wissensspeicher" (R, 264), while in the latter, the normal course of life is subordinated to the smooth circulation of information (R, 206). Both are presented as possible ways of imagining the future, not as blueprints for Utopia. The complexity of city life towards the end of the twentieth century is such that Rosei is neither willing nor able to provide easy solutions to its problems.

"Phalansterra" recalls Fourier's utopian vision, developed in *Theorie des quatre mouvements* (1808) and later works. He envisaged a world in which people would be organized into economic units consisting of 1,620 members, who would live communally in the "phalanstery." Like Fourier's Utopia, the "Phalansterra" in *Rebus* is described as a place based on self-sufficiency, where each person can live in direct contact with the soil. Social relations are to be based on love, and all property is to be collectively owned.

The status of the ownership of property signals a major difference between "Phalansterra" and the "Umspannwerk." In the latter, private ownership is the norm. Observing this never-to-be-finished construction from its margins, we (the narrative form is the third person plural at this point) are witnessing the globalized world laid bare. This world cannot be understood in terms of social relations or of national identity. It can only be grasped "von seiner Betrieblichkeit her, die an eine Verflechtung gigantischer Konzerne erinnert" (R, 206). Although this world is apparently based on the ideal of coherence and the transcendence of the opposition between interior and exterior (R, 204–5), the carnival-like atmosphere of an interior based on the endless play of difference (R, 207) contrasts starkly with the description of the landscape around the "Umspannwerk," with which the chapter ends:

> [. . .] dort, über Einschnitte und Mulden verstreut, rasten die Ausgestoßenen. Es sind die Ungebrauchten und Unbrauchbaren, die sich hier umtreiben. Durch eine Art negativer Energie, aus Verzweiflung und Enttäuschung gemacht, scheinen sie miteinander und auch mit dem Umspannwerk verbunden. (R, 209)

The final sentence of this passage holds the key to understanding Rosei's Vienna. Above all, his concern is to enable the reader to trace the correspondences between the fragments of city life presented in the text. The role of "correspondances" in writing about the city can be traced back through Benjamin to Baudelaire, whose work also exerted a fascination for Altenberg (Simpson, 3). Writing about Vienna a century apart, Altenberg and Rosei make use of similar methods to come to similar conclusions (Altenberg, *Briefe*). This fact should not surprise us, however, for in writing about the city in the latter part of the twentieth century, Rosei is bringing to his novels not only his subjective experience of the city, but also his reading of the already written city — which includes the writings of Baudelaire and Altenberg, Simmel, Benjamin and Kracauer, as well as a multitude of other literary, theoretical, and practical documents. The written city, at any given point in history, is always a palimpsest.

Notes

[1] Cited in *Die Wiener Moderne,* edited by Gotthart Wunberg (Stuttgart: Reclam, 1981), 99–104.

[2] Emperor Franz Josef first announced his plan to allow the military space of the glacis to be used for civilian purposes in 1857, and the first major building on the Ringstrasse, the Votivkirche, was conceived as a celebration of his escape from an assassination attempt (Schorske, 30).

[3] Stadt Wien, *Der Strategieplan für Wien,* http://www.magwien.gv.at/stadtentwicklung /07/01/02/strategieplan.htm (accessed 23 July 2001).

[4] There were five City Dialogues in total: "Made in Vienna. Erfolgreich im Wettbewerb der Metropolen," "Techno im Dreivierteltakt. Freizeit, Kultur und Wiener Klassiker von Morgen," "Science City — Job Factory Vienna. Wissen, Forschung und Innovation," "Das Gesicht der Stadt,'" and "Wiener Melange. Miteinander leben — voneinander lernen." For further details see: http:// www.stadtdialog.at/main_stadtgesprach.html (accessed 23 July 2001).

[5] In an interview, Rosei remarked of *Rebus* that he made use of Vienna as far as it was appropriate. However, he did not shy away from building in characteristics of other cities (Bartens, 150). Interview cited in Schwarz, *Gespräche in Kanada,* 16–17.

[6] In *Land ohne Eigenschaften,* Robert Menasse mourns the lack of a genuine Austrian *Großstadtroman* (102). Bartens (95) argues that had he had known of *Rebus,* he would have revised his opinion.

[7] For an extended discussion of the role of fashion in displaying and disguising difference in Vienna at the beginning of the twentieth century see Stewart, 98–130.

[8] The fascination with nerves, neuraesthenia and art at the turn of the twentieth century is recounted by Michael Worbs in his book, *Nervenkunst.*

Works Cited

Adorno, Theodor, and Max Horkheimer. *Dialektik der Aufklärung.* Frankfurt am Main: S. Fischer, 1988.

Altenberg, Peter. *Wie ich es sehe.* Berlin: S. Fischer, 1896. [WS]

———. *Ashantee.* Berlin: S. Fischer, 1897. [A]

———. *Was der Tag mir zuträgt.* Berlin: S. Fischer, 1902. [WT]

———. *Prodromos.* Berlin: S. Fischer, 1905. [P]

———. *Peter Altenberg: Die Auswahl aus meinen Büchern.* Berlin: S. Fischer, 1908. [PA]

———. *Bilderbögen des kleinen Lebens.* Berlin: Reiß, 1909. [B]

———. *Märchen des Lebens.* Berlin: S. Fischer, 1911. [ML]

———. *Neues Altes.* Berlin: S. Fischer, 1911. [NA]

———. *Fechsung.* Berlin: S. Fischer, 1915. [F]

————. *Nachfechsung.* Berlin: S. Fischer, 1916. [NF]

————. *Vita Ipsa.* Berlin: S. Fischer, 1918. [VI]

————. *Mein Lebensabend.* Berlin: S. Fischer, 1919. [LA]

————. *Der Nachlass,* edited by Alfred Polgar. Berlin: S. Fischer, 1925. [N]

Altenberg, Peter et al. "Unveröffentlichte Briefe über die dichterische Inspiration." *Die Literarische Welt* 8/23, 1932.

Baedeker, Karl. "Wien 1892." In *Die Wiener Moderne,* edited by Gotthart Wunberg. Stuttgart: Reclam, 1981.

Barker, Andrew. *Telegrammstil der Seele.* Vienna: Böhlau, 1998.

Barker, Andrew, and Leo Lensing. *Peter Altenberg: Rezept die Welt zu sehen.* Vienna: Braumüller, 1995.

Barlösius, Eva. *Naturgemäße Lebensführung: Zur Geschichte der Lebensreform um die Jahrhundertwende.* Frankfurt am Main/New York: Campus, 1997.

Bartens, Daniela. "Stadt ist, wo noch keiner war. Stadt und städtische Strukturen im Werk Peter Roseis." In *Peter Rosei,* edited by Gerhard Fuchs and Günther A. Höfler. Graz/Vienna: Droschl, 1994.

Beck, Ulrich. "Risikogesellschaft." In *Auf dem Weg in eine andere Moderne.* Frankfurt am Main: Suhrkamp, 1986.

Benjamin, Walter. *Gesammelte Schriften Vol. 1.* Edited by Rolf Tiedemann and Hermann Schweppenhäuser. Frankfurt am Main: Suhrkamp, 1974.

————. *Gesammelte Schriften Vol. 5.* Edited by Rolf Tiedemann and Hermann Schweppenhäuser. Frankfurt am Main: Suhrkamp, 1982.

Buck-Morss, Susan. *The Dialectics of Seeing: Walter Benjamin and the Arcades Project.* Cambridge, MA: MIT Press, 1989.

Cacciari, Massimo. *Architecture and Nihilism: On the Philosophy of Modern Architecture.* Translated by S. Sartarelli. New Haven/London: Yale UP, 1993.

de Certeau, Michel. *The Practice of Everyday Life.* Translated by Steven Rendall. Berkeley/London/Los Angeles: U of California P, 1988.

Fourier, Charles. *Oeuvres completes,* 12 vols. Paris: Anthropos, 1966–69.

Frisby, David. *Fragments of Modernity.* London: Polity Press, 1985.

————. *Sociological Impressionism: A Reassessment of Georg Simmel's Social Theory.* London: Routledge, 1992.

Kracauer, Siegfried. *Aufsätze 1927–1931. Schriften, vol. 5.2,* edited by Inka Mülder-Bach. Frankfurt am Main: Suhrkamp, 1990.

Le Corbusier. "Article X / In the East / A Few Impressions. Vienna." Translated by Clare Charters, in *Abroad in Austria: Travellers' Impressions from Five Centuries,* edited by Heinz Lunzer and Victoria Lunzer-Talos. Vienna: Austrian Federal Ministry of Foreign Affairs, 1997.

Loos, Adolf. *Ins Leere gesprochen.* Edited by Adolf Opel. Vienna: Prachner, 1981.

———. *Trotzdem.* Edited by Adolf Opel. Vienna: Prachner, 1982.

Marx, Karl. *Manifest der Kommunistischen Partei.* Stuttgart: Reclam, 1989.

Menasse, Robert. *Land ohne Eigenschaften: Essay zur österreichischen Identität.* Vienna: Sonderzahl, 1992.

Mülder, Inka. *Siegfried Kracauer — Grenzgänger zwischen Theorie und Literatur: Seine frühen Schriften 1913–1933.* Stuttgart: J. B. Metzler, 1985.

Nenno, Nancy. "Femininity, the Primitive, and Modern Urban Space: Josephine Baker in Berlin." In *Women in the Metropolis: Gender and Modernity in Weimar Culture,* edited by Katharina von Ankum. Berkeley/Los Angeles: U of California P, 1997.

Rahm, Klaus J. "Das Rätsel Wien." In *Peter Rosei,* edited by Gerhard Fuchs and Günther A. Höfler. Vienna: Droschl, 1994.

Rilke, Rainer Maria. *Moderne Lyrik.* In *Sämtliche Werke 5: Worpswede. Rodin. Aufsätze.* Frankfurt/M: Insel, 1965.

Rosei, Peter. *Die Milchstraße.* Salzburg: Residenz, 1981.

———. *15000 Seelen.* Salzburg: Residenz, 1985.

———. *Rebus.* Stuttgart: Klett-Cotta, 1990.

———. *Try your Luck!* Translated by Kathleen E. Thorpe. Riverside, CA: Ariadne, 1993.

Salten, Felix. *Wurstelprater.* Vienna/Leipzig: Rosenbaum, 1911.

Schorske, Carl. *Fin-de-siècle Vienna: Politics and Culture.* New York: Vintage Books, 1987.

Schwarz, Wilhelm. *Peter Rosei: Gespräche in Kanada.* Frankfurt am Main: Lang, 1992.

Simmel Georg. "Die Großstädte und das Geistesleben." In *Aufsätze und Abhandlungen 1901–1908, I. Georg Simmel Gesamtausgabe, vol. 7,* edited by Rüdiger Kramme, Angela Rammstedt and Otthein Rammstedt. Frankfurt am Main: Suhrkamp, 1995.

Simpson, Josephine M. N. *Peter Altenberg: A Neglected Writer of the Viennese Jahrhundertwende.* Frankfurt am Main: Lang, 1987.

Sitte, Camillo. *Der Städtebau nach seinen künstlerischen Grundsätzen.* (1889) 3rd ed. Vienna: Graeser, 1901.

Stadt Wien. *Der Strategieplan für Wien.* http://www. magwien.gv.at/ stadtent wicklung /07/01/02/strategieplan.htm (accessed 23 July 2001).

Stewart, Janet. *Fashioning Vienna: Adolf Loos's Cultural Criticism.* London: Routledge, 2000.

Tester, Keith. *The Flâneur*. London: Routledge, 1994.

Thurnher, Armin. *Das Trauma, ein Leben: Österreichische Einzelheiten*. Vienna: Zsolnay, 1999.

Wagner, Otto. *Moderne Architektur*. Vienna: Anton Schroll, 1895.

———. *Die Großstadt: Eine Studie über diese*. Vienna: Anton Schroll, 1911.

Worbs, Michael. *Nervenkunst: Literatur und Psychoanalyse in Wien der Jahrhundertwende*. Frankfurt am Main: Athenäum, 1988.

Österreichische Postsparkasse, designed by Otto Wagner and built in 1904–1906. Photograph courtesy of Annemarie Schamal.

Town hall of Vienna.
Photograph courtesy of Annemarie Schamal.

Notes from the Counter-World: Poetry in Vienna from Hugo von Hofmannsthal to Ernst Jandl

Rüdiger Görner

IN HIS SATIRICAL POEM "Goethe und Hofmannsthal" Karl Kraus (1874–1936) suggested, somewhat misleadingly, that the gap of one century between both poets had been of no stylistic consequences.[1] Thus, Kraus concluded, the reader could not tell one poet from the other. Given their impeccable (read: sterile) poetic form Goethe and Hofmannsthal, Kraus predicted, would in future become even more interchangeable.

It seems, however, that much, perhaps everything, has changed since 1900 — in Vienna and elsewhere. Would anyone nowadays feel tempted to follow Kraus's example and write a poem on Hofmannsthal and Ernst Jandl (1925–2000)? What is left for instance of Hofmannsthal's language in today's poetry? Or are we to ask how much Austrian consciousness was and is present or left, if not lost, in Viennese poetic modernism and postmodernism?

The question of what the year 1900 actually stands for has been the subject of countless intellectual explorations and debates. Some insist on associating this penultimate turn of a century with Vienna and nothing but Vienna,[2] while others wish to de-localize, as it were, this unique blending of Symbolism, Naturalism, the atmosphere of the *fin de siècle* and early Expressionism.[3] And there are others who would single out one particular non-literary phenomenon that conditioned this period such as the crisis of political Liberalism in Austria around 1900 which resulted in an overall sense of crisis and acute sensitivities amongst (predominantly bourgeois) intellectuals as regards their own position in society.[4]

In language it is poetry that articulates such sensitivities most effectively. But whether we review the poetry of 1900 or any other time there is one thought that we ought to emphasize at the outset of this essay: any genuinely great poem represents a turning point in language independent from any turns of centuries. Poems of significance are demarcations within language. They set up boundaries and transcend them at the same time, boundaries between traditional notions of speech and hitherto unexplored territories of linguistic expression. Poems mark turning points but these are points of frequent returns; for they need to be revisited in order to be understood.

Between Hofmannsthal and Jandl there were the poetic counterworlds of Paul Celan (1920–1970), Ingeborg Bachmann (1926–1973) and Christine Lavant (1915–1973), to mention but a few; but these poetic landscapes were full of deep ruptures and void spaces yet filled with unheard of rhythms, harsh melodies and haunting images only to be perceived by what Lavant called "Aber-Augen" ("eyes of the But" and in the old meaning of the word "Aber" as part of a compositum: "plentiful eyes").[5] These poems of alienation reflected the soulscape of a tormented century. It seems though that both of its poles, the years 1899–1900 and 1999–2000, were — in lyric terms — conditioned by a type of poetry that encouraged self-referential poetic reflection. Yet, whether such reflection generated, in turn, a particular form of poetry is, perhaps, more difficult to prove. In Hofmannsthal's case this self-referential reflection referred, in the first place, to the very material of poetry, namely words. It included, perhaps surprisingly, the gradual "elimination of the Self" as a gesture of the poet by which he indicated an acute sense of identity crisis.[6]

This said, the poetry that emerged at both ends of the last century is related to aesthetic discourses that were not altogether too dissimilar. In both cases a plurality of styles was prevalent, albeit in different degrees. This very plurality corresponded with a dissolution of particular traditions, a tendency which was evidently opposed already by the young Hofmannsthal through his insisting on the classical canon of poetic forms.

One of the most intriguing texts to consider in this case is Rainer Maria Rilke's lecture "Moderne Lyrik" given in Prague in March 1898. The important issue is that in his lecture, Rilke recognized the significance of early Hofmannsthal as a poet whose approach to poetry was informed by a remote world of magic, Romanticism and French symbolism, by dreams and fairy-tale like dispositions. Rilke did not associate him, however, with Viennese modernism. According to him, the first voice of modern Vienna was Peter Altenberg (1862–1919) with his poems in prose. Altenberg's sketches or miniatures revealed the "inner elements of Vienna" with all its architectural nuances, its at the same time hermetic and worldly atmosphere, its fashions and eccentricities. In a sense, Altenberg was building with his miniatures a second Vienna next to the existing one.[7] The actual conception of modernism behind Rilke's characterization of Altenberg's art suggested that neither poetry nor prose nor 'poetic prose' should attempt to emulate reality. Rilke did not portray Altenberg as a narrator who was mimetically describing what he saw. On the contrary, Rilke saw Altenberg as a poet who had taken minutes of the city, as it were, even "mit der größten Pünktlichkeit" (with greatest diligence and exactitude). Rilke added that this way of depicting the city resulted in creating some primitive beauty ("unsagbare primitive Schönheit").

The use of the word "primitive" here is puzzling. We are not to confuse this with, say, the evocative simplicity of Paul Gauguin's art which Rilke had not yet encountered.[8] Altenberg's "primitiveness" referred in Rilke's reading of these poems in prose to their elementary character and sheer sobriety. Rilke found them so fascinating because of their contrast to the voluptuous world of the *fin de siècle* but also bourgeois coziness, the ever festive street life and the serene façades of the houses (Rilke actually calls them "Häuserstirnen" — the house's foreheads, thus creating a metaphor reminiscent of Altenberg!).

As regards his own development Rilke's essay "Moderne Lyrik" represented but a foretaste of his own "breakthrough to Modernism" which occurred, according to general consensus, between 1906 and 1910 with the *Neue Gedichte* and *Die Aufzeichnungen des Malte Laurids Brigge*.[9]

The interesting point about Rilke's early reflections on modern poetry is, however, his fascination with Altenberg's anti-mimetic approach to writing. Nowadays, we view this approach as a first step towards the autonomy of the lexemes and with it the establishing of hermetic poetry. Some even argue that one main feature of modernist poetry around 1900 was its emphatic incomprehensibility.[10] One example for this verdict is Gotthart Wunberg's comment on Hofmannsthal's poem "Lebenslied"[11] which reads as follows:

> Ein Gedicht wie Hofmannsthals 'Lebenslied' beispielsweise ist schlechterdings unverständlich. Es vermittelt aber den Eindruck, daß, wer den Wohlklang von 'Adler, Lamm und Pfau,' das Salböl aus den Händen der toten alten Frau' usw. auch nur hört, diesen Text bereits versteht oder doch verstehen könnte.[12]

Even if we accepted this view we would still need to investigate *why* Hofmannsthal's poem represented this ultimate challenge to hermeneutics or, to put it more crudely, we would have to try to comprehend the poem's incomprehensibility, the reasons for it and the very function of a deliberately, or at least seemingly, incomprehensible poetic composition.

Wunberg has argued that Hofmannsthal's and Georg Trakl's (1887–1914) contemporaries, such as Ludwig Wittgenstein (1889–1950) and Robert Musil (1880–1942), employed the notion of incomprehensibility early on to modernist poetry. Wittgenstein, for instance, wrote on Trakl's poems: "Ich verstehe sie nicht. Aber ihr Ton beglückt mich";[13] and Musil referred to Hofmannsthal's poem as a "sinnloses Gedicht."[14]

Yet, Wittgenstein's comment on Trakl comes close to Hofmannsthal's original intentions, too. Clarifying Hofmannsthal's poetic position toward what he called in one of his early speeches "Poesie und Leben" (1896) the young poet emphatically pronounced that the only thing that mattered in a poem was its tone.[15] To young Hofmannsthal content or meaning was but one element of the lyrical atmosphere or *Stimmung* that emanated from a poem. The true element of poetry, Hofmannsthal argued further, was formed by evermore ambiguous words which he saw "dangling between God and creature."

In this essay Hofmannsthal regarded words as the sheer material of any poetry; furthermore, a poem was to him but a weightless texture of words.[16] This presupposition of poetic modernism is significant for it contradicts the image of Hofmannsthal the pure aesthete who had indulged in disregarding the social and historical conditions, or presuppositions, of art.

Hofmannsthal's emphasis on the materiality of poetry was to find echoes in Gottfried Benn (1886–1956) and, eventually, Ernst Jandl. In his essay "Das Gedicht zwischen Sprachnorm und Autonomie" (The poem between language norm and autonomy, 1976) Jandl stated that poems knew of but one material, namely language. He demanded from the poem to be, or become, identical with a particular experience ("Erlebnis") thus defining the poem as a linguistic event.[17] But is Hofmannsthal's "Lebenslied" not a similar event, just as comprehensible or incomprehensible as any poem by Jandl?

So what about the "Lebenslied"? If we are to read it as an exemplary poem of Viennese Jahrhundertwende which it undoubtedly is we might examine the question what sort of event it represents for us today. This famously controversial poem reads as follows:

Lebenslied

Den Erben laß verschwenden
An Adler, Lamm und Pfau
Das Salböl aus den Händen
Der toten alten Frau!
Die Toten, die entgleite,
Die Wipfel in dem Weiten —
Ihm sind sie wie das Schreiten
Der Tänzerinnen wert!

Er geht wie den kein Walten
Vom Rücken her bedroht.
Er lächelt, wenn die Falten
Des Lebens flüstern: Tod!
Ihm bietet jede Stelle
Geheimnisvoll die Schwelle;
Es gibt sich jeder Welle
Der Heimatlose hin.

Der Schwarm von wilden Bienen
Nimmt seine Seele mit;
Das Singen von Delphinen
Beflügelt seinen Schritt:
Ihn tragen alle Erden
Mit mächtigen Gebärden.
Der Flüsse Dunkelwerden
Begrenzt den Hirtentag!

Das Salböl aus den Händen
Der toten alten Frau
Laß lächelnd ihn verschwenden
An Adler, Lamm und Pfau:
Er lächelt der Gefährten. —
Die schwebendunbeschwerten
Abgründe und die Gärten
Des Lebens tragen ihn.[18]

To begin with, both the poem's relevance to our own post-modern experience and its intrinsic comprehensibility are striking. For we are sufficiently post-modern to understand only too well what it means to have an heir as the subject of a poem who squanders the unction from the hands of a dead lady on symbols of power, peace and vanity. Are we not facing a similar sense of the past and the dead gliding away whilst we can only appreciate their legacy in aesthetic terms like the heir of the poem who perceives them as dancers? Do we not pretend like this very heir, who has no conception of the significance of his heritage, that nothing is threatening us and that we acknowledge with a feeble smile when certain aspects of life signal to us that death is upon us? We, who have lost any notion of a firm point of view, we know what it means when the heir beliefs every place where he finds himself to be a threshold or transition towards yet another event, or wave of fashionable thought. Like Hofmannsthal's heir we simulate a close relationship with nature but, in fact, we have lost our intimate connection with her. We can indeed recognize ourselves in the carefree smile of this turn of the century heir and identify with his eminently bearable lightness of being which turns even abysses into places of light-hearted entertainment. What is, perhaps, less comprehensible for us today is the fact that Hofmannsthal still had sufficiently naïve concepts and rhymes at his disposal to express this complex conception of what it means to waste one's own (cultural) heritage.

In contemporary Austrian poetry it was evidently the late Ernst Jandl who came closest to this combination of sophistication and supposed naivety. Hofmannsthal had observed in his "Lebenslied" the growing darkness of rivers ("der Flüsse Dunkelwerden") as a boundary for the ever unfolding pastoral of a — pretended — carefree "Hirtentag" (day of the herdsman); and we find a distant reverberation of this notion in one of Jandl's last poems on a "dark day" which reads as follows: "dunkler tag / es ist ein dunkler tag vom wetter her / und von innen ist er es noch mehr / ach ließe das herz sich doch abschalten."[19]

Or are we to argue that any such similarities between poetic conceptions in Austrian poetry around 1900 and 2000 are but fallacies? Is it not true that virtually all social and political parameters and, consequently, their aesthetic transformations have changed beyond recognition? Are we therefore not better advised to look for the effects of these radically different "conditions poétiques" on the actual poem then and now?

One striking difference between 1900 and 2000 is the fact that mankind has experienced what it means to live through, or rather survive a "siècle de la fin,"[20] a century that defined itself by a series of "finalities," including its most unspeakable one, the so-called "final solution." At the various ends of such finalities we now discover words that serve like intellectual synapses, to use Durs Grünbein's appropriate phrase. We speak of the "Anschlußfähigkeit" (potential of continuation) of particular words or ends of verses; but we are equally aware of the deep fractures than run right across our perception of the cultural heritage that informs our myths and images. The principle question is whether poetry can retain under such circumstances its traditionally seismographic function, detecting and reflecting socio-cultural fractures, or whether it has become subject to raptures itself. Can we really rely on the unbroken faculty of poetry to create neologisms through which it opens up new cognitive and emotional "spaces" as the poet and translator Raoul Schrott suggests.[21]

If we attempted to define the specificity of Austrian poetry in 1900 and 2000 then one might refer to a certain melancholic expressiveness which is, for example, much in evidence in the second famous — and emphatically comprehensible — "Lebenslied" of the early twentieth century by Franz Werfel (1890–1945).

Ein Lebenslied

Daß einmal mein dies Leben war,
Daß in ihm jene Kiefer standen,
Und Ufer schlafend sich vorüberwanden,
Daß ich in Wäldern aufschrie, sonderbar,
Daß einmal mein dies Leben war!

Wo Ufer schlafend sich vorüberwanden,
Was trug der Fluß mit Schilf und Wolk' davon?
Wo bin ich, — und ich höre noch den Ton
Von Ruderbooten, wie sie lachend landen,
Wo Ufer schlafend sich vorüberwanden.

Wo bin ich, — und ich höre noch den Ton
Von Equipagen, dicht im Kies verfahren,
Kastanien- und Laternensprache waren
Noch da und Worte, — doch wo sind sie schon?
Wo bin ich, — und ich höre noch den Ton.

Kastanien- und Laternensprache waren
Noch da und Atem einer breiten Schar,
Und mein war ein Gefühl von Gang und Haaren.
Oh Ewigkeit! — Und werd ich es bewahren,
Daß einmal mein dies Leben war?

It is a poem about experiencing life in retrospect. Life is but a memory the poem seems to suggest. But this memory begins to alienate the poet from his own past. He finds it difficult to associate himself with the landscape and atmosphere of his origins. Yet, he is not estranging himself completely from his past; for he can still perceive the very sound of his former life. The entire third stanza is dominated by the question "where am I" — in relation to the own past, its words, images and sounds. The evident evocativeness and expressiveness of the poem is matched by a deep sense of melancholy which originates in the unsettling question whether the poet will be able to retain his memories of his own past at all. Or, to be more precise, will he in future still identify these recollections as part of his own life or dissociate himself from them?

But how do such experiences relate, if at all, to contemporary (Austrian) poetry? When the periodical *Text + Kritik* invited Durs Grünbein, Thomas Kling, Barbara Köhler, Friederike Mayröcker, and Peter Waterhouse to select fifty poems which would in their view represent aspects of the twentieth century[22] they opened their anthology symptomatically enough with a poem written around 1800 and one of the finest ever created in the German language: Friedrich Hölderlin's (1770–1843) "Hälfte des Lebens." With this choice the poets suggested, it seems, that any turn of a century begins some hundred years earlier. In this anthology we find, among others, the following poets: Hofmannsthal's poem "Unendliche Zeit," Rilke's "Alkestis," "Archäischer Torso Apollos," as well as the eighth of his *Duineser Elegien,* Trakl's "Grodek" and "Landschaft." We re-encounter poems by Jandl, H. C. Artmann, Ingeborg Bachmann ("Wahrlich"), Celan, Franz Tumer ("Sätze von der Donau") and Mayröcker. Together, they complement what Hermann Korte calls afterward in his essay "Energie der Brüche";[23] for these poems represented in this anthology reflect the very raptures that have conditioned the twentieth century but also the "energy" they have released. The fractures in question are, for instance, the discrepancies between the remnants of mythology (Rilke's "Alkestis") and the ordinariness of daily life, between landscape as a breeding ground for death and the indifference toward its sheer beauty and between language as an instrument of meaningful communication and the inadequacy of words. While, for instance, in Rilke's poetry metamorphosis was still treated like a genuine experience with the implication that the world as such could turn and change, Jandl would only consider mere words not worlds to turn — around themselves inviting the reader to indulge in unashamed self-referentiality but without being able to change anything at all in social terms.

Perhaps this is the moment to ask whether the label Austrian or even Viennese poetry that can claim to be more than just poem written in the Viennese dialect is in any way appropriate or helpful. Is there anything typically Viennese about Hofmannsthal's "Lebenslied" or Peter Waterhouse's poem "Der gemeinte Mensch"? The latter poem opens, at least, with an explicit reference to the "Kaffeehaus" as a place where you "cough into your newspaper" and become part of a society in which you avoid socializing however.

In some of his poems in the Viennese vernacular Jandl encountered the problem of having had to write the poem twice, first in Viennese and then in German translation.[24]

Writing in Vienna like in any other place can mean to purposely avoid local subjects and concerns. The more prevalent approach has been, however, to use local flair — and not only that of the Kaffeehaus — and turn it into an expression of the human condition as such. Ilse Aichinger's poems on Vienna, such as "Gonzagagasse" and "Das Geburtshaus," prove the point.[25] Her Vienna is veiled by memory which, in turn, commands such a poignant immediacy that the reader takes it for a poetic snapshot of today's Vienna.

Perhaps Vienna inspires in poets a deeper and at once more playful sense of surrealism than many other cities given the overpowering presence of the past at virtually every corner. Whether the supposed 'incomprehensibility' of some poems by Hofmannsthal was an early expression of the surreal atmosphere in Vienna or whether this impression emerged first in proper poetic terms from the Wiener Gruppe in the 1950s around Oswald Wiener (b. 1935), Konrad Bayer (1932–1964), H. C. Artmann and Gerhard Rühm (b. 1930) is open to debate. But this surrealism is real and alive in Viennese poetic texts in 2000 through, say, Friederike Mayröcker, Franzobel (b. 1967) and, up to a point, Elfriede Jelinek (b. 1946). It is a surrealism "between the established discourses"[26] but distinctly different from, say, Ingeborg Bachmann's self-asserting "Ich" that escaped Viennese surrealism by opting for "emigration" to Rome. It seems though that Bachmann's myth-like impact on contemporary poets today is much exaggerated.[27] It would be difficult, in fact, to trace any aspect of Bachmann's poetic legacy in recent poetry from Vienna or indeed Austria on the whole. Instead the Jandl/Mayröcker version of poetic surrealism is more prevalent amongst contemporary Austrian poets.

But what about poetic form in 1900 and 2000? To begin with, there is only a handful of poets who have never aspired to creating a large poem. Hofmannsthal belonged to those very few. His poetry, not to speak of Altenberg's minimalism, looks like an opposition to the great canvasses and large-scale symphonies of his time — a manifestation even against the oversized work of art. From today's perspective, the intimacy in Hofmannsthal's poems and small-scale pieces for stage stand against the claim of composers and painters to encompass an entire world through their art. His Beethoven, for example, was not the Beethoven of the *Ninth Symphony* which is evidenced by his two speeches on the composer of "the third Leonore *Overture,* (only!) the second movement of the third symphony, the adagio of the Appassionata, opus 57, opus 111, opus 130"; it was a Beethoven reduced to chamber-size, as it were, the composer with his "empty room, a piano and violin and the four instruments of the quartett."[28] And Hofmannsthal's Schubert was not the composer either who was striving toward writing his grand symphony, a desire that had to wait for Anton Bruckner, Hans Rott, and Gustav Mahler to be fulfilled. Hofmannsthal's modernism was obliged to comparatively modest scales, in musical terms closer to late Brahms and even Anton von Webern. He could not trust the medium of language in particular and artistic forms in general any longer and therefore doubted whether such fragmented language, increasingly deprived of meaning, would be suitable for expansive epic enterprises that depended on coherence.

Yet, the ambition to generate a poetic cosmos had not vanished. Rilke realized it in his *Duineser Elegien;* and even today, this ambition is alive and has led to remarkable results. Mayröcker's early experimentalism made her, too, write long poems. Julian Schutting is another prominent contemporary poet in mind who continues this tradition.[29] But the very poem that captures this expansionist mood most comprehensively is Christoph Ransmayr's (b. 1954) four-part epic lyrical composition *Strahlender Untergang* (1982–2000), which he simply calls "a letter."[30] The fact that this poem was first published some twenty years ago and is now reprinted in unaltered form seems to signify more than a publisher's ploy to continue to draw the readers' attention to one of his most important but by conventional standards rather modestly productive authors. My impression is that the decision to re-publish this poem in the year 2000 should enable it to make the impact it deserves; for *Strahlender Untergang,* Ransmayr's very first publication, represents an astonishing attempt on writing an epic poem on contemporary concerns. As such, it stands with Botho Strauss's "Diese Erinnerung an einen, der nur einen Tag zu Gast war" (1986), which owes much to Rilke and T. S. Eliot, and Jürgen Becker's epic poem *Das Gedicht von der wiedervereinigten Landschaft* (1988).

Ransmayr's poem describes a project that turns into a plea to drain a huge area and thus create a super-desert, or "mother of all deserts." In this poem Eliot's "waste land" with its cultural deprivation has lost its melancholic, if not elegiac, undertones. Instead it has a become *the* ultimate project and prophecy. The poem has a protagonist who actively champions this very project which he refers to as an "anticipation of the future." In addition to the 'desertification' of whole areas this project involves the disappearance of Man. Ransmayr's protagonist, or project leader, calls a new science into being but, with it, life as such into question. This *scienza nuova* is purely designed to organize a large-scale disappearance of all things and beings. It creates as the protagonist says the conditions for the dissolution of the Self (35). What needs to be produced is final sterility on earth and the self-abolition of life.

I read Ransmayr's *Strahlender Untergang* not only as a shockingly serene message on the conception of self-annihilation, in other words, a message from a genuine and horrifying counter-world but as *the* major counter-poem to both Hofmannsthal's and Werfel's "Lebenslied." The poet's point is that the character of the poem and its message do not depend on a particular location; he stresses that the poem was written in Vienna and at the cliffs of Trachila on the southern Greek peninsula Mani and mildly revised at the coast of West Cork in Castletownshend. In fact, this assembly of locations in addition to the desert between Adrar and Bordj Moktar where the poem is actually located endows *Strahlender Untergang* with an ubiquitous flair and underlines the universality of its message. Though being so closely associated with provincial towns at two different more or less dramatic coastlines Vienna appears to be dislocated, as it were, pushed towards the periphery and, in the case of Trachila, a potential abyss. The poet had decided to desert Vienna in order to associate the entire city ultimately with the limitless of the sea, the ocean and — the desert.

In conclusion, only the obvious can be stated: 1900 is not a rhyme for 2000, neither in Viennese nor any other poetry. Yet, there are somewhat surprising thematic affinities and resemblances both in terms of metaphor and poetic style. But no such affinity could, or should, conceal the fact that this monstrous century between Hofmannsthal and Jandl consisted of several worlds at once that separated one poet from the other. In view of the scale of the linguistic problems in general and the pitfalls of poetic expression in particular the question of whether there is a specifically Viennese solution to them seems almost redundant. The key-question that needs to be addressed, time and again, is how poetry in the German language is trying to come to terms with what had prepared the "lingua tertii imperii," to use the title of Victor Klemperer's famous investigation,[31] and how poetry in German tried to cope with the aftermath of this unspeakable distortion of its language. This was, for example, Celan's poetic and existential concern. But this problem is reflected, too, in the poets who had to emigrate. Viennese poetry in 1900 and 2000 is as much epitomized by Hofmannsthal and Jandl as it is by the exiled poet Theodor Kramer (1897–1958) with his inconsolable melancholy, even if his fate represents the very middle of the last century. But is was, after all, a melancholy that owed as much to the *fin-de-siècle* miniaturism of Altenberg as to Hofmannsthal's growing skepticism about the trustworthiness of language. Furthermore, Kramer's melancholy influenced a condition of writing that is, in parts, still present in Austrian poetry today. (Erich Fried, for example, countered such melancholy by inspiring a "poésie engagée."[32])

Kramer's tragic example illustrates that 1900, or what he called with Joseph Roth and other emigrants "die alte Welt," truly ended only in 1938. "Es ging die alte Welt um mich zugrunde" is the first line of one of Kramer's most famous and immensely touching poems ("An der Wende").[33] Yet, this old world did not perish within himself. He took it with him into his exile.

This old world in spite of all its questionable values was still present in poets as different as, say Alexander Lernet-Holenia (1897–1976), Bachmann and Thomas Bernhard (1931–1989); and some may even detect remnants of this old world, Kramer was referring to, in contemporary poets like Franz Josef Czernin (b. 1952) and Julian Schutting (b. 1937) given the sheer linguistic voluptuousness of their poetic language. Others, like Celan or Erich Fried (1921–1988), had, once and for all, rejected and overcome this legacy.

In 2000 though, (Austrian) poets are faced with a plurality of poetic legacies and their virtual presences. With the notable exception of Raoul Schrott it seems that, by and large, fewer Austrian than German poets seek to escape from these legacies by taking refuge in a more science-oriented way of writing poetry. One wonders whether Friederike Mayröcker's analogy between her childhood and a dark chamber[34] might help towards finding an explanation for this difference. Is it fair to say that Austrian (and especially Viennese) poets are, perhaps, more conscious of myths and "dark legacies" than their German (and Swiss) contemporaries? However, the need for creating poetic counter-worlds to the profanity of an ever intensifying materialism was overwhelming both in 1900 and, arguably even more so, in 2000. We are today, however, less concerned with developing a new symbolist poetry or a renewed "poésie pure"; furthermore, we tend to have reservations about a moralizing "poésie engagée." The pure and engaged type of poetry may be dead; but, luckily, a purely engaging poetry is alive again — in Vienna and elsewhere.

Notes

[1] In Karl Kraus, *Magie der Sprache,* edited by Heinrich Fischer (Frankfurt am Main: Suhrkamp, 1979), 312–13.

[2] To mention but one volume that represents this approach: Jürgen Nautz/Richard Vahrenkamp, eds., *Die Wiener Jahrhundertwende: Einflüsse — Umwelt — Wirkungen* (Vienna/Cologne/Graz: Böhlau, 1993).

[3] This is documented in volume VII of *Hansers Sozialgeschichte der Deutschen Literatur:* York-Gotthart Mix, ed., *Naturalismus. Fin de Siècle. Expressionismus 1890–1918* (Munich/Vienna: Hanser, 2000).

[4] See for example Jens Malte Fischer, "Ahnung und Aufbruch. Der junge Gustav Mahler und das Wien um 1870," in *Neue Zürcher Zeitung,* 2–3 June 2001, 49.

[5] In Christine Lavant, *Gedichte,* edited by Thomas Bernhard (Frankfurt am Main: Suhrkamp, 1988), 37.

[6] This point was first made by Gotthart Wunberg, *Der frühe Hofmannsthal: Schizophrenie als dichterische Struktur* (Stuttgart/Berlin/Cologne/Mainz: Kohlhammer, 1965), 11. It was followed up by Rolf Tarot, who coined the phrase "Tendenz zur Eliminierung des Ich" in *Hugo von Hofmannsthal: Daseinsform und dichterische Struktur* (Tübingen: Niemeyer, 1970), 227.

[7] In Rainer Maria Rilke, *Werke. Kommentierte Ausgabe in vier Bänden* (= KA), edited by Manfred Engel, Ulrich Fülleborn, Horst Nalewski, August Stahl. *Schriften* vol. 4 (Frankfurt am Main/Leipzig: Insel, 1996), 81–83.

[8] The first reference to Gauguin is in his 1907 "Briefe über Cézanne," in KA, 595 and 635.

[9] Cf. Ulrich Fülleborn, "Rilke 1906 bis 1910: Ein Durchbruch zur Moderne," in *Rilke heute: Der Ort des Dichters in der Moderne,* edited by Vera Hauschild (Frankfurt am Main: Suhrkamp, 1997), 160–80. By 1906 Rilke had also overcome his apprehension against poems in prose.

[10] One of the propagators of this thesis is Gotthart Wunberg. For further reference see his volume *Jahrhundertwende: Studien zur Literatur der Moderne* (Tübingen: Narr, 2001), 46–84 and 111–45.

[11] Wunberg states rather categorically: "Ein Gedicht wie Hofmannsthals 'Lebenslied' beispielsweise ist schlechterdings unverständlich," in Gotthart Wunberg, *Jahrhundertwende,* 49.

[12] Wunberg, *Jahrhundertwende,* 49.

[13] Quote from Gotthart Wunberg, *Jahrhundertwende,* 49 (footnote 18) — letter to Ludwig von Ficker of 28 November 1914.

[14] Gotthart Wunberg, *Jahrhundertwende* (Musil in 1931).

[15] In Hugo von Hofmannsthal, *Gesammelte Werke. Reden und Aufsätze I (1891–1913),* edited by Bernd Schoeller (Frankfurt am Main: S. Fischer, 1979), 17.

[16] Hugo von Hofmannsthal, *Gesammelte Werke,* 15 ("…das Material der Poesie sind Worte" . . . "ein Gedicht ist ein gewichtloses Gewebe aus Worten").

[17] In Ernst Jandl, *Die schöne Kunst des Schreibens* (Darmstadt: Luchterhand, 1976), 52.

[18] In Hugo von Hofmannsthal, *Gedichte,* edited by Hansgeorg Schmidt-Bergmann. (Frankfurt am Main/Leipzig: Insel, 2000), 18–19.

[19] Ernst Jandl, *Letzte Gedichte,* edited by Klaus Siblewski (Munich: Luchterhand, 2001), 109.

[20] Cf. my essay "Unterwegs zu einem neuen Fin de Siècle," in Rüdiger Görner, *Mauer, Schatten, Gerüst: Kulturkritische Versuche* (Tübingen: Klöpfer & Meyer, 1999), 181–85 and "Auf dem Weg ins fraktale Zeitalter," in Rüdiger Görner, *Mauer, Schatten, Gerüst,* 186–90.

[21] Raoul Schrott, "Der Katalog der Poesie oder über die Funktionalität ihrer Formen," in Joachim Sartorius, ed., *Minima Poetica: Für eine Poetik des zeitgenössischen Gedichts* (Cologne: Kiepenheuer & Witsch 1999), 37–43.

[22] In Heinz Ludwig Arnold, ed., *Lyrik des 20. Jahrhunderts.* Text + Kritik. Sonderband XI/1999. (Munich: Edition text + kritik, 1999), 5–62.

[23] Heinz Ludwig Arnold, ed., *Lyrik des 20. Jahrhunderts,* 63–106.

[24] This is most prominent in his penultimate volume of poetry *peter und die kuh: Gedichte* (Munich: Luchterhand, 1996), 48.

[25] In Ilse Aichinger, *Verschenkter Rat: Gedichte* (Frankfurt am Main: S. Fischer, 1991), 58 and 72.

[26] See Sibylle Cramer, "Von weiblicher Autorschaft zu feministischer Literatur. Das Beispiel österreichischer Autorinnen," in *Literarische Moderne: Europäische Literatur im 19. und 20. Jahrhundert,* edited by Rolf Grimminger, Jurij Murasov, Jörn Stückrath (Reinbek: Rowohlt, 1995), 662–89.

[27] To a most recent survey (*Einsam sind alle Brücken: Autoren schreiben über Ingeborg Bachmann,* edited by Reinhard Baumgart and Thomas Tebbe [Munich/Zürich: Piper, 2001] only one contemporary Austrian writer, Franzobel, contributed an essay — one with a decidedly surrealistic title: "Fische in der Bachmann. Eine österreichische Suppe," 101–7.)

[28] Hugo von Hofmannsthal, *Reden und Aufsätze II (1914–1924),* 69 (Zürcher Rede auf Beethoven, 1920).

[29] For reference see his volume *Aufstörung: Zwei Prosagedichte* (Hamburg: Rospo, 1999).

[30] Christoph Ransmayr, *Strahlender Untergang: Ein Entwässerungsprojekt oder Die Entdeckung des Wesentlichen* (first published in 1982; reprint Frankfurt am Main: S. Fischer, 2000).

[31] Viktor Klemperer, *LTI (Lingua tertii imperii): Notizbuch eines Philologen* (Berlin: Aufbau-Verlag, 1947).

[32] See Paul Hoffmann, "Poesie und Engagement — Paul Celan und Erich Fried," in P. H., *Das erneuerte Gedicht* (Frankfurt am Main: Suhrkamp, 2001), 69–98.

[33] In Theodor Kramer, *Die Wahrheit ist, man hat mir nichts getan: Gedichte,* edited by Herta Müller (Vienna: Zsolnay, 1999), 19.

[34] Friederike Mayröcker, *Ein Gedicht und sein Autor: Lyrik und Essay,* edited by Walter Höllerer (Munich/Vienna: Hanser, 1969), 251.

Works Cited

Aichinger, Ilse. *Verschenkter Rat: Gedichte.* Frankfurt am Main: S. Fischer, 1991.

Arnold, Heinz Ludwig, ed. *Lyrik des 20. Jahrhunderts.* Text + Kritik Sonderband XI/1999. Munich: edition text + kritik, 1999.

Becker, Jürgen. *Das Gedicht von der wiedervereinigten Landschaft.* Frankfurt am Main: Suhrkamp, 1988.

Cramer, Sibylle. "Von weiblicher Autorschaft zu feministischer Literatur. Das Beispiel österreichischer Autorinnen." In *Literarische Moderne: Europäische Literatur im 19. und 20. Jahrhundert,* edited by Rolf Grimminger, Jurij Murasov, Jörn Stückrath. Reinbek: Rowohlt, 1995. 662–89.

Fischer, Jens Malte. "Ahnung und Aufbruch. Der junge Gustav Mahler und das Wien um 1870." *Neue Zürcher Zeitung,* June 2–3, 2001, 49.

Franzobel. "Fische in der Bachmann. Eine österreichische Suppe." In *Einsam sind alle Brücken: Autoren schreiben über Ingeborg Bachmann,* edited by Reinhard Baumgart and Thomas Tebbe. Munich/Zurich: Piper, 2001. 101–7.

Fülleborn, Ulrich. "Rilke 1906 bis 1910: Ein Durchbruch zur Moderne." In *Rilke heute: Der Ort des Dichters in der Moderne,* edited by Vera Hauschild. Frankfurt am Main: Suhrkamp, 1997. 160–80.

Görner, Rüdiger. "Auf dem Weg ins fraktale Zeitalter." In R. G., *Mauer, Schatten, Gerüst: Kulturkritische Versuche.* Tübingen: Klöpfer & Meyer, 1999. 186–90.

———. "Unterwegs zu einem neuen Fin de Siècle." In R. G., *Mauer, Schatten, Gerüst: Kulturkritische Versuche.* Tübingen: Klöpfer & Meyer, 1999. 181–85.

Hoffmann, Paul. "Poesie und Engagement — Paul Celan und Erich Fried." In P. H., *Das erneuerte Gedicht.* Frankfurt am Main: Suhrkamp, 2001.

Hofmannsthal, Hugo von. *Gedichte*. Edited by Hansgeorg Schmidt-Bergmann. Frankfurt am Main/Leipzig: Insel, 2000.

———. *Gesammelte Werke. Reden und Aufsätze I (1891–1913)*. Edited by Bernd Schoeller. Frankfurt am Main: S. Fischer, 1979.

Jandl, Ernst. *Letzte Gedichte*. Edited by Klaus Siblewski. Munich: Luchterhand, 2001.

———. *peter und die kuh: Gedichte*. Munich: Luchterhand, 1996.

———. *Die schöne Kunst des Schreibens*. Darmstadt: Luchterhand, 1976.

Klemperer, Viktor. *LTI (Lingua tertii imperii): Notizbuch eines Philologen*. Berlin: Aufbau-Verlag, 1947.

Kramer, Theodor. *Die Wahrheit ist, man hat mir nichts getan: Gedichte*. Edited by Herta Müller. Vienna: Zsolnay, 1999.

Kraus, Karl. *Magie der Sprache*. Edited by Heinrich Fischer. Frankfurt am Main: Suhrkamp, 1979.

Lavant, Christine. *Gedichte*. Edited by Thomas Bernhard. Frankfurt am Main: Suhrkamp, 1988.

Mayröcker, Friederike. *Ein Gedicht und sein Autor: Lyrik und Essay*, edited by Walter Höllerer. Munich: Hanser, 1969.

Mix, York-Gotthart, ed. *Naturalismus. Fin de Siècle. Expressionismus 1890–1918*. Munich/Vienna: Hanser, 2000.

Nautz, Jürgen, and Richard Vahrenkamp, eds. *Die Wiener Jahrhundertwende: Einflüsse — Umwelt — Wirkungen*. Vienna/Cologne/Graz: Böhlau, 1993.

Ransmayr, Christoph. *Strahlender Untergang: Ein Entwässerungsprojekt oder Die Entdeckung des Wesentlichen*. Frankfurt am Main: S. Fischer, 2000.

Rilke, Rainer Maria. *Werke. Kommentierte Ausgabe in vier Bänden*. Edited by Manfred Engel, Ulrich Fülleborn, Horst Nalewski, August Stahl. *Schriften*, vol. 4. Frankfurt am Main/Leipzig: Insel, 1996.

Strauß, Botho. *Diese Erinnerung an einen, der nur einen Tag zu Gast war*. Munich/Vienna: Hanser, 1985.

Schutting, Julian. *Aufstörung: Zwei Prosagedichte*. Hamburg: Rospo, 1999.

Tarot, Rolf. *Hugo von Hofmannsthal: Daseinsform und dichterische Struktur*. Tübingen: Niemeyer, 1970.

Werfel, Franz. *Gedichte aus den Jahren 1908–1945*. Frankfurt am Main: S. Fischer, 1993.

Wunberg, Gotthart. *Der frühe Hofmannsthal: Schizophrenie als dichterische Struktur*. Stuttgart/ Berlin/ Cologne/Mainz: Kohlhammer, 1965.

———. *Jahrhundertwende: Studien zur Literatur der Moderne*. Tübingen: Narr, 2001.

Austrian Women and the Public: Women's Writing at the Turn of the Centuries

Dagmar C. G. Lorenz

A T FIRST GLANCE, THE DIFFERENCE BETWEEN the role of women in
the public sphere in 1900, at the *fin de siècle,* and in 2000, at the
millennium, appears tremendous. In terms of fashion, educational opportunities, employment, legal and civil rights, participation in the dominant culture and gender role expectations, the long-skirted, corseted
suffragettes seem light years apart from women who take their active and
passive voting rights for granted, see nothing unusual in single motherhood and abortion, and dress whichever way they choose, in skirts, pants,
shorts, suits, and gowns.[1] Yet writings of contemporary avant-garde,
Marie-Thérèse Kerschbaumer (b. 1936), Elfriede Jelinek (b. 1946), and
Marlene Streeruwitz (b. 1950) as well as somewhat more conservative
women authors, Anna Mitgutsch (b. 1948) and Barbara Frischmuth (b.
1941), reveal that serious issues remain unresolved. Male-female relationships continue to be unequal in the home, in politics, and on the job
market. Women are still barred from top positions and denied equal
access in the social arena. Even more problematic is the fact that the
prevailing mentality in the dominant culture, internalized by women at
a young age, continues to relegate girls and women to a secondary role
and thus prevents them from living up to their potential. The outside
pressures on women to be submissive and women's internalization of the
socially accepted roles reinforce one another.

The works of women writers since 1945 — Ingeborg Bachmann
(1926–73) in the unfinished novel *Der Fall Franza* (1979, translated by
Peter Filkins as *The Book of Franza,* 1999), Elfriede Jelinek in the novel
Die Liebhaberinnen (1975, translated by Martin Chalmers as *Women as
Lovers,* 1994), and Marlene Streeruwitz in *Lisa's Liebe* (1997, Lisa's
Love) — point to more subtle strategies of oppression after the Shoah
and in the postmodern era. Less transparent than the blunt exploitation
and disenfranchisement of women a hundred years earlier, misogynist
cynicism and brutality are harder to recognize and resist.[2] Ute Gerhard,

noting the inter-relatedness of feminist theory and sociological analysis, observes that gender roles became again the focus of late twentieth century critical discourse because culturally based gender difference is a constitutive aspect, perhaps even the foundation of bourgeois society and capitalism.[3] Not coincidentally, there has been a renewed interest in the works of women writers of the *fin de siècle* and the interwar period. The recent publications of almost forgotten and neglected works make an impact on contemporary writing, just to mention Veza Canetti's oeuvre published in the 1990s, the letters and prose writings of Lou Andreas-Salomé (1861–1937), and the Theresienstadt memoir of the prominent *fin-de-siècle* dramatist Elsa Bernstein (1866–1949), better known as Ernst Rosmer, at the turn of the millennium.[4] The journalist and film-maker Ruth Beckermann (b. 1952), throughout her career, Marlene Streeruwitz in her novel *Nachwelt* (1999, Posterity) by thematizing the life of Gustav Mahler's daughter, the sculptor Anna Mahler, in the United States, and Anna Mitgutsch in her novels *Abschied von Jerusalem* (1995, translated as *Lover, Traitor,* 1997) and *Haus der Kindheit* (2000, House of Childhood), examining the uncertainty of loyalties and identity as a result of the history of persecution and exile in Austria, Israel, and the United States, have explored and examined the links between past and present.[5]

The turn of a century usually does not coincide with periods of cultural and social history or perceived "movements," although "magic" dates such as the Year 2000 are often declared new beginnings. Processes identified with a new century or millennium already have a history that gradually unfolds. Generally an era's achievements are assessed in retrospect; so-called periods are usually assigned after the fact. Thus the prose writer and dramatist Veza Canetti (1897–1963) is of particular interest in this article because her writings epitomize progressive *fin-de-siècle* Viennese thought at a time when the victory of Austro-Fascism and National Socialism is imminent. Looking back from vantage point of the early twenty-first century, the trends around 1900 appear more clearly defined than they would have been to those living them. Yet, even in the case of the *fin de siècle* the sharp long-range image becomes diffuse when the achievements of individual authors come under scrutiny. Their careers often span decades and encompass a wide variety of styles and ideas. Moreover, women writers in particular have responded and continue to respond to events and social developments not specific to Austria but affecting the situation of women worldwide. One might mention the global anti-white-slavery efforts of the conservative Jewish social reformer and activist Bertha Pappenheim (1859–1936) and the role of Bertha von

Suttner (1843–1914), a member of the Verein zur Bekämpfung des Antisemitismus (Association for the Struggle against anti-Semitism), in the international peace movement.

Obviously, Austrian women's writing evolved within the wider framework of Austrian culture which, since the collapse of the Holy Roman Empire during the Napoleonic Wars, defined itself as distinct from Germany. The awareness of Vienna's history as the capital of a multi-nation empire continued to shape Austrian identity after 1918, and it reverberates even in the twenty-first century when Catholicism and the legacy of the Counter-Reformation are still important aspects of the Austrian mentality. Indeed, Marlene Streeruwitz's collages in the collection of texts, images, and excerpts *Und. Sonst. Noch. Aber. Texte I* and *Und. Überhaupt. Stop* suggest that the Enlightenment with its concept of the autonomous secular individual which is fundamental to the bourgeois values underlying other Western societies, has made few inroads into the Austrian public discourse, hence her preoccupation with the role of the Christian tradition in contemporary culture.[6] In her dramas and prose works Streeruwitz confirms the assessment of the philosopher and postwar feminist Simone de Beauvoir (1908–1986), whose early reception in Austria by Marlen Haushofer (1920–1970) brought new impulses into Austrian women's writing. According to Streeruwitz, authoritarian, religiously based views on gender and sexuality rather than rational, enlightened thought determine the psychological makeup of girls and women.[7]

By opening the private and intimate sphere to scrutiny contemporary feminist writing reveals that, despite some progress in the public arena, fundamental issues pertaining to sexual and emotional relationships, motherhood and women's work, sickness, aging and dying have not begun to be seriously discussed. Neither have the dilemmas of the "post-feminist" era, as revealed in Streeruwitz's *Lisa's Liebe*. Dressed up as a trivial romance the narrative reveals that access to gainful employment; mobility and the freedom to travel and engage in unrestricted sexual activity provide the basis for emancipation, as Streeruwitz argues. Yet in a patriarchal setting they guarantee neither an acceptable quality of life nor emotional comfort because society is not ready to accept and validate autonomous women. Worse yet, women themselves, brainwashed by the dominant discourse, have difficulty coming to terms with their new uncharted roles. They remain dependent on familiar patterns and male validation. The daily insult, as Streeruwitz calls it, the disregard for a woman's abilities and desires, continues to pose insurmountable barriers to gender equality. Placing her protagonists of *Nachwelt* and *Lisa's Liebe* in Austrian as well as in settings in the United States, Streeruwitz shows the variations of misogyny in two different Christian capitalist societies.

As elsewhere in Europe, the emancipation of women, Jews, and the working class emerged as pivotal issues in nineteenth century Austria when women and Jews participated increasingly in shaping Austria's high culture, and the proletariat began to rebel against class privileges. Critical intellectual impulses emanated from these disadvantaged groups challenging the *status quo* on all fronts. Women demanded equal rights as citizens and questioned the deeply ingrained patterns of male and Christian hegemony, criticized the militarist ethos essential to nationalism and ethnocentrism, and denounced vivisection and socially sanctioned animal abuse. As in Great Britain and the United States around 1900 women took an active part in animal protection issues. For example the journalist and fiction writer Emilie Mataja (1855–1938) was a regular contributor to publications supporting animal protection such as the publication of the Verlag des Tierschutzvereins (Humane Society), and she protested against the indiscriminate killing of song birds for food purposes in Northern Italy. She also pleaded for better treatment of farm animals.[8] The interest in animals is also evident from the empathetic portrayal of domestic and wild animals in narratives of that period, including Marie von Ebner-Eschenbach's *Die Spitzin* (1901, The Pomeranian) and *Der Fink* (1897, translated by Helga H. Harriman as "The Finch," 1986).[9] By the *fin de siècle* Vienna had attracted a sizeable Jewish population which together with other ethnic groups from the provinces of the Empire was turning the city into the ethnic melting pot so vividly portrayed in Veza Canetti's novel *Die gelbe Straße* (1932–33, translated as *Yellow Street*).[10] Canetti's novel suggests that it was in the urban metropolis, if anywhere, that opportunities for change were created. At the same time, the progress achieved by the formerly disenfranchised groups in the late nineteenth and early twentieth century evoked strong reactions, epitomized by anti-Semitic and anti-feminist movements. The disparities in Austria's capital are best illustrated by the fact that Herzl's Zionism as well as Hitler's National Socialism were conceived in Vienna, so was Bertha von Suttner's and Karl Kraus's pacifism opposing the militarism cultivated by the privileged classes. Otto Weininger's treatise on the inferiority of women and Jews, *Geschlecht und Charakter* (1903, translated as *Sex and Character*), where the coalescence of misogyny and anti-Semitism is almost complete, is a reflection of a wide-spread sentiment at the *fin de siècle*.[11] This is obvious from the countless editions the book had reached by 1933.

At the end of the nineteenth century feminism had evolved in a European and American context into a powerful movement which interacted with the major representatives of Western critical thought. Chris Weedon mentions the impact Nietzsche had on early feminists — despite his misogynist views, he offered feminists "a platform from which to criticize existing bourgeois moral and social norms and to advance women's right to full self-development as individuals."[12] The impetus Nietzsche's work provided women, despite his undeniably misogynist statements, was a basis from which to attack traditional Christian morals and the notion that the established family structures were ordained by God. Nietzsche's iconoclasm, especially his proclamation that God was dead, was viewed as an encouragement by rebellious spirits. It is no coincidence that some of his most ardent supporters were independent women such as the writer and free spirit Lou Andreas-Salomé and, like the writer and art critic Malwida von Meysenburg, one of Nietzsche's friends.

Equally important impulses came from Socialism — Marx, Engels, and Bebel. At the same time, the "classical" authors of the eighteenth and nineteenth centuries and the Humanist visions of Goethe and Schiller, Grillparzer and Stifter continued to inform the works of Austrian women writers. So did the writings of other women — each new generation built on and expanded the women's discourse established by earlier authors. Important was also the association with the larger artistic and literary movements of their age. Participants in the *fin-de-siècle* bohème, *l'art nouveau,* and expressionism, they associated with the avant-garde of Berlin, Munich, Zurich, Paris, and London.[13] Many women intellectuals, including the social reformer and writer Bertha Pappenheim, were interested in the politically and educationally more advanced situation of women in the United States and established contacts with American feminists. Veza Canetti traveled frequently to England and had connections in Berlin as well.

The rapid progress made in the development of new technologies such as film provided Austrian women authors international career opportunities. The bestseller author Vicki Baum (1888–1960) emigrated to Hollywood in 1932 where the film version of her novel *Menschen im Hotel* (1929, translated by Basil Creighton as Grand Hotel, 1930, and filmed as *Grand Hotel* in 1932) made her a world success.[14] Likewise, in the postwar era women availed themselves of the modern technological media. Ilse Aichinger and Ingeborg Bachmann made a name for themselves as authors of radio plays. Elfriede Jelinek co-authored the award winning film adaptation for Ingeborg Bachmann's novel *Malina* (1971, translated by Philip Boehm as *Malina*, 1990) and the film script for her novel *Die Ausgesperrten* (1985, translated by Michael Hulse as *Wonderful, Wonderful Times*, 1990) based on her novel by the same title.[15]

The networking characteristic of women intellectuals of the end of the twentieth century takes place on an even larger scale under the auspices of an unprecedented globalization, including the use of the Internet. Elfriede Jelinek, for example, makes an extensive display of her work and views on a highly professional website.[16] Authors become involved in the filming of their works and write for radio and television. Ruth Beckermann is equally proficient in the media of film, essay, and photo documentary. A prominent contemporary author unfamiliar with a number of cultural codes and without worldwide contacts would be hard to find. This is particularly true for intellectuals whose families were affected by the political and racial persecution and the genocide during the Nazi era and lived outside of Austria as well as for feminists who established links with writers, critics, and academics in the wake of the 1970s women's movement. Authors of different generations such as Ilse Aichinger (b. 1921), Barbara Frischmuth, Elfriede Jelinek, Anna Mitgutsch, Ruth Beckermann, and Marlene Streeruwitz have taught or lectured outside of Austria on a regular basis. As a result of the collaboration between academics and writers and the activities of different cultural agencies, there exist especially strong ties between Austrian authors and universities and colleges in the United States.

Women's writing, whether or not deliberately political, expands the range of expression and the conceptual possibilities pertaining to the lives and experiences of women. It brings women's perspectives to the interpretation of human interactions and social conditions, thereby transforming the way reality is conceptualized and discussed. By the end of the nineteenth century women as different as Marie von Ebner-Eschenbach (1830–1916), Rosa Mayreder (1858–1936), Emilie Mataja (1855–1938), who wrote under the pseudonym Emil Marriot, Elsa Bernstein, whose pen name was Ernst Rosmer, and Lou Andreas-Salomé had produced an extensive body of literature that reveals gender specific, woman-centered, attitudes toward culture and society. They described, scrutinized, and criticized the male dominated patterns structuring their world that limited the opportunities and options of women. This is the case in numerous works of fiction, for example, in Mataja's critical examination of the clergy in her novel *Der geistliche Tod* (1884, Spiritual Death), in Ebner-Eschenbach's novel *Unsühnbar* (1890, translated by Vanessa van Ornam as *Beyond Atonement*, 1997) dealing with the tyranny of marriage under patriarchal law, and in Bernstein's dramas *Wir drei* (1893, We Three) and *Witwen* (1901, Widows) which suggest that within the traditional social structures emancipated women are not allowed to prosper.[17] These women authors also opened unprecedented vistas into the traditional women's spheres of family, housework, articulated women's desires in regardless which in literary genre they wrote (Weedon 112). Moreover, explicitly or implicitly, their diaries, letters, biographical writings, novels, essays and short stories contained without fail a feminist point of view. This is true for von Suttner's challenging the military aspirations of nation states, Andreas Salomé's taking issue with Freud and Nietzsche, and the feminist Socialist Canetti, who at a time when the major demands — suffrage and legal equality — were met, reexamines the concerns raised by *fin-de-siècle* feminists.

Some of Veza Canetti's works were first published in the early 1930s. They show the unmistakable influence of nineteenth century women's realism and in their journalistic approach, the impact of the sober, unsentimental style of *Neue Sachlichkeit* characteristic of progressive interwar literature. Canetti's focus on the economic and social situation of lower middle class and working women is inspired on the one hand, by Socialist thought, on the other by Ebner-Eschenbach's women protagonists, for example in the novel *Božena* (1876) and in the narration *Lotti, die Uhrmacherin* (1880, Lotti, the Watch-Maker).[18]

Moreover, the experience of Jewish marginalization allows Canetti to examine the social mainstream from an outsider's point of view, while her Viennese socialization gives her access to an insider's perspective. Sensitized to the plight of women from her own family background, Canetti displays a keen awareness of the plight of abused women which is absent even in pro-feminist male writing. Her works provide insights into the emotional traumas of double binds that prevent the oppressed from taking advantage of their legal and material opportunities. Canetti's fiction and drama still reflect the *fin-de-siècle* debates on Socialism, feminism, and pacifism as well as the criticism of the prevailing anthropocentrism voiced by anti-vivisectionists and animal protectionists of that era. All of these concerns continued to be controversial issues in the First Republic.[19] When Canetti published short stories and several of the narratives that make up part of her novel *Die gelbe Straße* the Weimar Republic and the First Austrian Republic were already undergoing cataclysmic changes. The short period of liberalization after World War I that had brought equal rights to women, Jews, and the working class came to an end.[20] Because women and Jews were pushed out of the public sphere already under Austro-Fascism, Canetti's later works, the drama *Der Oger* (1991, The Ogre) and the novel *Die Schildkröten* (1999, translated as *The Tortoises,* 2001), were not published during her life-time.[21] Like Canetti, other authors such as Gina Kaus (1894–1985) and Vicki Baum lived abroad, unable to return to or visit their country of origin during the Nazi years. Others were deported to concentration camps, such as Elsa Bernstein. Between 1934 and 1945 oppositional discourses, be it in the public, be in literary and academic writing or in film and radio were not tolerated.

For Austrian women's writing at the turn of the millennium major aspects of in the oeuvres of Canetti and her peers are still highly pertinent, including the feminist thematic, the social critical perspective, the confrontation with fascism, and the call for gender equality as the only possible foundation of a viable society. All of these issues are present in the works of post-Shoah authors such as Jelinek, Mitgutsch, and Streeruwitz.[22] Veza Canetti, like most Austrian women writers of the last two centuries, worked with and against the language of her conservative environment. By portraying experiences such as woman and child abuse, anti-Semitism, and the exploitation of female workers by male and female capitalists contributed significantly to establishing textual conventions appropriate to women's perceptions. In fact, feminist literature intersects with other critical writing, Marxist and post-colonial theory as well as pacifist, anti-fascist, civil rights, minority, and animal rights discourses for example. Positioned between the pioneers of the nineteenth century and the postwar and post-Shoah generations, Canetti worked alongside authors who forged a progressive literary tradition with which authors could connect after the demise of National Socialism.

The modernist writings by socially aware women authors affiliated with the *Arbeiter-Zeitung* provided a platform to discuss the plight of women in the First Republic. Their textual legacy was rich in concepts and language to confront the residues of misogyny, racism, Austro-fascism, and National Socialism, and enabled authors after 1945 to produce a highly articulate. Let's go with literature and visible feminist literature of specifically Austrian dimensions.[23] Articulating women's concerns and revealing their everyday experience within Austria's patriarchal Catholic tradition and against what was left of Nazi authoritarianism and ethnocentrism was an important project to which Austrian women writers and even some male writers devoted their creative energies. Opposing the increasing xenophobia after the 1986 Waldheim scandal and the validation of Austria's fascist past and rightwing extremism fostered by Jörg Haider's Freedom Party, women intellectuals are taking a public stand alongside like-minded men of all walks of life, voicing their opposition in the media, at demonstrations, and on the internet.

Since its beginning women's literature in Austria emphasized the worldly and the mundane. In the Age of Enlightenment Vienna had become a center for women intellectuals. In the absence of an extensive convent culture a significant tradition of religious women's poetry had not developed. Major momentum was gained in the salon-era when, as in Berlin, women's literature evolved from letters, diaries, auto-biographies, and epistolary novels. These genres continue to play an important role in women's writing in addition to the forms of expression of which women availed themselves in the nineteenth century, poetry, narrative prose, and drama. With few notable exceptions, however, women dramatists rarely prevailed in the traditionally male bastion of the theater. This situation remains unchanged despite the notoriety of Jelinek's and Streeruwitz' dramas at Austrian and international theaters the productions of which are almost sure to give rise to widespread controversy (Kraft, xii).

When the bourgeois revolutionaries of 1848 ridiculed the notion women's emancipation, Austrian feminists formed associations to pro-mote women's educational and professional opportunities, including an association for female authors and artists that offered insurance and a pension fund. Yet, well into the twentieth century many women writers felt it necessary to protect their private sphere by using male or female pen names. The prose writer and dramatist Bernstein, for example, pub-lished under the pseudonym of Ernst Rosmer and the feuilletonist, poet, and novelist Emilie Mataja under that of Emil Marriot. Also Veza Ca-netti wrote under a variety of assumed names, including Veronika Knecht and Veza Magd. Women intellectuals of the Second Republic are far less hesitant to enter the public arena under their own names and to take an active part in negotiating the interests of male and female writers — Anna Mitgutsch, for example, serves as Vice President of the "Interes-sensgemeinschaft Autorinnen Autoren."

Notwithstanding their stylistic and philosophical differences the dis-tinguishing trait of Austrian women writers of this and the last turn of the century has been a remarkable political and social astuteness. Aus-tria's most notable nineteenth century woman author, Marie von Ebner-Eschenbach explored in her dramas and realistic social fiction the role and status of women within the family and as professionals. Because of her interest in the plight of the disempowered, critics described her as "the social conscience of her class."[24] Ebner-Eschenbach's works empha-size the importance of financial independence for a woman as well as her rights and responsibilities as a productive member of society. They take issue with the arranged marriages of the upper class as well as the fashionable romantic love matches celebrated in trivial literature. Stressing a woman's intellectual capabilities as well as strength and determination as positive traits, Ebner-Eschenbach thematizes work ethics and motherly traits, advocating, if need be, single or surrogate motherhood, as in *Božena*.[25] In her animal stories the author demonstrates her interest in the relationship between humans and non-humans and holds authoritarian, unilateral relationships up to criticism even on this level. Thus her popular dog story *Krambambuli* (included in *Dorf- und Schloßgeschichten*, 1883, translated as *Krambambuli*, 1908) lends itself to be read as a critique of "woman in a patriarchal society" (Rose/Kraus, 129).[26]

Ebner-Eschenbach and her peers developed a linguistic register to express women's wishes, feelings, and hopes. The early naturalistic writings by the proletarian poet and prose writer of the same era, Ada Christen (1844–1901), fascinated the *fin-de-siècle* readership because of their advocacy of free love and the open articulation of women's erotic desires. The Nobel Peace Prize winner Bertha von Suttner, known for the radical pacifism in her novel *Die Waffen nieder!* (1889, translated by Alice Asbury Abbott as *Ground Arms*, 1908 and by Andrea Hofer-Proudfoot as *Disarm, Disarm!*) tackled major ethical and social issues in her essays and prose fiction, including anti-Semitism, the exploitation of workers and women. Bertha Pappenheim, better known as Freud's *Anna O.*, published travel accounts, didactic dramas, autobiographical prose, and translations of religious and secular texts in the service of her mission to help Jewish women, fight the international trade in girls and women as well as prostitution, and rehabilitate unwed Jewish mothers and homeless girls. Especially for the latter two women their intellectual prowess and social activism went hand in hand. They were brilliant orators and teachers noted for their journalistic skills.

By the *fin de siècle* women journalists and critics had moved into the cultural forefront Adelheid Popp (1869–1939), the editor of the *Arbeiterinnenzeitung* (1892), the women's paper of the Social Democratic Party, for example. Together, Rosa Mayreder (1858–1938), Auguste Fickert (1855–1910), and Marie Lang (1855–1934) founded the journal *Dokumente der Frauen* (1899) as a forum for women's concerns. Mayreder, who examined the concept of femininity and decried the culturally and economically marginal position of women in her essays *Kritik der Weiblichkeit* (1905, translated as *A Survey of the Woman Problem*) and her critical response to Otto Weininger, *Geschlecht und Kultur* (1923, Sex and Culture), belonged to the radical wing of the feminist movement and was a member of the *Erster Allgemeiner Österreichischer Frauenverein*. After the First World War she took an active part in the Peace

Movement. Also her friend Bertha Zuckerkandl Szeps (1863–1945), a maverick who wrote about architecture, the arts, and international affairs as well as society gossip, was a well-known journalist. Another high-profile journalist and photographer was Alice Schalek (ps. Paul Michaely, 1874–1956). Best-known and satirized by Karl Kraus in the vast drama *Die letzten Tage der Menschheit* (1918–19, The Last Days of Mankind) for her activities as a war reporter during the First World War, her works include travel literature and novels.

The first generation of politically emancipated women played an important role in the first Austrian Republic and its thriving literary and political coffeehouse culture. Career opportunities for women writers and journalists were especially good in Austria's Social Democratic capital, "Red Vienna." Women were represented in all styles and genres, in the avant-garde or, like the novelist, dramatist, and film author Vicki Baum, in popular literature. Conservative writers such as the author of religious historical dramas and novels, Enrica von Handel-Mazzetti (1871–1955), the novelist Imma von Bodmershof (1895–1982), the prose writer and poet Martina Wied (1882–1957), and the poet Erika Mitterer (1906–2001), adhered to traditional forms and contents. Uncomfortable with modernity, urban culture, and ethnic diversity some of these author's were not overly offensive to the Nazi authorities. Apparently politically neutral, they continued to publish during the Nazi era and beyond.

Women writers and ideological pioneers who had taken issue with the masculine heroic discourse, favored by conservatives and fascists alike, or questioned the racial ideology fell on hard times. Mela Hartwig (1895–1963) had criticized the androcentrism of Freud's psychoanalysis in her novella *Das Verbrechen* (1923, The Crime) and opposed the assumption that women were defined by their biology (e.g., her novellas *Ekstasen* [1928, Ecstasies]).[27] In novella *Das Wunder von Ulm* (1936, The Miracle of Ulm), which appeared in Paris, she criticized the persecution of the Jews.[28] After the Nazi takeover in 1938 unwelcome authors, dissenters, and Jews were barred from publishing, forced into exile, imprisoned or murdered, and their works were outlawed. Veza Canetti, at risk as a Jew, a Socialist and a feminist, took exile in England together with her husband in 1938 and lived there, writing but not publishing, until her death in 1963. Until her departure from Austria she had been active in helping to save persecuted individuals.

The interwar period had begun auspiciously for those who had hoped for change. In the young republic it seemed possible to realize the dreams for which *fin-de-siècle* women intellectuals had struggled. Gender equality, at least on paper, was achieved; after the defeat of Germany and

Austria in 1914 pacifism had become a strong force; the Social Democratic party prevailed, at least in Vienna, and an extensive social safety net, a model for other European metropolitan centers, was being constructed. Veza Canetti, born into an assimilated family of Bosnian Sephardic descent, carried on the legacy of the progressive forces of *fin-de-siècle* Vienna. She had a keen social conscience and an eye for the suffering of others, both of which are manifest in her works. The graduate of a public college preparatory school, she provided tutoring services to needy children and as an intellectual she became a respected member of the Viennese avant-garde. She had a particularly strong affinity for Karl Kraus, already a pacifist before the First World War, whose moralistic fervor and rigorous stance as an ethicist resembled her own idealism. Canetti's own utopian vision is rooted in Vienna's urban culture and motivated by the promise of social justice held out by Social Democracy articulated in treatises like August Bebel's *Die Frau und der Sozialismus* (1879, translated as *Woman under Socialism*, 1904) and Friedrich Engels's in *Vom Ursprung der Familie, des Privateigentums und des Staats* (1884, translated as *The Origin of the Family, Private Property and the State,* 1902). The influence of women's writing is evident in her representation of reality, which is unsentimental, like that of von Ebner-Eschenbach, with whom she also shares the conviction that financial independence and the free choice of a partner are absolute necessities for a woman. The Iger episode in *Die gelbe Straße* as well as the drama *Der Oger* call to mind Engel's central thesis that in the nuclear family the wife and children are placed in the role of the proletariat, while the husband acts as the bourgeois capitalist.[29] For Canetti, the economic autonomy of the disempowered is the single most important condition for normalizing the relationship between men and women. This conviction places her outside bourgeois feminism whose representatives adhered to the concept of basic constitutional gender differences and a proclaimed "separate but equal" gender roles as expressed in Mayreder's *Kritik der Weiblichkeit* or Andreas-Salomé's writings. As is the case with the majority of women's writers of her age, Canetti seems convinced that once the obvious ideological and material barriers between the sexes are abolished, men and women will be able to enter equal partnerships. In contrast, authors after 1945, including Haushofer, Bachmann, Jelinek and Streeruwitz question that equality, let alone love and partnership, are a real option. Some authors doubt that the constitutional differences between men and women will allow for successful inter-gender interaction, while others suggest that the emotional and ideological patterns established through education, the media, and social influences are impossible to overcome. In other words, the happy endings concluding many of the literary battles of the sexes in *fin-de-siècle* literature seem no longer appropriate.

The devastation of two world wars, the dismantling of the political Left and the feminist movement between 1934 and 1945, the cultural influences of the United States and the closeness to the former eastern bloc necessitated constant rethinking of political positions, including gender roles. The reorganization of Central and Eastern Europe and the devaluation of Marxist and Socialist models led to an search for alternative structures to global capitalism with its accompanying threat to individual and cultural autonomy. With nationalism and cultural conservatism gaining currency in wide segments of the population, gender equality is anything but an issue of the past. On the contrary, the gender debates have become more complex precisely because many obstacles in the political and social arena were removed in the wake of the women's movement of the 1970s. In today's Austria as elsewhere in the Western world, the feminist discourse is less concrete and single-minded than it was in the past because the complexity of the gender problem has become obvious.

Veza Canetti and her peers advocating basic social change by modifying gender and class structures were convinced that the active social and political involvement of women and economically oppressed groups would finally produce an egalitarian democratic society. The happy ending of her drama *Der Oger,* which predates the Nazi invasion of Austria and the Holocaust, is based on an optimistic view of human nature and social possibilities. While in her novel *Die gelbe Straße* only women characters are shown to be capable of genuine kindness, *Der Oger* suggests no fundamental psychological difference between male and female characters. The differences between the sexes are caused by the misogynist culture bolstered by the class hierarchy and the political and legal system. Clearly, Canetti's work is inspired by the belief in progress. She considered the chaos of the modern metropolis a destabilizing force that provided an opportunity for fundamental change through social reform.

Growing up after the war in an era of restrictive gender roles and political conservatism Elfriede Jelinek rebelled early against her cultural environment only to experience the disillusionment of her generation after the disintegration of the 1968 movement. The daughter of a leftist Jewish father who had survived the Nazi era as a forced laborer, Jelinek was also painfully aware of the failure of the utopian Socialist project of the interwar era and the demise of the first feminist movement. Already in her earliest works she criticizes the promotion of uncritical consumerism through the language of capitalism: pop-culture and advertisement. Through language criticism she reveals the predicament of externally "liberated" women who, exposed to constant conditioning by the cliché-ridden language of their parents and teachers and lured by the mass media are rendered incapable of identifying the sources of their suffering. In *Die Liebhaberinnen* and *Die Klavierspielerin* Jelinek reveals how domestication and submission are effected through the media of the post-war mass culture by means that Herbert Marcuse, one of the most acclaimed thinkers of the German New Left, refers to in his study *A Critique of Pure Tolerance* as the "systematic moronization of children and adults."[30] Jelinek had taken part in the debates about ideology and politics conducted in the Austrian literary journal *manuskripte* since the late 1960s. Having lived in Berlin in 1972, she was influenced by the social criticism articulated by leftist intellectuals in the sixties and early seventies. In 1974 she married Gottfried Hüngsberg, a computer scientist associated with the avant-garde filmmaker Rainer Werner Fassbinder, and joined the Communist Party (KPÖ). In her works of this period Jelinek portrays the victims of capitalist society: oppressed women and underprivileged men lacking communication skills and incapable of critical thought. Not only the advertisement industry and the mass media, but also the authorities, including parents and teachers, prevent Jelinek's protagonists from developing their intellectual potential. Rather, they are socially conditioned to act against their own interests. As if in a dialogue with earlier feminists who considered gainful employment the remedy for women's oppression, Jelinek portrays women enslaved by the dead-end jobs typically accessible to them, the plight of married women abused by husbands, and the oppression of daughters by mothers who act as the enforcers of their patriarchal culture. She debunks the myths of free love and partner choice — with or without the benefit of marriage; the sexual relations of her protagonists end up being sado-masochistic power games as the lovers reproduce the interaction between fathers and mothers, fathers and daughters, daughters and sons in the nuclear family. Jelinek also exposes the social disapproval along with the inner conflicts and mental disturbance that paralyze women trying to break with the norm.

Ruth Beckermann, deliberately linking up with the progressive interwar tradition, focuses on the mentality of average Austrians, mostly men, and their profound connection to the Nazi past. For her, the interviewees in her film and book *Jenseits des Krieges* (1997, translated as *East of War*), veterans of the Second World War and their wives and children represent the radical other.[31] Beckermann reveals the impact the veterans' interpretations of their experiences have on the mentality of present day Austria, a country that elected president a man with a proven Nazi record (Kurt Waldheim) and allowed into the government a party lead by a politician known for his racist views (Jörg Haider). In the recent film *Ein flüchtiger Zug nach dem Orient* (1999, subtitled as *A Fleeting Passage to the Orient,* 1999) she reflects on the extreme marginalization as a woman and a Jew not only in contemporary Austria but also in a global context.

Jenseits des Krieges (1997) reveals that the *Volksgemeinschaft,* the national community, forged by the Nazi propaganda machine still exists.[32] With few exceptions Beckermann's older interviewees derive a positive sense of identity from the memory of the Second World War because the national community has successfully transmitted the experiences of the 1930s and 1940s, including their values, attitudes, and body language, to the following generations. Questions about past atrocities elicit frowns and a defensive crossing of the arms, common memories left unspoken evoke gestures of camaraderie and laughter, and insistent questions are answered with a raised voice or by stepping into the querent's body space. The reactions of the younger generations reveal solidarity with the fathers and grandfathers. Their loyalty is, to be sure, not without ambivalence and often unreflected. It results from close familial relationships with the veterans of Hitler's army and all of those in the prewar and war generations taken in by Nazi propaganda. It is automatic and spontaneous and reveals the long-range effects of the all-encompassing effort to brainwash and subdue the non-Jewish population. This intimacy between the generations precludes any critical judgment, let alone condemnation. Socialized in postwar Austria one of Beckermann's younger interviewees, a middle-aged woman, rejects the images and the content of the *Wehrmacht* exhibition held in Vienna in 1995 by denying that her relatives could possibly have been accomplices or perpetrators of Nazi atrocities. "Aber das hier, das macht uns glauben, daß unsere Onkel, unsere Väter Mörder sind. Denn sie stellen es ja als Mord hin oder nicht? . . . Das kann ich nicht glauben, denn sonst müßte ich mich aufhängen" (71). Through this and similar instances Beckermann's film and book reveal that Austrians have constructed a cultural memory that is acceptable to them, a memory that disenfranchises her, a Jew and a woman.

In the past two decades an increasing number of women authors have engaged in a search for Austria's Jewish tradition, its representatives and its legacy, as the major alternative tradition opposing and transforming the dominant culture in the interwar period. Streeruwitz's *Nachwelt* deals with such a memory mission: a Vienna dramatist conducts research about Gustav Mahler's daughter, Anna Mahler (1904–1988), a gifted but almost forgotten sculptor. The search for the other is at the same time a quest for self-affirmation on the part of the woman protagonist left by her lover and faced with the public indifference that crushed the name of Anna Mahler in the annals of art history.

Streeruwitz's search through the radically other for self assertion amidst destruction and violence, also thematized in *Majakowskiring* (2000), is also the motif of Beckermann's discursive film *Ein flüchtiger Zug nach dem Orient.*[33] The film revolves around the almost mythical Empress Elisabeth of Austria who wanted to travel the world and live as a stranger. The fast initial sequence transporting the viewer across the ocean from a snow covered Austria to modern Cairo underscores the relativity of the European experience and the marginality of Jewish culture in Europe and the Middle East. Through her voice-over Beckermann creates a ethereal site of remembrance and interconnects the loneliness of the Austrian Empress, assassinated at the age of sixty-one, with the isolation of a Jewish woman in the Arab world. The places Elisabeth visited on her journey to Egypt do not show a trace of the monarch. Similarly, the modern visitor from Austria will make no lasting impact on the Egyptians with whom she interacts in public places such as bazaars and market places. As the narrative evokes the elusive memory of the empress by showing her youthful pictures — Sisi had not allowed any pictures to be taken of her after the age of thirty-one — and quoting from her notes and letters, the multiple marginalization of the filmmaker is revealed. Beckermann's affinity for Austrian *fin-de-siècle* culture that held out to Jews and women the promise of equality is a distinguishing trait of the small Jewish intellectual community that emerged in the 1980s.[34] The descendent of Viennese and East European Jews and survivors of the Holocaust, Beckermann indicates through her images and her ephemeral narrative position at an age of reemerging anti-Semitism and anti-feminism, that the only workable position she can assume is one based in language and conveyed through her voice. The retreat to voice and language effects a transubstantiation of geographic locations and the material world into sound and fleeting images. Compared to the stability enjoyed by those who belong to nation states, especially if they are men, Beckermann's space is elusive and transitional. Similar to Streeruwitz's *Nachwelt*, with its unsuccessful search for traces of the Jewish tradition of the interwar era, and the almost constant confrontation with pervasive misogyny in the United States, Beckermann's earlier film *Nach Jerusalem* (1991, subtitled *To Jerusalem*, 1991) and *Ein flüchtiger Zug nach dem Orient* do not point their way to a viable alternative to the oppressive situation in contemporary Austria. Mitgutsch, likewise combining Jewish and women's themes in *Abschied von Jerusalem* and *Haus der Kindheit* comes to a similar conclusion. Both novels, the former set in Jerusalem, the latter in the United States and small-town Austria, trace the dilemma of Jewish-women, descendants of the destroyed Austro-Hungarian culture torn by the legacy of the Nazi era and the Shoah. Positioned between several cultures, Austrian, Jewish, European, Israeli, and American, the members of the second post-Shoah generation, and the women characters in Mitgutsch's novels wind up in a tragic impasse because they are incapable of getting a grip on reality because of their multiple marginalization and exclusion.

It is not coincidental that feminists — Jelinek and Streeruwitz — are at the forefront of the current political debates, together with men associated with Jewish traditions, Doron Rabinovici and Robert Schindel. Since the election of Kurt Waldheim in 1986 and even more since the Freedom Party became part of the government in February 2000, the situation in Austria has given cause for international concern. When the new government took their oath of office a pro-democracy mass demonstration held against racism and neo-fascism was represented by some Austrian media, particularly the television reports in the ORF and papers such as *Kurier* and the *Kronen Zeitung,* as the ravings of extremists, thereby showing the disregard in which they hold dissidence and democratic action. Yet, the opposition of the small, determined minority could not be silenced and informal demonstrations continue to take place. The numbers of those silently disagreeing with the regime are much larger than the numbers of dissidents, as recent elections have shown. In addition to the conventional media, the Internet plays a decisive role in the activities of the Human Rights and Civil Rights initiative SOS-Mitmensch, which publicizes information about activities against racism, poverty, and announces related arts events and meetings, of the *Demokratische Offensive,* an internet-connected forum established in opposition to the current Austrian government, and the *Republikanischer Club* which provides a forum for democratic debates by organizing meetings and encourages discussion by producing and distributing informational materials such as brochures and pamphlets, and by maintaining a sophisticated web page with announcements, documentation of activities and opinions.[35]

The participants in the oppositional civil society come from ideologically heterogeneous groups, as is obvious from the names in a representative collection of essays edited by Isolde Charim and Doron Rabinovici, *Österreich: Berichte aus Quarantanien* (2000, Austria: Reports from Quarantania).[36] The volume is exemplary for the type of open exchange of opinions the new civil society advocates. The process of argumentation and the multitude of voices make the volume a counter-model to Haider's monolithic Freedom Party. Streeruwitz discusses the political crisis in conjunction with the erosion of language, warning that in light of the Nazi past, Haider's metaphors must not be mistaken for mere figures of speech.[37] Jelinek, who barred further performance of her plays on Austrian stages, discusses the similarity between the conservatives who helped Hitler into office and those who did the same for the Freedom Party. Focusing on speech and thought patterns now and then she raises doubt that the conservatives will be able to control rightwing extremism in the future. "Während sie noch an ihre Fähigkeit zur Kontrolle glauben, reißt es sie schon fort."[38] Describing the current party constellations as the end of democracy, Jelinek maintains that any involvement by intellectuals against the overwhelming power of the government-dominated media is futile (104). Yet, despite her pessimism concerning the effectiveness of literary language against the language of totalitarianism void of self-criticism or doubt,[39] Jelinek continues to write and speak out against the situation in Austria.[40]

Supraregional discussions reaching beyond the national and European continental framework and innovative forms of interaction have become an integral part of feminism and other oppositional political and cultural initiatives such as the global peace and ecological movements and post-Shoah Jewish writing. Already in the 1980s Marie-Thérèse Kerschbaumer explored basic conditions for life and survival in physical, psychological and creative terms and stated the interdependence of all forms of live.[41] Authors with far-reaching international connections and experiences such as Beckermann and Mitgutsch have pointed to the necessity of multiple linguistic and cultural literacy in order to achieve justice in a cosmopolitan context. Former leftists such as Jelinek discuss the dangers of cultural imperialism by way of the indiscriminate dissemination of Western pop culture. Another critical discussion pertains to the attempts to regulate and control the world wide web. Global democracy would presuppose a value basis that includes other than Western ideas, acknowledges multiple identities and legalizes multiple citizenship.[42] The contemporary post-colonial and diasporic identities call for cosmopolitan, intercultural patterns appropriate to the needs of all cultures, a pluralism that integrates the wisdom of all ethnicities and the most varied modalities of knowledge, including those derived from literature. The works of Austrian women writers at the turn of the millennium reveal how far out of reach these goals still are.

Notes

[1] *Die Frau im Korsett: Wiener Frauenalltag zwischen Klischee und Wirklichkeit 1848–1920* (Vienna: Eigenverlag der Museen der Stadt Wien, 1985).

[2] Ingeborg Bachmann, *Der Fall Franza* (Munich: dtv, 1981); Elfriede Jelinek, *Die Liebhaberinnen* (Reinbek: Rowohlt, 1975), Marlene Streeruwitz, *Lisa's Liebe* (Frankfurt am Main: S. Fischer, 2000).

[3] Ute Gerhard, "'Frauenfrage' und Geschlechterdifferenz — Krisenanzeigen der Moderne: Feministisch Perspektiven auf die Kulturwissenschaften," in *News: Internationales Forschungszentrum Kulturwissenschaften* 1 (2001), 17.

[4] Elsa Bernstein, *Das Leben als Drama: Erinnerungen an Theresienstadt* (Dortmund: ebersbach, 1999). Lou Andreas-Salomé, *Fenitschka / Eine Ausschweifung* (Frankfurt am Main: Ullstein, 1993); *Briefwechsel. Rainer Maria Rilke, Lou Andreas-Salomé* (Frankfurt am Main: Insel, 1989); *Ma* (Frankfurt am Main: Ullstein, 1996); *Friedrich Nietzsche in seinen Werken* (Frankfurt am Main: Insel, 2000); *Sigmund Freud and Lou Andreas-Salome: Letters by Sigmund Freud* (New York: Norton, 1985).

[5] Ruth Beckermann, dir., *Jenseits des Krieges* (Vienna: filmladen, 1997). See also the book *Jenseits des Krieges* (Vienna: Döcker, 1998); Marlene Streeruwitz, *Nachwelt* (Frankfurt am Main: S. Fischer, 1999); Anna Mitgutsch, *Abschied von Jerusalem* (Berlin: Rowohlt, 1995) and *Haus der Kindheit* (Munich: Luchterhand, 2000).

[6] Marlene Streeruwitz, *Und. Sonst. Noch. Aber., Texte I 1989–1996; Und. Sonst. Noch. Aber., Texte II 1996–1998* (Vienna: edition selene, 2000); *Das Bibel Projekt: Das Evangelium des Matthäus*, introduction by Marlene Streeruwitz (Frankfurt am Main: S. Fischer, 2000).

[7] Dagmar C. G. Lorenz, "Marlen Haushofer — eine Feministin aus Österreich," *Modern Austrian Literature* 12, 3–4 (1979), 1–192.

[8] Emilie Mariott, "Der Vogelmassenmord in Südtirol," *Neues Wiener Tagblatt*, September 22, 1892 and *Erbarm dich deines Viehes* (Innsbruck: Verlag des Thierschutzvereins, 1891).

[9] Marie von Ebner-Eschenbach, *Die Spitzin* (Vienna: Bibliothek der Provinz, 1994).

[10] Veza Canetti, *Die gelbe Straße* (Frankfurt am Main: S. Fischer, 1993). Published in part in the *Arbeiter-Zeitung* (Vienna) 1932 and 1933. Edited by Elias Canetti in 1989.

[11] Otto Weininger, *Geschlecht und Charakter* (Munich: Matthes and Seitz, 1980). Weininger's treatise, originally his doctoral dissertation at the University of Vienna, abounds with blanket characterizations such as the following: "Die Kongruenz zwischen Judentum und Weiblichkeit scheint eine völlige zu werden, sobald auf die unendliche Veränderungsfähigkeit des Juden zu reflektieren begonnen wird" (429) and "Der Jude ist ewig wie das Weib, ewig nicht als Persönlichkeit, sondern als Gattung" (430).

[12] Chris Weedon, "The Struggle for Emancipation: German Women Writers of the *Jahrhundertwende*," in *A History of Women's Writing in Germany, Austria and Switzerland*, edited by Jo Catling (Cambridge: Cambridge UP, 2000), 111–27. Here: 114.

[13] Sabine Werner-Birkenbach, "Trends in Writing by Women, 1910–1933," in *A History of Women's Writing in Germany, Austria and Switzerland,* 128–45. Here: 128.

[14] Vicki Baum, *Menschen im Hotel: Ein Kolportageroman mit Hintergründen* (Berlin: Ullstein, 1929).

[15] Elfriede Jelinek et al. *Malina* (RCA/Columbia Pictures International Video 1990). Brigitta Lorenzoni, *Die Ausgesperrten,* Schriftenreihe des Österreichischen Filmarchivs 15 (Vienna: Österreichisches Filmarchiv, 1986).

[16] http://ourworld.compuserve.com/homepages/elfriede/fLepus.htm contains essays, polemics, photographs, and bibliographical information.

[17] Emil Marriot, *Der geistliche Tod* (Vienna: Hugo Engel, 1884). See Helga Kraft, *Ein Haus aus Sprache* (Stuttgart: Metzler, 1996), 77–78.

[18] Marie von Ebner-Eschenbach, *Lotti, die Uhrmacherin* (Stuttgart: Reclam, 1999); *Božena* (Stuttgart/Berlin: J. G. Cotta, 1911).

[19] The last polemic sentence in *Die gelbe Straße* calls into question the notion of human superiority. After a violent mass attack on a little girl it reads: "Denn der Mensch schreitet aufrecht, die erhabenen Zeichen der Seele ins Gesicht gebrannt" (168).

[20] Jacqueline Vansant, *Against the Horizon* (New York: Greenwood, 1988), 16, places the historical demarcation lines somewhat differently. According to her the years 1918 to the early 1920s coinciding with the control of the Socialist party are an era of "sweeping reforms" that ended in 1920 with the demise of Social Democracy. "Still," she writes, "support for women's rights did not cease," noting that the SPÖ put forth the most radical demands in 1926. In her dissertation, *Feminism and Austrian Women Writers in the Second Republic* (Diss. University of Texas, Austin 1986), Vansant specifies that sweeping reforms after World War I brought women the passive and active voting rights (21), and that at least in theory, the constitution of 1920 guaranteed women sexual equality, although the belief persisted that childcare and housework were women's work (22).

[21] Veza Canetti, *Der Oger* (Munich/Vienna: Hanser, 1991); *Geduld bringt Rosen* (Munich/Vienna: Hanser, 1992); *Die Schildkröten* (Munich/Vienna: Hanser, 1999).

[22] For example Elfriede Jelinek, *Die Ausgesperrten* (Reinbek: Rowohlt, 1985) and the author's extensive internet activity in protest against Haider's Freedom Party; see also Marlene Streeruwitz, *Nachwelt* (Frankfurt am Main: S. Fischer, 1999).

[23] Vansant in *Feminism and Austrian Women Writers in the Second Republic* notes that the 1970s feminist movement had minimal impact on "conservative Austrian society and on the Austrian consciousness" and wonders if Austria and feminism is a contradiction in terms (1).

[24] Ferrel Rose and Linda Kraus Worley, "Marie von Ebner-Eschenbach (1830–1916)," in *Women Writers in German-Speaking Countries,* edited by Elke P. Frederiksen and Elizabeth Ametsbichler (Westport: Greenwood, 1998), 125–33. Here: 127.

[25] Ester Riehl, "Marie von Ebner-Eschenbach's Božena: A Czech Maid and the Future of Austria," in *Austria in Literature,* edited by Donald G. Daviau (Riverside, CA: Ariadne, 2000), 19–30.

[26] Marie von Ebner-Eschenbach, *"Die Kapitalistinnen" und zwei andere Novellen* ["Der Muff," "Krambambuli"] (New York: F. S. Crofts, 1928); *Krambambuli und andere Erzählungen* (Stuttgart: Reclam, 1965).

[27] Sigrid Schmid-Bortenschlager, "Der zerbrochene Spiegel. Weibliche Kritik der Psychoanalyse in Mela Hartwigs Novellen," *Modern Austrian Literature* 12 (1979), 77–95.

[28] Mela Hartwig, *Das Wunder von Ulm* (Paris: Éditions du Phénix, 1936).

[29] Friedrich Engels, *Der Ursprung der Familie, des Privateigenthums und des Staats* (Hottingen-Zürich: Schweizerische Genossenschaftsbuchdruckerei, 1884). August Bebel, *Die Frau und der Sozialismus: Die Frau in der Vergangenheit, Gegenwart und Zukunft* (Stuttgart: Dietz, 1891).

[30] Herbert Marcuse, *A Critique of Pure Tolerance* (Boston: Beacon, 1965), 83.

[31] Ruth Beckermann, dir., *Jenseits des Krieges* (Vienna: filmladen 1997). *Jenseits des Krieges* (Vienna: Döcker, 1998).

[32] Eduard von Borsody, dir., *Wunschkonzert* (Indianapolis, IN: International Historic Films, 1984); Veit Harlan, dir. *Jud Süss* (Chicago: IHF Productions, 1988); Fritz Hippler, dir., *Der ewige Jude* (Tamarelle International Films, 1986); Leni Riefenstahl, dir., *Triumph des Willens* (Chatsworth, CA: Timeless Video, 1996).

[33] Marlene Streeruwitz, *Majakowskiring* (Frankfurt am Main: S. Fischer, 2000). Ruth Beckermann, *Ein flüchtiger Zug nach dem Orient* (Zurich: First Hand Films, 1999). (Aichholzer Filmproduktion). Nurith Aviv was the camera woman for Beckermann's film *Nach Jerusalem* (Vienna: filmladen, 1991).

[34] See Matti Bunzl, "Counter-Memory and Modes of Resistance: The Uses of Fin-de-Siècle Vienna for Present-Day Austrian Jews," in *Transforming the Center, Eroding the Margins: Essays on Ethnic and Cultural Boundaries in German-Speaking Countries,* edited by Dagmar C. G. Lorenz and Renate Posthofen (Columbia, SC: Camden House, 1998), 169–84.

[35] http://www.demokratische-offensive.at/wir_ueber_uns/index.html; http://www.sos-mitmensch.at/; http://www.repclub.at/.

[36] *Österreich: Berichte aus Quarantanien,* edited by Isolde Charim and Doron Rabinovici (Frankfurt am Main: Suhrkamp, 2000).

[37] Marlene Streeruwitz, "Alles, was falsch ist," in *Österreich: Berichte aus Quarantanien,* 123–33. Here: 125.

[38] Elfriede Jelinek, "Moment! Aufnahme! 5. 10. 1999," in *Österreich: Berichte aus Quarantanien,* 100–109. Here: 100.

[39] Elfriede Jelinek, "Meine Art des Protests," in *Der Standard,* February 2, 2000. Also: http://ourworld.compuserve.com/homepages/elfriede.HTM

[40] See: "Rotz. Rede gehalten am 16. 3. 2001 auf der Antirassismus-Kundgebung der Demokratischen Offensive in Vienna (Stephansplatz)": "Wir müssen hier wieder einmal ein kleines Stück unsrer Lebenszeit hergeben, um für etwas einzustehen oder,

mehr noch, gegen etwas zu stehen, das anderen wie brauner Schleim, einfach so, ganz natürlich, wie es in den Körpern, den bierseligen wie den Hochmütigen an der Kreissäge, im Kreißsaal oder in der Vorstandsetage, die jetzt auch dazugehören und sich für vieles zu fein sind, von dem sie profitieren, aus den Mündern quillt. Sie müssen nicht nachdenken, wir aber müssen es, leider, und zwar um auf sie zu reagieren." http://ourworld.compuserve.com/homepages/elfriede/

[41] Marie-Thérèse Kerschbaumer, *Für mich hat Lesen etwas mit Fließen zu tun — Gedanken zum Lesen und Schreiben von Literatur* (Vienna: Wiener Frauenverlag, 1989); *Der Schwimmer* (Salzburg: Winter, 1976).

[42] Engin F. Isin and Patricia K. Wood, *Citizenship and Identity* (London: Sage, 1999), 118, 121, 159.

Works Cited

Anderson, Harriet. *Vision und Leidenschaft: Die Frauenbewegung im Fin de Siècle Wiens.* Vienna: Deuticke, 1994 (translated as *Utopian Feminism: Women's Movements in Fin de Siècle Vienna.* New Haven: Yale UP 1992).

Brix, Emil, and Lisa Fischer. *Die Frauen der Wiener Moderne.* Vienna: Verlag für Geschichte und Politik, 1997.

Brugger, Ingried. *Jahrhundert der Frauen: Vom Impressionismus bis zur Gegenwart, Österreich 1870 bis heute.* Salzburg: Residenz, 1999.

Das Schreiben der Frauen in Österreich seit 1950, edited by the Walter Buchebner Literaturprojekt. Vienna: Böhlau, 1991.

Die Frau im Korsett: Wiener Frauenalltag zwischen Klischee und Wirklichkeit 1848–1920. Vienna: Eigenverlag der Museen der Stadt Vienna, 1985

Frauenliteratur in Österreich von 1945 bis heute. Edited by Carine Kleiber and Erika Tunner. Bern/Frankfurt am Main/New York: Peter Lang, 1986.

Frederiksen, Elke. *Women Writers of Germany, Austria, and Switzerland: An Annotated Bio-Bibliographical Guide.* New York: Greenwood Press, 1989.

Marcuse, Herbert, *The One-Dimensional Man.* Boston: Beacon, 1965.

Modern Austrian Literature 12 (1979), no. 3/4, edited by Donald Daviau (Special Issue on Austrian Women Writers).

Schmidt-Bortenschlager, Sigrid, and Hanna Schmidt-Benicek, *Österreichische Schriftstellerinnen 1880–1938.* Stuttgart: Dietz, 1982.

Dreams of Interpretation: Psychoanalysis and the Literature of Vienna

Thomas Paul Bonfiglio

From Dream Life to Dream Work

THE FIRST EDITION OF *Die Traumdeutung* (translated as *The Interpretation of Dreams*, 1913) bears a publication date of 1900, although it actually appeared in Vienna in November 1899. This is consistent with the pivotal temporality of a work that looks retrospectively into the nineteenth century and prospectively into the twentieth. In 1931, Freud said of his first and arguably most important book, "It contains, even according to my present-day judgement, the most valuable of all the discoveries it has been my good fortune to make."[1] In terms of the influence not only on his later publications, but also on humanistic inquiry in general, this judgment certainly rings true. In 1924, however, Freud noted that the study had received little attention in professional journals when it first appeard.[2] This observation is borne out by surprisingly meager initial sales figures. In the first six years of publication it sold an average of only fifty-nine copies per year (Gay 1988, 3). These are remarkably low numbers, especially in view of the considerable presence of the work in the twentieth century and beyond. If few were purchasing it, one may indeed ask what the nature and significance of *Die Traumdeutung* really was at the onset of the twentieth century. The most fruitful model for approaching this question is one that views psychoanalysis in a symbiotic relationship with its environment, as both an emergence from and an influence upon its era.

The work is introduced with an epigraph from book seven of the Aeneid: "flectere si nequeo superos, Acheronta movebo" (*GW 2/3*: 283) (If I cannot bend the higher powers, I will move Acheron). Acheron is the river in Hades across which Charon ferried the dead. This citation indicates a directional change; the impossibility of bending the superior downward yields the alternative of moving the inferior upward. It is also a transgression, a boundary crossing that brings the border closer to the surface, and the relocated cargo is that of unconscious behavior. One may characterize Freud's general project as the demonstration of the continual intrusion of the unconscious into consciousness and as the establishment of a science that makes the unconscious present and observable. This is reflected even in the first review of *Die Traumdeutung*, published in *Die Zeit* (Vienna) on January 6, 1900, which praised the work as "ein modernes Traumbuch" and lauded its scientific nature.[3]

It is important to clarify Freud's concepts of "consciousness" and "the unconscious." The terms in German are, respectively, *das Bewusstsein* and *das Unbewusste*. The first term is a substantive meaning "the being aware," which indicates a condition or state. The second term is an adjectival noun meaning "that which is not conscious." The most important aspect of these two terms is that they do not indicate spaces or places.

In Freud's writings, *das Unbewusste* and *Unbewusstes* are interchangeable. The title of the first section of *Das Ich und das Es* (1923, *The Ego and the Id*) is "Bewusstsein und Unbewusstes" (*GW* 13: 29), and it is in the use of the latter term that the meaning becomes clear: the unconscious is a collection of things that are not part of consciousness. They are repressed, blotted out, and excluded by the active psychological mechanisms of denial, displacement, inversion, projection, transference, and so on. For Freud, consciousness — the condition of being aware — is predicated upon such repressive mechanisms. The energy required to keep things out of consciousness, however, is not infinite, and the repressed eventually passes into wakefulness; this causes us to slip, to blunder, to misspeak, to misperceive. The repressed is always present in varying degrees of partial, and often total eclipse, but there nonetheless. Consequently, Freud used the German terms *latent* and *manifest* to distinguish the unconscious and conscious elements of the text of the dream (*GW* 2/3: 283).

Freud was a great demystifier, and romantic notions of a mysterious, otherworldly unconscious were as anathema to him as religion itself. He sees no clairvoyance in dreams; their images are constructed by psychological mechanisms. They do betray secrets of the dreamer, but in the form of a parallel language, not a parallel reality. *Die Traumdeutung* is a work of science intended to make the dream processes observable, and it crowns a tradition that was concerned with the quotidian function of dream. The central part of the text is *Die Traumarbeit* (the dream work), a term that adds a strong dimension of reality to the endeavor — it is work, and connotes a technical description.

Thus, Freud's relocation of Acheron is a metaphor for his endeavor of making unconsciousness visible, of demonstrating its existence in waking life. The psychic structures delineated in *Die Traumdeutung* inform the works that Freud wrote subsequently: *Zur Psychopathologie des Alltagslebens* (1901, translated as *The Psychopathology of Everyday Life*), *Der Witz und seine Beziehung zum Unbewussten* (1905, translated as *Jokes and Their Relation to the Unconscious*), and *Bruchstück einer Hysterie-Analyse* (1905, translated as *Dora, An Analysis of a Case of Hysteria*). All of these works instantiate dream-as-life and are constructed by four master tropes: condensation (*Verdichtung*), displacement (*Verschiebung*), overdetermination (*Überdeterminierung*), and secondary revision (*sekundäre Bearbeitung*), the functions of which were described in chapter six of *Die Traumdeutung* (*GW 2/3*: 283–513). The first process that Freud discusses is that of condensation: the images in the text of the dream are synthetic compressions that display multivalent allusions to many facets of the dreamer's experiences. These are arranged, however, in a displaced narrative. The initial story is charged with psychic anxiety; consequently, it becomes repressed and shifted to a theme that is sufficiently different to escape repression but sufficiently similar to be read as an allegory of the original narrative. The fact that the images are multivalent and the theme allegorical renders the dream an inexhaustible fund of interpretation, a condition that Freud chose to call overdetermination. Moreover, the processes of displacement and condensation are still operative in the renarration of dream; this is the secondary revision that problematizes the discussion of dream itself.

The interest in dream in the intellectual and cultural life of nineteenth-century Vienna culminated in the generation of a certain configuration of dream at the *fin de siècle*. The image of the dream had been present in Judeo-Christian culture since the Old Testament story of Joseph, whose ability to read dreams aided in his survival, and Freud's work stands in a prominent place in this ancient tradition. It had been present in European literature since Calderón's play *La vida es sueño* (1635) and had profoundly informed the German Romantic movement, where it was viewed as a missionary of "higher" neo-idealist truth, as a kind of visionary condition of holy madness. The German Romantics tended to view the mind as split bicamerally, which was expressed metaphorically in images of the diurnal versus the nocturnal. On the one hand, there was a postlapsarian waking consciousness that sees only superficial images of existence; on the other, there was a higher oneiric state of consciousness that sees the hidden truth beyond the quotidian realm. Human existence was seen as plagued by an apparent irreconcilable division between these two spheres, and German Romantic poets, such as Novalis, postulated a time of reconciliation, a marriage of night and day, wherein repressed dream structures reclaim reality and dominate over the diurnal. This applies, however, to German, not Austrian literature. There was no Austrian Romanticism as such, and Austrian literature can be largely viewed as postidealist. The end of the age of Goethe in Germany is oddly coeval with the beginnings of literature in Austria, and the first writers to identify themselves as distinctly Austrian, such as Grillparzer, Nestroy, Raimund, and Stifter, wrote after the larger German neo-idealist project was spent. They constitute a different generation in a different country that had little retrospective or nostalgic relationship to the ideology of Classicism and Romanticism.

Two hundred years after Calderón wrote *La vida es sueño,* Franz Grillparzer published *Der Traum ein Leben* (1834, translated as *A Dream is Life*), the brilliance of which is reflected in its title. The conventional German translation of Calderón's work is *Das Leben, ein Traum;* Grillparzer's title, however, effects a fluid transposition of the constituent elements. There is no verb, no copula. Whereas Calderón's Spanish title presents an equation: life is a dream, the structure of this equation inadvertently sets up a division with dream on one side and life on the other, which ultimately foils the equation itself. Grillparzer's fluid title omits the copula and circumvents the problem of division. There is neither equation, nor comparison, nor simile, nor metaphor; simply: the dream a life. There is also no punctuation to separate the terms, which thus effects an identification of realms. Moreover, dream is presented as the general term and life as the singular, which grants universality to the dream and makes life an example thereof. In an odd act of perhaps involuntary resistance, many editors have "normalized" the title by inserting a comma: *Der Traum, ein Leben.* Most editions, however, preserve the original syntax.

Beginning with Grillparzer, the Romantic dualism of dream and reality, which had existed in near mutual exclusivity, seems almost anachronistic, and the distinction between noumena and phenomena is overcome. The entire psychic theater has been diurnalized, and one is left with the phenomenality of dream. If one removes the mystified notions of omnipotence of thought from the Romantic movement, one is left with the presence of a helpless subject in a world of mind. Viennese writers of the *fin de siècle,* such as Hofmannsthal, Schnitzler, and Beer-Hofmann, continued the tradition established by Grillparzer. A good example is Hofmannsthal's poem "Terzinen III" (1894) which begins by alluding to Shakespeare's characterization of humans as dream-stuff and concludes, "Und drei sind Eins: ein Mensch, ein Ding, ein Traum."[4] This is a clever allusion to the Catholic doctrine of the Holy Trinity, which demands belief in the mystery of *an identity* of three. The inclusion of an object into the triad not only objectifies the other elements, but also communicates the themes of aesthetic iconicity, identity, and insularity seen in the symbolist poetry of such writers as Hofmannsthal and Rilke. In 1910, Hofmannsthal's uncompleted play *Das Leben ein Traum,* written between 1901 and 1904, was published. The fragment alludes to both Calderón and Grillparzer and represents the protagonist Sigismund within an experiential identity of inner psyche and external world. This aspect of Hofmannsthal's plays appealed to Freud. He saw them as excellent illustrations of the return of the repressed, of the play of unconscious motivations along the border of consciousness (Worbs 1983, 259–69). This applies especially to Freud's reaction to Hofmannsthal's dramas *Elektra* and *König Oedipus.*

The historian Carl Schorske situates the emergence of psychoanalysis within the demise of liberal politics in Vienna in the second half of the nineteenth century, which has considerable import for Freud, as his sociocultural origin was that of Viennese bourgeois liberal Jewry. The defeat of the liberals in Vienna in the 1890s was accompanied by the emergence of the anti-Semite Karl Lueger, who became mayor of Vienna, and the rise of socialism, especially Christian socialism. Schorske sees these disappointments as leading Viennese intellectuals, a very large proportion of whom were Jewish, to a social and political withdrawal and a general cultural flight into aesthetics. He notes that "the life of art became a substitute for the life of action" (8) and thus situates *Die Traumdeutung* as a liberal solution to the political crisis of absolutism versus socialism. He says that the work "constitutes an incomplete but autonomous subplot of personal history" (181). This phenomenon can be seen as an intellectual retreat into the inner and lower circles of mind, in which interaction is either a highly private one between analyst and analysand or solely personal, as exemplified by Freud's proclivity to analyze his own dreams and base his theories upon those analyses.

This psychic withdrawal was exacerbated by Freud's feelings of exclusion. In his "Selbstdarstellung," a self-portrait written in 1924, Freud claimed that, in the first decade of his independent career in Vienna, he had no supporters, was completely isolated, shunned in Vienna, and ignored abroad (*GW* 14: 74). Recent scholarship has shown, however, that this was not the case, and that Freud was not as isolated as he would have us believe in the early years of psychoanalysis (Tichy and Zwettler-Otte 1999, 33–34). He was, in fact, much discussed, as is the case with all seminal thinkers. But the unappreciated outsider is the central character in Freud's self-portrait. Gay observes that Freud was ambivalent about Vienna itself, avoided the contemporary café culture, and rarely went to the opera. Most of his remarks on the city are disparaging; he complained of antisemitism and tended to romanticize his birthplace of Freiberg in Moravia (Gay 1988, 9–10, 30). Here, the words of Gustav Mahler seem relevant: "Ich bin dreifach heimatlos: als Böhme unter den Österreichern, als Österreicher unter den Deutschen und als Jude in der ganzen Welt" (Worbs, 20).

This marvelous model of triple alienation can also apply to the Moravian-born Freud. Here, the nuclear problem is one of Jewish marginalization within a fragmented empire that can only dream the Habsburg myth of unity. This alienation was exacerbated by the death of Freud's father in 1896, an occurrence that contains ominous echoes of the particular political configuration of the Austrian bourgeoisie, which, according to Schorske, "did not succeed either in destroying or in fully fusing with the aristocracy . . . it remained both dependent upon and deeply loyal to the emperor as a remote but necessary father-protector" (7). Freud's attainment of a professorship in 1902 was a transitional point for him as well as for psychoanalysis; in the same year, the Wednesday Society began to meet at Freud's home. This was the circle of psychoanalysts, artists, and intellectuals that is seen as the point of dispersion of psychoanalysis, the source of its rise to the status of an intellectual force in the café culture of the Viennese intelligentsia.[5] One of the analysts in the Wednesday Society, Wilhelm Stekel, based parts of his theory on Grillparzer's *Der Traum ein Leben.*

In addition to this cult of isolation among the Viennese intelligentsia, Schorske also sees the emergence of a "bourgeois culture of feeling" (9). He says, "Liberalism's collapse further transmuted the aesthetic heritage into a culture of sensitive nerves, uneasy hedonism, and often outright anxiety" (10). This was a phenomenon with not only cultural, but also philosophical manifestations. In 1886, Ernst Mach published *Beiträge zur Analyse der Empfindungen,* which restated British empiricist notions of self within the consciousness of the *fin de siècle* and characterized human existence as a series of sense impressions. Mach saw the self as a construct abstracted from those sense impressions, a fictive collection that is sensual, thus bodily in origin, which then blurs the distinction between the psychological and the physiological.

There arose in Vienna a pronounced aesthetics of anxiety, a phenomenon that Worbs characterizes as *Nervenkunst,* literally "nerve art." Central to these developments was the Young Vienna circle ("Junges

Wien"), which began in the late 1880s in reaction to the naturalist movement. Its leader was Hermann Bahr, whose essay *Die Überwindung des Naturalismus* (1891), holds among other things that mental processes begin not with the senses, but with the nerves. The topos of neuroses, which are, literally, nervous disorders, had a seminal presence in this movement from its onset.

A good example of this is Hofmannsthal's discussion of the novel *Niels Lyhne* (1888) by the Danish writer Jens Peter Jacobsen. He notes that, whereas the older psychological novels, among them *Werther*, simply represented the contents of psychic life, Jacobsen represents their form in psychiatric detail: the promiscuous confusion of thoughts, illogic, the perturbations of mind, and the immediacy of impression, all of which he terms a "neuropathic idealism" (Worbs, 65). This neologism replaces traditional transcendent idealism with one of a pathology of nerves that yields a new aesthetics, a kind of psycho-impressionistic *Nervenkunst*. Again, it is important to emphasize that this new aesthetic orientation was informed by factors of ethnicity. With only a few exceptions, the intellectual circle of the Young Vienna movement was Jewish (Freud, Felix Dörmann, Jakob Julius David, and Felix Salten, for example). In their works one finds psychoanalytic themes used to mediate ethnic marginalization.

The emergence of these ideas in Vienna at the advent of the twentieth century has been aptly labeled "the Viennese Enlightenment" (Francis 1985), a characterization that serves as an ironic counterpoint to the conventional understanding of eighteenth-century Enlightenment as a clearing up or bringing to light. Here, it is the realm of non-clarity, of non-consciousness that is contributing to the understanding of the human condition.

The discourse of psychoanalysis even encompassed its ostensible opponents. Karl Kraus (1874–1936), the satirist and editor of the influential journal *Die Fackel* (1899–1936), is traditionally seen as a violent opponent of Freud. Recent studies, however, have shown that Kraus and Freud had much more in common than is believed (Timms 1986). Kraus shared Freud's criticisms of Victorian sexuality, never once criticized Freud in *Die Fackel,* and had high praise for *Die Traumdeutung.* His differences lay with the scientific and deaestheticized aspects of psychoanalysis and especially with the practice of psychotherapy. Even here, however, one sees parallels. Kraus's famous statement that psychoanalysis is the disease whose cure it purports to be (1913, 21) is itself open to interpretation. He also said that in psychoanalysis it is hard to tell the patient from the doctor; the disease is the therapy and the therapy is the disease; sane people become patients, and patients become doctors (1924, 149). While this is ironically critical of psychoanalysis, it also succeeds in representing the phenomenon as inseparable from the cultural milieu that generated it. And it is certainly consonant with Freudian notions of transference, counter-transference, and secondary revision, with Freud's frequent analysis of his own dreams and errors, with his view of culture as fundamentally neurotic, and with the basic notion of the psychopathology of everyday life.

The Viennese writer most closely associated with the aesthetics of dream is clearly Arthur Schnitzler, whose works are an excellent example of the influence of the culture of dream at the *fin de siècle*. While Freud and Schnitzler were clearly in contact with one another, it is safe to say that Schnitzler had begun developing his unique idiom of dream aesthetics before the publication of Freud's major work on dreams. Schnitzler kept a daily journal and mentions reading *Die Traumdeutung* on 26 March 1900 (Martens,[6] 144), but his use of dream is evident already in his 1890 play *Alkandis Lied,* in which the dream presents the hero with information on his own repressed wishes. In a telling ploy, Schnitzler uses an image of the hero sleepwalking, thus dream walking, thus in a kind of dream-waking that implies the presence of dream in consciousness. The 1898 play *Paracelsus* concerns similar themes about the superior value of psychic reality via the pan-psychist ideas of the alchemist and mystic Theophrastus von Hohenheim (1494–1541).

An excellent example of the presence of dream work in the waking mind can be found in Schnitzler's novella *Leutnant Gustl* (1900). Clearly influenced by *Die Traumdeutung,* the work makes use of dream patterns in the devices of interior monologue and free association in order to represent the thought processes of Gustl, who is a symbol of the state of empire in decline, the political fragmentation of which mirrors his own fragmented thought patterns. In the psychoanalytic model, free association is never free, just as errors are never random; the connections made in free association are the same displacements and condensations that one finds in dream. Gustl's associative leaps from one theme to another can be seen not only as displacements, but also as literary metonymies. They inform his interior monologue, which can be viewed as a daydream of angst and wish fulfillment, of the fear of the decline of empire, and of the desire for military and political order. Schnitzler's play *Der Schleier der Beatrice* (1899, The Veil of Beatrice) also confuses dream and reality. Finally, *Traumnovelle* (1926, translated as *Rhapsody: A Dream Novel)* is so effective in leaving the question unanswered as to what is dream and what not that critics cannot agree as to which is which. Other Viennese authors, such as Richard Beer-Hofmann, are similarly preoccupied with such confoundings. Beer-Hofmann's, *Der Tod Georgs* (1900, The Death of Georg) is a novella that "obscures the transition between waking reality and dream" (Martens, 139). The narrative strategy of this *fin-de-siècle* novella is to fool the reader into believing that the dream is real. It often uses the same sentences to describe dream and waking life. In what may be the first novella to use interior monologue in German, dream is also depicted here as a superior condition.

The Freudian model of dream work and the literature associated with it share more than a common cultural origin; they have a similar relationship to language. There are strong structural elements in both and a definite idea of nonreferentiality and internal linguistic play. Beginning at the *fin de siècle,* there emerged from Austria a notion of the inadequacy of language, exemplified by Fritz Mauthner in his *Beiträge zu einer Kritik der Sprache* (1901–1902) and by Ludwig Wittgenstein in his *Tractatus* (1922). These early pragmatic philosophers were skeptical of the efficacy of language and viewed it as a limited medium, a closed system that could not describe things outside of itself, and that should be viewed at best as self-referential. This view of language resulted in a philosophy of linguistic pragmatism, which continues today in the poststructuralist tradition, especially in the works of Richard Rorty. This postromantic and postidealist conception of language makes no claims to any mediative or transcendent function. Language, in this conception, has no access to any "higher truth." These ideas emerged from the linguistic pluralism of Austria-Hungary, an empire whose hegemonic language was spoken by only a third of its inhabitants. Mauthner, for instance, grew up in a trilingual environment in Prague. Even the capital of the empire was, in 1910, mostly populated by those not born in Vienna. This can be seen as a sociopolitical factor that contributed to the linguistic aesthetics of the period. The poets who operated within this system thematized the nonreferentiality of language in their literary production.

This approach can be seen in Hofmannsthal's poem "Weltgeheimnis" (1894), which represents language as originating in the moment of non-understanding. In the prelapsarian state, knowledge is mute. The condition of knowing is the condition of being silent; there is no need for language. In the postlapsarian state, however, language emerges as an expression of dislocation, as a neurotic substitute for knowledge. This culminates in the concluding line that describes the human condition: "Nun zuckt im Kreis ein Traum herum" (*GW* 2: 15). Here, dream recirculates as a kind of nervous twitch. In this repetitive state, dream, language, and neurosis become, in effect, coterminous. Among Austrian writers of the *fin de siècle,* such ideas effected a general acceptance of the nonreferentiality of language as a given, as a base of aesthetic operations. This is evident in Hofmannsthal's "Ein Brief" (*GW* 12: 7–20) (1902, translated as "Letter of Lord Chandos"), which outlines three stages of language: first, there is iconicity, then unrepresentability, and finally a celebration of the symbolist presence and potential of the sign, ideas that he shared with Baudelaire. In his "Gespräch über Gedichte" (*GW* 12: 80–96) (1903, The Conversation on Poetry), Hofmannsthal celebrates poetry as that which uses words for the sake of words; that is, poetry is a linguistic closed circuit. The symbolist poets' configuration of poetry as a plastic art — the ideas of the "Dinggedicht" and "Kunstding" — fit well into this schema.

A model emerges from this particular configuration of language, one that resembles a hysterical conversion of psyche into soma: it is the literal use of metaphor, the conversion of language into object.[7] This generates images that operate as the rebuses of dream work, or as visual puns. The plays of Oskar Kokoschka are a case in point. His *Hiob* (1917, Job) abounds in such rebus-like literalizations of metaphor. A character takes off his dog's costume and utters the phrase from Goethe's *Faust,* "Ich bin des Pudels Kern!" (151), and he also complains of the "Hundewetter" (151). Job's patience continues even as he literally loses his head (156). Kokoschka's *Sphinx und Strohmann* (1913, Sphinx and Strawman) operates in a similar fashion: A straw man is a stand-in or representative, and the central character is literally a straw head, which also puns on the metonymy of a "head" of an organization. To the 1913 edition of *Sphinx und Strohmann* are appended some of Kokoschka's prints and sketches of heads, called portraits, in psycho-expressionist disfigurement. Kokoschka thus presents not only a drama, but also a physiognomy of the psyche, in which the distortive nature of language and the ineluctability of metaphor are reflected in the asymmetry of mind and body. Similarly, in Beer-Hofmann's drama *Der Graf von Charolais* (1905, The Count of Charolais), notions of totemism, guilt, and patriarchy assume literal and macabre incorporation in a patrimony issue: creditors repossess the body of the dead father, and it is the responsibility of the son to settle the debt and redeem the corpse.

Thus emerged from Vienna at the first *fin de siècle* a new configuration of the human condition: one of alienation, reverie, and neurosis. This perspective arose in distinction to traditional idealism, which also continued into the twentieth century. This new world-view is fundamentally adualistic, with no Neo-Platonist divisions between a derivative lower world and an ideal higher one. There is only the psychophysical world, in which language is configured as corporeal and iconic, not with higher meaning or supra-personal referentiality, but instead as the verbal structure and instantiation of neurosis.

In the course of the twentieth century, psychoanalysis migrated beyond Austria, beyond Europe, and even into nonwestern cultures. It was appropriated and fortified by two important intellectual movements: poststructuralism and critical second-wave feminism. In mid-century, the French psychoanalyst Jacques Lacan observed that the dream mechanisms of displacement and condensation corresponded to the literary devices of metaphor and metonymy, and that there were strong similarities between the vocabulary of literary tropes and that of psychological defense mechanisms. Along with Jacques Derrida, he brought hermeneutics to a linguistic and symbolic understanding of Freudianism. In the last quarter of the twentieth century, French and Anglo-American feminists (Luce Irigaray, Sara Kofman, Jane Gallop, and Juliet Mitchell, for example) came to a similar symbolic reading of psychoanalysis, especially as a delineation of the origin and structure of patriarchy. These international revisions of Freud also reinformed and revitalized Viennese literature.

Systemic Reverie:
Psychoanalysis and Literature at the Second *Fin de Siècle*

On October 12, 1999, the Viennese writer Elfriede Jelinek, one of the foremost authors writing in the German language, gave the honorary lecture at the reopening ceremonies for the Wiener Psychoanalytisches Ambulatorium. In this address, she invokes the name of the novelist and poet Hermann Broch (1896–1951) as a model of the use of autopsychoanalysis to reach a higher state of intricate self-awareness. Corporealizing a metaphor for introspection, she represents Broch as one who tried surgically to remove his ego, as if it were a bloody organ, but simultaneously to retain it. For Jelinek, it is the responsibility of the artist to reflect upon self and culture, and she sees psychoanalysis as the optimal reflexive medium for realizing this obligation.

The fact that a feminist writer should inaugurate the reopening of a psychiatric institute is indicative of the symbiosis of psychoanalysis and literature in contemporary Vienna, where one event after the other demonstrates that psychoanalysis is very much in the public eye. Most are functions of the Sigmund Freud Museum, which presents Vienna as one of the three major international centers, along with Washington and London, for the study of psychoanalysis. Although the archival and research facilities of these other metropolises would justify classing them with Vienna in importance, the presence of Washington needs to be reconsidered. The Freud Museum may be reacting to the recent exhibit "Freud: Conflict and Culture" (15 October 1998 to 16 January 1999) at The Library of Congress. While the exhibit was clearly significant, it was marred by the complications of the schizophrenic American reception of Freud. Objections to the exhibit caused it to be postponed and reconfigured for a period of several years, which resulted in a very problematic product. Each major stage in the development of Freudianism was displayed in a separate booth and framed by a collage of quotations pro and contra. Thus the exhibit was influenced, in part, by the American resistance to Freud, which has three basic origins: Puritanism, noncritical feminism, and experimental psychology. The puritan strain in American culture rejected *a priori* the notions of the basic sexuality of human existence. Some of the early manifestations of second wave feminism took the ideology of penis envy at face value and could not make the inductive leap to the more recent feminist criticism of phallocentrism, criticism that would have been impossible without Freud. American psychology, which is dominated by the ideologies of behaviorism and quantitative experimentation, teaches little Freud, in many cases none at all, and rejects his ideas as "unscientific," in ignorance of the fact that, in other western cultures, the term *science* applies to methodical and methodological inquiry in general. American technocracy has reduced the semantic field of the term *science* to the process of predictable and reproducible experimentation alone. In doing so, it suppresses the study of psychoanalysis.[8]

This is clearly not the case in Austria, where psychoanalysis was never subject to the superficial rejection that it underwent in the United States.[9] In 1997, The Institut für Wissenschaft und Kunst in Vienna held a symposium called "Die Wiener Psychiatrie im 20. Jahrhundert," which involved a collaboration of psychiatrists, physicians, social scientists, and humanists that would be difficult to imagine in the United States. There were papers on the history of psychoanalysis, war neuroses, psychiatry under National Socialism, the history of involuntary institutionalization, alcoholism, psychiatric ethics, psychiatry in the context of rhetoric and communication, and many others.[10] In 2000, the institute held the symposium "Traum, Logik und Geld," which was a confluence of economics, psychoanalysis, and analytic philosophy that celebrated the hundredth anniversary of Freud's *Die Traumdeutung*, Husserl's *Logische Untersuchungen*, and Simmel's *Philosophie des Geldes*. Co-funded by Bank Austria, the symposium presented papers on a multitude of topics including the logic of dream interpretation, instincts and financial markets, and Wittgenstein and Freud.

The library at the Sigmund Freud Museum in Vienna amasses interdisciplinary books on psychoanalysis in many languages. Its allied organization, the Sigmund Freud-Gesellschaft, has numerous events combining psychoanalysis and other disciplines. It sponsored the lecture series "Die Psychoanalyse nach Freud" and, in November 2000, heralded that month's theme of psychoanalysis and music with the event "Freud deutet Träume," which involved a performance and discussion of Otto Brusatti's musical composition of the same name. Brusatti, the music library director of the Library of Vienna (Wiener Stadt- und Landesbibliothek), sees *Die Traumdeutung* as "eine Wort-Klangreise ins Innere der Seele" and chose to set the work to music. Events such as these in Vienna are sterling examples of the contemporary pervasiveness of psychoanalysis.[11]

The presence of psychoanalysis in the aesthetic project, especially as a fruitful reflective activity for the writer, invokes the general theme of the therapeutic value of writing, that is, writing itself as a kind of psychotherapy. This may be the most reasonable way to approach the recent prose works of Werner Kofler, *Üble Nachrede — Furcht und Unruhe* (1997, Evil Slander, Fear, and Unrest) and *Manker: Invention* (1999), in which the author thematizes his involvement in a libel suit, a break-in in his apartment, and his own reception of the radio play version of *Üble Nachrede — Furcht und Unruhe*. He sets up an infinite regress of mirror images of himself within a postmodern confusion of artist, spectator, and media figure, so that the reader wonders if this is writing as an avoidance or instantiation of schizophrenia. Making public the psychological entrails of writing, he is at once writer, consumer, and consumed who introduces *Manker: Invention* with an epigraph saying that he dreamed of a magician whose art consisted in eating himself [sich selbst zu verspeisen]. Kofler's interest in schizophrenia, identity, and psychotherapy was evident in the 1978 novel *Ida H.: Eine Krankengeschichte* (Ida H.: A Medical History), reissued in 2000. This work can be generically situated in relation to Freud's "Krankengeschichten," such as those of Anna O. (1895) (*GW* 1: 75), the "Rat Man" (1909) (*GW* 7: 379), and the "Wolf Man" (1918) (*GW* 12: 27).

A fine example of the continuation of the Freudian tradition can be seen in the works of Paulus Hochgatterer (b. 1961), a Viennese psychiatrist and novelist whose professions recall the image of Arthur Schnitzler. In 1993, he published *Über die Chirurgie* (On Surgery), which is an oneiric, absurd, and often grotesque examination of the interplay of psyche and soma. The work progresses in free associative narration through several series of operations, while a patient observes that free association is not at all free, but subject to strict aesthetic rules. Hysteria is treated by hysterical analysts. Operation protocols are interspersed with dinner menus. A sparkling miniature crystal hedgehog is found in one patient's abdomen (146). This is an ironic trope for Austria: when frightened, the hedgehog retracts into a ball, hides its head, and stiffens its bristles. Most absurdly, however, but also most tellingly, a message in a bottle is found in the rectum of a patient. It is a full bottle of twelve-year-old Dimple Scotch, and the message reads, "Die Psychoanalyse hält den Tod für ein Phänomen des Widerstandes . . . gegen die Psychoanalyse" (168–69). This can be seen as a reification, a hysterical and hyperbolic conversion of neurosis into body and language, in which the patient literally has "Freud up the ass." Thereupon follows a series of rhetorical questions to Freud as to why he had a vasectomy, why he had thirty-two mouth cancer operations, and why he spent sixteen years dying, cigar by cigar. The interrogation concludes by inverting the message found in the rectum: psychoanalysis is a phenomenon of resistance to death (169–73). There is also another punning reification present here that does not work in English: "Freud ist im Arsch," which means that psychoanalysis is no longer working; it has reached its "end," where the conversion of psyche into soma is stopped dead in the face of physical reality.

In 1999, Hochgatterer published *Caretta Caretta,* which continues the themes of anality, telling of an orphaned fifteen-year old gay male prostitute who embarks on a search for the father. Similarly, his *Wildwasser* (1997, Rapids), tells of a seventeen-year-old whose father has also disappeared, and who embarks upon an odyssey to find him. Each of the six chapters begins with a citation from Catholic liturgy evoking the search for God the Father: kyrie eleison; gloria in excelsis deo; credo in unum deum; sanctus dominus; agnus dei; requiem aeternam dona eis. The crises of identity and language within the dissolution of empire at the first *fin de siècle* are mirrored in Hochgatterer's Vienna of the second *fin de siècle* as an ongoing search for the father and for order under an American cultural colonialization that is written in a Creolized blend of German and English.

In 2000, Josef Haslinger published the novel *Das Vaterspiel* (The Father Game), which contains two parallel narratives that approach each other so closely that the reader has increasing difficulty keeping them apart. One narrative deals with the decline of a prominent family of social democrats, the other with the nightmarish horrors lived by a Lithuanian Jewish family during the Holocaust. The respective sons narrate both novels in the first person. The Austrian is working on a computer game called "Vaternichtungsspiel," which he eventually sells in English as "The Father Game." The Jew searches for a Nazi war criminal. This story clearly deals with the Oedipal problem, as well as the repression of Austrian complicity in the Holocaust. It also takes place partly in New York, and one of the chapters is entitled "Losing My Religion," after the song by R.E.M. The preface to the novel contains a lengthy list of characters that reads like a random romp through history: Adolf Hitler, Marcello Mastroianni, Oswald Spengler, Ovid, Goethe, Bill Clinton, Neil Young, etc. It deals with the problems of Austria at the second fin de siècle, which is cracking under the failures of the politics and history of the twentieth century and American cultural colonization. But it does so in a manner humorous in its absurd irony: the patricidal game becomes a bestseller. The psychoanalytic theme of patricide functions here as a condensation of the problematic heritage of the fatherland. Haslinger's earlier work is also heavily psychoanalytic: in 1987, he published the psychopolitical essay "Politik der Gefühle" (The Politics of Feelings), in which he investigates the dynamics of repression and denial that led to the election of Kurt Waldheim. Repression and displacement are also evident in his acclaimed novel *Opernball* (1995, Opera Ball), which is interspersed with cultural memories and historical descriptions of the Holocaust and of Bergen-Belsen. The narrator is the journalist Fraser, who is half Jewish and has an assumed name that hides his German origin.

One of the most postmodern, pyrotechnic writers in Vienna today is Stefan Griebl, who writes under the pen name Franzobel. His novel *Der Trottelkongreß. Commedia dell'pape. Ein minimalistischer Heimatroman* (1998, The Congress of Jerks. Comedia dell'pape. A Minimalist Heimatroman) is a parodistic montage of fabricated names of popes and Austrians taken from the Vienna phone book. Every other page contains a photo of a male singing club on parade, which is evocative of Nazi marches. This cognitive confusion ends with the image of Pope "Johann Paul Pürzelmeier" getting kicked in the behind by his successor and the final words, "und es wurde wieder Ich" (104). This tropes on Freud's famous statement, "Wo Es war, soll Ich werden" (*GW* 15, 86). Out of this mad pastiche of stream of consciousness puns, which he terms "écriture autocomique," a coherent self is to emerge via an identification with paternal images, or popes as father figures. The epigraph of the book is "habeamus papam mobile," which evokes *perpetuum mobile*, a perpetuity of popes, father figures that Austria is always seeking. Franzobel's other works are also structured by ludic oneiric associations. In 1997, he published the play *Kafka: Eine Komödie,* in which Max Brod speaks in Joycean compounds (e.g. "Riesenkafkadichterschreiberleben"

[7]). In a recent interview, Franzobel said that his purpose is to evoke associations in the reader that are external to the author's sphere of influence (Herzog 1997, 21).

In 1997, Friederike Mayröcker published the prose piece *Das zu Sehende, das zu Hörende,* (That to be Seen, that to be Heard), which develops a variation on the theme of Narcissus in a way that employs psychoanalysis as a given, as a self-evident structure in need of no formal justification. The central figure is the countertenor Narkissus, a mental patient and altered response to the mythical figure who, when seeing his own image, experiences not love at first sight, but instead desperation and guilt, and who eventually severs the interlocutor Echo. Here, the original moment of self-reflection is not one of narcissistic self-love, but self-doubt. Her novel *Lection* (1994) also works via oneiric transitions and connections, and *Brütt, oder, Die seufzenden Gärten* (1998, Brütt, or, The Sighing Gardens) is written in a diary form of free association and automatic writing that achieves an entwining of philosophy, art, and literature.

In Mayröcker, one also encounters the psychoanalytic use of language as a concrete form of dream work. Her short prose work *Magische Blätter V* (1999, Magical Leaves V) can be characterized as a conversion of art, dream, and image into life and a confounding of artist, art, and reality. Alternating between analysis and dream, the work consists largely of poetic reactions to visual art, a kind of *ut pictura poesis* that undoes the distinction between word and image. She asks the concrete poet Eugen Gomringer, "wie bist du konkret und wie konkret bist du" (21). The work occasionally reads like a screenplay containing the film director's instructions to the cameraman, as if concept, form, and content were one. Themes of the world as a fragmented psycholinguistic construct recur in Viennese literature and can be situated on a continuum beginning at the first *fin de siècle*. In 1999, the poet Ferdinand Schmatz published the novel *das grosse babel,n*, which effects a reworking of biblical narratives beginning with an original state of linguistic rupture, as indicated in the title. The work makes use of the Freudian ideas of fort/da (*GW* 13, 9–15) and says that since the fall, things are present (da) as words, but are not understood. These words clothe us, but we do not dress up, we dress forth (fort) (18).

Elfriede Jelinek's *Das Lebewohl* (2000, The Farewell), contains three short plays. The first, "Das Lebewohl," uses interior monologue to mirror the nonsensical paranoid associations of Jörg Haider. "Der Tod und das Mädchen II" (Death and the Maiden II) begins with the maiden saying: "Mein Dasein ist Schlaf" (51). It tropes on the fairy tale of Sleeping Beauty, compares Haider to Hitler, and sees Austria as a sleeping maiden. The book jacket includes a comment by Jelinek, in which she says, "Dornröschen, das ist auch das kleine, dicke, hübsche, unschuldige, harmlose Land, das vom Prinzen Haider wachgeküßt wird. So ein Kuß ist dem Land schon einmal passiert, und schon damals hat es sich bekanntlich willig hingelegt." Both Austria and Haider are depicted here as dreamers who dream of an older, innocent Austria, one that, however, has never existed.

In 1998, Jelinek published *er nicht als er* (he not as he), which consists of twelve monologic sketches and focuses on the fact that the writer Robert Walser (1878–1956) spent the last thirty years of his life in an insane asylum. She employs the traditional Viennese forms of interior monologue and dream work to elegize Walser and to represent his psyche during those years. She says that he is one of those poets who do not mean "I" when they say "I": his inner life is thus a collective that belongs to all (39). The work plays with the pronoun *er:* "Rob-er-t nicht als Wals-er, er nicht als er," indicating that he was not himself, he is not he, he is us, our psyche. This notion of the artist as one who reveals a collective psychology is further specified by the statement: "Der Unterschied zwischen Schlaf und Tod ist der Traum" (32). The last few pages discuss the difference among sleep, dream, and death, implying the postmortem presence of the poet in the collective dream. Here, the afterlife of the poet, who speaks from the asylum, exists in his works, between life and death, as waking dream.

Jelinek's novel *Gier* (2000, Greed) deals with a policeman who seeks a new wife and a new house, and the novel treats the two elements so similarly, that the narrator confesses confusion as to which is being discussed. It is as if the work parodies the Freudian symbolic dream equation of rooms and women (*Frauenzimmer*). The policeman's uncontrolled desire (his *Gier*) results in the brutal death of the women he pursues. Structured by displacements, condensations, and confusions of percept and dream, the novel deals symbolically with the national guilt for brutality against women and encourages the reader to think in larger terms about how symbols of authority are responsible for the contemporary milieu. In 1998, she published the play *Ein Sportstück* (A Piece on/of Sports), which examines athletics as sanctioned violence. It explores the relationship between sports and war and offers a psychology of the themes of violence in present culture. The work is structured as a tragedy, in which the Greek chorus wears Nikes, and it deals with the Freudian concepts of Oedipus and Elektra, again in heightened reflexive form: the first character presented is "Elfi Elektra."

Deconstructive psychoanalytic techniques often focus on the city of Vienna itself. They frequently critique the phenomenon of Viennese amnesia as it pertains to fascism and the Holocaust. This is especially true of Jewish writers. In 1997, Milo Dor published *Wien, Juli 1999* (Vienna, July 1999), the title of which anticipates the millennium. There are two *Doppelgänger* in the novel; one is the right wing extremist Haselgruber, a surrogate for Haider, whose establishment of a "Dritte Republik" (117) in Vienna marginalizes minorities and foreigners. The other *Doppelgänger* is Mladen Raikow, a surrogate for the author, who refuses to be discouraged by neo-conservatism, and who preserves "seinen Traum von einem freien, kosmopolitischen Wien gegen unsichtbare, aber allgegenwärtige Feinde" (119). This is a continuation of the dream of a united Austria, but one that opposes a nightmarish version of Haiderism. In his essay "Meine Reisen nach Wien und zurück" (1995, My Travels to Vienna and Back), Dor claims that he suffers from the disease of always returning to Vienna without knowing why; he has no interest in the opera, the art museum, or the Prater, and he has never seen the Wienerwald (149). He admires the innate ability of the Viennese persistently to ignore unpleasantness (148). He sees an ephemeral atmosphere in Vienna, the center of a nonexistent empire, whose walls were built to celebrate a victory that never happened, and he claims to like the Viennese because they find it difficult to take themselves seriously (150).

A similar use of Jewish memory is present in the novels of Robert Schindel (b. 1944). *Gott schützt uns vor den guten Menschen* (1995, God Saves Us from Good People) carries the subtitle "Jüdisches Gedächtnis — Auskunftsbüro der Angst" (Jewish Memory — Information Office of Angst). Schindel holds that a person with memory is rare in Austria. In the novel *Gebürtig* (1992, translated as *Born-where*), crass corporeality is used to show the embodiment of identity: "In Herz und Lunge sitzen Glaube und Aberglaube, welche sich im Hirn als Identität und Ichsein ausdrücken" (9). Employing Freud's theory that the ego is bodily in nature (*GW* 13: 253), Schindel deconstructs folkish notions of consanguinity and race by representing them as hysterical conversions of psyche into soma, where ethnicity is projected onto the body in the form of a corporeal distinction of race and blood, thus generating an ideology of identity. This is an identity based on a massive Austrian denial, one to which Schindel assigns the emblem "weder verwandt noch verschwägert" (9), written in banner-like majuscule letters.[12] Thematically similar corporeal conversions are found in Ivan Ivanji's remarkable novel *Der Aschenmensch von Buchenwald* (1999, The Ash Man of Buchenwald). Ivanji, himself a survivor of Buchenwald, writes of a *Dachdecker* — an excellent image of "covering up" — who, while working at the crematorium at Buchenwald, finds urns hidden under the roof that contain the ashes of seven hundred death camp victims. The ashes rise from the urns and form an *es*, which then takes on human form, hovers in the air above Weimar, and cries in seven hundred voices, acting as a gadfly to the conscience of those below. This is the return of the repressed as one massive celestial admonition, a conversion of both id and superego into corporeal form. This configuration recalls Freud's taxonomy of the psyche, in which id and superego can act in collusion against the ego.

Gerhard Roth's short prose work *Die zweite Stadt* (1991, The Second City) is an ironic psycho-archaeology of Vienna. Beneath a church, an archaeologist finds the skeleton of a man who died while trying to pry open a coffin. He terms this "einen Alptraum, der unbeabsichtigt die österreichische Zerrissenheit illustriere" (14): on the surface, there is an image of order, but internally, there is mortal angst. Roth presents Vienna as the city where Freud was forced to make the discovery that the truth is not obvious, but exists on a subterranean level. All of central Vienna is connected by underworld passages. Skeletons, history, and Habsburg intestines are buried beneath the capital. Vienna is "eine große Nekropole" (26) containing "den größten unterirdischen See Europas" (27), where Freud learned that the border between normality and insanity is "eine so fließende" (30). Roth's Vienna is an urban geography of repression, denial, and neurosis, one where forgetting is only apparent. Roth uses comic psychoanalytic images to illustrate that humor can be a technique for undoing repression. Also, his novel *Der Plan* (1998, The Plan) deals with the schizophrenia, psychosomatic asthma, and paranoia of the hero Feldt, who interprets his perceptions as rebuses.

In Marlene Streeruwitz's drama *New York. New York* (1993), the unrenovated men's room at the tram station at the Burggasse in Vienna becomes a tourist attraction. It still bears the original inscription "k. k. Piß- und Bedürfnisanstalt" as well as "ein Doppeladler in Schwarz-Gold" (10). The only character in the play who has maintained an identity is the bathroom attendant (8), and tours are given in awkward English for Japanese tourists: "Gentlemen, I want to show you . . . you are in an antique WC. This toilet is built 1910 and was opened by the last Emperor of Austria, Franz Joseph (*Fraantz Tschosef*). It is told that he pissed in here and said: 'It was very beautiful. I was very pleased.' He always said this" (19). Thereupon, a chorus of Japanese tourists repeats the emperor's words in English. While this seems to parody more the direction that Germany is taking with a "Sony Center" proudly in the middle of its capital, it is also a caricature of the linguistic and identity crises of second *fin-de-siècle* Vienna. It employs a complex of allusions to history and empire that are located in a psychoanalytic conversion to the physical, to the phallus and the bowels, which effects both an implicit critique of patriarchy and phallocentrism as well as an expulsion of monarchist ideology.

Peter Henisch's novel *Schwarzer Peter* (2000, Black Peter) begins with an ironic undercutting of the image of Vienna on the Blue Danube. He says that, in the first place, the Danube is not blue, and in the second place, Vienna is not on the Danube; actually, the Danube passes Vienna by. The city really lies on a lesser tributary, the Danube Canal, which is the color of pea soup, and nobody would ever compose a waltz about a canal. The narrator also imagines that he was conceived there (7). The title is also a locution for *scapegoat,* and so is the narrator, an outsider who is the son of a black American soldier and an Austrian. One of the themes of the novel is, again, the search for the father, as well as the search for identity. Peter loses his passport and cannot prove his citizenship; without his passport, he is not an Austrian.

Elisabeth Reichart's novel *Nachtmär* (1995, Night Tale) plays phonetically with the quasi-homophonous English *nightmare.* The work deals with the illusions of selfhood within a psychological collectivity and with the betrayal of a Jewish woman, Esther, the daughter of exiles, who became the object of the fickle emotions of Viennese friends. A major theme of the work is the fluidity of identity, which is juxtaposed with Austrian guilt and responsibility. *Nachtmär* can be seen as a working through of Third Reich guilt, in which reveric excursions into the past interrupt "das vertraute Nicht-Wissen-Wollen" (188).

The itinerant writer Leopold Federmair, who occasionally spends time in Vienna, wrote the novel *Das Exil der Träume* (1999, The Exile of Dreams), which tells the reader that one is permanently trapped between here and there, and that the spirit rests in a nowhere land, in the exile of dream. His collection of shorter prose works *Der Kopf denkt in Bildern* (1996, The Head Thinks in Pictures) begins with the story of Herr Kaiser, who, lying underneath an automobile, grabs onto his "steifes Glied" and uses it to vault himself above the detritus of the city and eventually above the globe. He is called "unser Herrscher," whose purpose is to shame us (7–8). Here, human thought is represented as symbolic, but in a random fashion that is also psychosexual, impressionistic, and episodic.

Gerhard Jaschke's *Illusionsgebiet Nervenruh* (1997, The Illusionary Area of Nerve Rest) is a collection of shorter prose works that takes its title from one minimalist anecdote: a first-person narrator, sitting on the toilet, is disturbed by the singing widow of a famous waltz composer who martyrs her voice for the church choir (45). Here, the figure of ostensible Austrian tranquility is deconstructed by a condensation of images of religion, culture, patriarchy, and history, which reveal the impossibility of privacy, even in the WC. Psychoanalysis has even influenced the Viennese popular detective novelist Wolf Haas. His *Ausgebremst* (1998, Boxed Out) is structured by themes of paranoia, delusions, persecution complexes, and conspiracy theories. And his recent detective trilogy *Auferstehung der Toten* (1996, The Resurrection of the Dead), *Der Knochenmann* (1997, The Skeleton), and *Komm, süßer Tod* (1998, Come, Sweet Death), uses motifs of the role of the unconscious in cognition, calculation, and problem solving. Similarly, Gert Jonke's *Es singen die Steine* (1998, The Stones Are Singing) is a meta-theatrical piece that uses dream devices to represent the multiple personalities of the protagonist Wildgruber, whose threefold identity threatens the political monarchic order.

Andreas Okopenko's prose work *Traumberichte* (1998, Dream Reports) is a good example of the ludic use of Freudian dreamwork. Okopenko offers a collection of dreams resembling the laconic descriptions of dream contents in Freud's *Die Traumdeutung*, but there is no subsequent attempt at interpretation. The absurd titles describe the dream contents succinctly and comically in rebus form: "Gebratenes Skelett und Meßbecher" (18) [Fried Skeleton and Measuring Cup], "Berg, Urin und die schöne Putzfrau" (166) [Mountain, Urine, and the Pretty Cleaning Lady], "Wohnbeete und heiße Gräber" (198) [Residential Plots and Hot Graves]. One chapter contains examples of writing while asleep. In the afterword, the authorial voice claims to be that of a realist, for whom dreams represent tangible prosaic reality (203). This use of rebuses self-consciously thematizes and ironizes the Viennese tradition of representing dream as empirical reality, which seeks to mirror the diurnal phenomena of mental catachresis. Peter Rosei's novel *Verzauberung* (1997, Enchantment) contains a similar attempt. The section "Rorschach-Text" narrates the author's family life as a boy within a discourse of plain descriptiveness, but it does so via rebus-like dream images presented to the reader as Rorschach figures to be interpreted. The narrator supplies, however, no interpretive guidance.

Thus, one can argue for the presence of a psychoanalytic tradition in the literature of Vienna that proceeds on a continuum from the turn of the twentieth century to the turn of the twenty-first. The view of the human condition as one of dream, neurosis, and language that emerged from Vienna at the first *fin de siècle* persists through the second, although the modes of representation tend to differ. Whereas the psychoanalytic aspects tended to be thematized in the literature of 1900, they have become fully systemic in the literature of 2000. They are part and parcel of the syntax of aesthetic discourse, are activated without preface, and serve as intertexts in need of no introduction. Never absent, they have returned from an odyssey through poststructuralism, feminism, and Holocaust studies to reinform language and to move the world from linguistic to psycholinguistic construct. This construct is, however, represented in a hyper-reflexive,[13] ironic, and ludic manner. Moreover, the earlier notion that life consists in fundamental catachreses, in random sequences of dislocation and dissonance, is even more salient, if not dominant, and tends to be expressed in more radical form. This odyssey also recovers the basic iconicity of language by resituating it in the context of dream symbolism, which foregrounds the allusive and associative operations of displacement and condensation. The literalizing devices of hysterical conversion from the symbolic to the corporeal are manifested in a way that is even more macabre than was the case in 1900 and occasionally take on scatological[14] form, but they still tend to be playfully and comically configured.

In 1999, Armin Thurnher published the collection of essays *Das Trauma, ein Leben: Österreichische Einzelheiten* (The Trauma, A Life: Austrian Particulars), which is fragmented, impressionistic, and dreamlike in its associativeness. Thurnher plays with the homophony of *Traum* (dream) and trauma, saying that the latter has replaced the former in Austrian consciousness. Each essay is introduced by a quote from Grillparzer's *Der Traum ein Leben,* but Thurnher inserts a comma that was not there originally. (Was he aware of this rupture?) He says of Austria, "Es ist auch ein verträumtes Land, es träumt noch immer den Traum von jener Größe, die ihm in einem traumatischen Ersten Weltkrieg genommen wurde" (26). Thus the dream of the first *fin de siècle* is replaced by the trauma of the second. Austria itself becomes a dream construct, from which there remain only isolated fragments, visible in the subtitle *Einzelheiten* (particulars). These fragments can only be connected by secondary revisions, by suppressing gaps and making metanarratives out of what Freud called "Fetzen und Flicken" (*GW* 2/3, 493). Such metanarratives can yield but dreams of interpretation.

Notes

[1] Sigmund Freud, *The Standard Edition of the Complete Psychological Works of Sigmund Freud,* 24 vols. (London: Hogarth Press, 1953–1974), vol. 4: xxxii. Freud wrote this in English for the introduction to the 1932 publication of *The Standard Edition.* There is no German version.

[2] Sigmund Freud, *Gesammelte Werke,* 18 vols. (Frankfurt am Main: S. Fischer, 1960), vol. 14, 74. All German quotations are taken from this edition, referred to as *GW.*

[3] Max Eugen Burckhard, review of *Die Traumdeutung* by Sigmund Freud, in *Die Zeit* (Vienna), 6 January 1900, 9. Burckhard was director of the Burgtheater in Vienna.

[4] Hugo von Hofmannsthal, *Gesammelte Werke in Einzelausgaben,* 15 vols. (Frankfurt am Main: S. Fischer, 1953–1966), vol. 2, 18. All quotations are taken from this edition, referred to as *GW.*

[5] See Elias Canetti, *Die Fackel im Ohr, Lebensgeschichte 1921–1931* (Munich/ Vienna: Hanser, 1980), 137–39.

[6] Martens's masterful study *Shadow Lines: Austrian Literature from Freud to Kafka* offers some of the most intelligent readings of psychoanalysis and literature to date. Her paradigm is dualistic, however, whereas this study seeks to discuss the more probable presence of an adualistic structure in the discourses of psychoanalysis and aesthetics.

[7] Both Martens and Anders discuss the concretization of metaphor in Kafka's *The Metamorphosis* and *The Penal Colony.*

[8] Another marginalizing influence was exerted by the post-war New Criticism, which eschewed psychoanalytic studies.

[9] This excludes, of course, the persecution of psychoanalysis during the Nazi period.

[10] Publication of the conference proceedings is forthcoming with Picus Verlag, Vienna.

[11] Outspokenly negative critiques of Freud are rare in Vienna. See Karl Reitter, *Der König ist nackt: Eine Kritik an Sigmund Freud* (Vienna: Verlag für Gesellschaftskritik, 1996), which was not well received. Even the Forum Anti-Psychiatrischer Initiativen Wien (FAPI Wien) has as its opponent not psychoanalysis, but biological behavior modification in general. They oppose brain surgery, shock therapy, and psychopharmacology and recommend treating patients with analysis and homeopathic medicines. Perhaps not coincidentally, the organization meets on Wednesday evenings.

[12] Slibar sees Freud's *Das Unbehagen in der Kultur* (1930, *Civilization and Its Discontents*) as the basis for representations of memory and Holocaust in the writings of Schindel and Ruth Klüger.

[13] One factor contributing to the hyperreflexivity of contemporary Viennese literature is the extensive academic preparation of many of its authors. Federmair, Haas, Haslinger, Hochgatterer, Menasse, Reichart, and Schmatz all hold the doctoral degree

in literary or related studies, and extensive pre-doctoral work was done by Franzobel, Dor, Henisch, and many others. Such academic training situates aesthetics in a dialog with literary and cultural history.

[14] The paramount example of the identification of language, body, and psyche is found in the works of the late Styrian author Werner Schwab (1958–1994), especially in his *Fäkaliendramen* (Graz: Droschl, 1991) (Feces Dramas).

Works Cited

Anders, Günther. *Franz Kafka*. London: Bowes and Bowes, 1960.

Bahr, Hermann. *Die Überwindung des Naturalismus*. Dresden: C. Pierson, 1981.

Beer-Hofmann, Richard. *Gesammelte Werke*. Frankfurt am Main: S. Fischer, 1963.

Burckhard, Max Eugen. Review of *Die Traumdeutung* by Sigmund Freud, in *Die Zeit* (Vienna) 275 (6 January 1900), 9.

Brusatti, Otto. *Freud deutet Träume*. Performance, Sigmund Freud Museum, Vienna, 7 November 2000.

Calderón de la Barca, Pedro. *La vida es sueño*. Madrid: Edimat Libros, 1998.

Canetti, Elias. *Die Fackel im Ohr, Lebensgeschichte 1921–1931*. Munich/Vienna: Hanser, 1980.

Dor, Milo. "Meine Reisen nach Wien und zurück." In *Wien erzählt*, edited by Jutta Freund. Frankfurt am Main: S. Fischer, 1995, 146–50.

———. *Wien, Juli 1999*. Vienna: Zsolnay, 1997.

Federmair, Leopold. *Das Exil der Träume*. Vienna: edition selene, 1999.

———. *Der Kopf denkt in Bildern*. Klagenfurt/Vienna: Ritter, 1996.

Francis, Mark. *The Viennese Enlightenment*. New York: St. Martin's Press, 1985.

Franzobel. *Kafka: Eine Komödie*. Klagenfurt: edition selene, 1997.

———. *Der Trottelkongreß. Commedia dell'pape. Ein minimalistischer Heimatroman*. Klagenfurt/Vienna: Ritter, 1998.

Freud, Sigmund. *Gesammelte Werke*. 18 vols. Frankfurt am Main: S. Fischer, 1960.

———. *The Standard Edition of the Complete Psychological Works of Sigmund Freud*. 24 vols. London: Hogarth, 1953–1974.

Gay, Peter. *Freud: A Life for Our Time*. New York/London: W. W. Norton, 1988.

Grillparzer, Franz. *Sämtliche Werke: Ausgewählte Briefe, Gespräche, Berichte*. 4 vols. Munich: Carl Hanser, 1965.

Haas, Wolf. *Auferstehung der Toten*. Reinbek: Rowohlt, 1996.

————. *Ausgebremst*. Reinbek: Rowohlt, 1998.

————. *Der Knochenmann*. Reinbek: Rowohlt, 1997.

————. *Komm, süßer Tod*. Reinbek: Rowohlt, 1998.

Haslinger, Josef. *Opernball*. Frankfurt am Main: S. Fischer, 1995.

————. *Das Vaterspiel*. Frankfurt am Main: S. Fischer, 2000.

Henisch, Peter. *Schwarzer Peter*. Salzburg/Vienna: Residenz, 2000.

Herzog, Andreas. "Gespräch mit Franzobel." *Neue Deutsche Literatur* 45/512 (1997): 11–21.

Hochgatterer, Paulus. *Caretta Caretta*. Vienna: Deuticke, 1999.

————. *Über die Chirugie*. Vienna: Deuticke, 1993.

————. *Wildwasser*. Vienna: Deuticke, 1997.

Hofmannsthal, Hugo von. *Gesammelte Werke in Einzelausgaben*. 15 vols. Frankfurt am Main: S. Fischer, 1953–1966.

Ivanji, Ivan. *Der Aschenmensch von Buchenwald*. Vienna: Picus, 1999.

Jaschke, Gerhard. *Illusionsgebiet Nervenruh*. Vienna: Sonderzahl, 1997.

Jelinek, Elfriede. *er nicht als er*. Frankfurt am Main: Suhrkamp, 1998.

————. *Gier*. Reinbek: Rowohlt, 2000.

————. *Das Lebewohl*. Berlin: Berlin Verlag, 2000.

————. *Ein Sportstück*. Reinbek: Rowohlt, 1998.

————. "Zur Wiedereröffnung des Wiener Psychoanalytisches Ambulatorium." Lecture, Wiener Psychoanalytisches Ambulatorium, 12 October 1999.

Jonke, Gert. *Es singen die Steine*. Salzburg/Vienna: Residenz, 1998.

Kofler, Werner. *Manker: Invention*. Vienna: Deuticke, 1999.

————. *Üble Nachrede — Furcht und Unruhe*. Reinbek: Rowohlt, 1997.

Kokoschka, Oskar. *Dramen und Bilder*. Leipzig: Kurt Wolff, 1913.

————. *Vier Dramen. Orpheus und Eurydike. Der brennende Dornbusch. Mörder, Hoffnung der Frauen. Hiob*. Berlin: Paul Cassirer, 1919.

Kraus, Karl. *Die Fackel* 376/77 (1913), 668/75 (1924). Vienna: Verlag "Die Fackel," 1899–1936.

Lacan, Jacques. *The Four Fundamental Concepts of Psychoanalysis*. New York: Norton, 1978.

Mach, Ernst. *Beiträge zur Analyse der Empfindungen*. Jena: G. Fischer, 1886.

Mann, Thomas. *Der Tod in Venedig*. Frankfurt am Main: S. Fischer, 1997.

Martens, Lorna. *Shadow Lines: Austrian Literature from Freud to Kafka*. Lincoln: U of Nebraska P, 1996.

Mauthner, Fritz. *Beiträge zu einer Kritik der Sprache.* Stuttgart: Cotta, 1901–1902.

Mayröcker, Friederike. *Brütt, oder, Die seufzenden Gärten.* Frankfurt am Main: Suhrkamp, 1998.

———. *Lection.* Frankfurt am Main: Suhrkamp, 1994.

———. *Magische Blätter V.* Frankfurt am Main: Suhrkamp, 1999.

———. *Das zu Sehende, Das zu Hörende.* Frankfurt am Main: Suhrkamp, 1997.

Okopenko, Andreas. *Traumberichte.* Linz: Blattwerk, 1998.

Reichart, Elisabeth. *Nachtmär.* Salzburg/Vienna: Otto Müller, 1995.

Rosei, Peter. *Verzauberung.* Frankfurt am Main: Verlag der Autoren, 1997.

Roth, Gerhard. *Der Plan.* Frankfurt am Main: S. Fischer, 1998.

———. "Die zweite Stadt." In *Eine Reise in das Innere von Wien: Essays.* Frankfurt am Main: S. Fischer, 1991. 14–31.

Roth, Michael S., ed. *Freud: Conflict and Culture.* New York: Knopf, 1998.

Schindel, Robert. *Gebürtig.* Frankfurt am Main: Suhrkamp, 1992.

———. *Gott schützt uns vor den guten Menschen.* Frankfurt am Main: Suhrkamp, 1995.

Schmatz, Ferdinand. *das grosse babel,n.* Innsbruck: Haymon-Verlag, 1999.

Schnitzler, Arthur. *Gesammelte Werke in Einzelausgaben.* Frankfurt am Main: S. Fischer, 1977–1979.

Schorske, Carl. *Fin-de-siècle Vienna: Politics and Culture.* New York: Knopf, 1980.

Slibar, Neva. "Anschreiben gegen das Schweigen: Robert Schindel, Ruth Klüger, die Postmoderne und Vergangenheitsbewältigung." In *Jenseits des Diskurses: Literatur und Sprache in der Postmoderne,* edited by Albert Berger and Gerda E. Moser. Vienna: Passagen Verlag, 1994.

Streeruwitz, Marlene. *New York. New York. Elysian Park. Zwei Stücke.* Frankfurt am Main: Suhrkamp, 1993.

Thurnher, Armin. *Das Trauma, ein Leben: Österreichische Einzelheiten.* Vienna: Zsolnay, 1999.

Tichy, Marina, and Sylvia Zwettler-Otte. *Freud in der Presse: Rezeption Sigmund Freuds und der Psychoanalyse in Österreich 1895–1938.* Vienna: Sonderzahl, 1999.

Timms, Edward. *Karl Kraus, Apocalyptic Satirist.* New Haven/London: Yale UP, 1986.

Wittgenstein, Ludwig. *Tractatus Logico-Philosophicus.* London: Routledge & Kegan Paul, 1961.

Worbs, Michael. *Nervenkunst: Literatur und Psychoanalyse im Wien der Jahrhundertwende.* Frankfurt am Main: Europäische Verlagsanstalt, 1983.

Venice as Mediator between Province and Viennese Metropolis: Themes in Rilke, Hofmannsthal, Gerhard Roth, and Kolleritsch

John Pizer

IN A MANNER SIMILAR TO VIENNA, the historical, social, and aesthetic contradictions of Venice have led to its engagement as both backdrop and narrative subject by writers for centuries. German literature's most famous treatment of the Italian city's bifurcated character, its oscillation in a subject's perceptual field between ornate, elaborately staged beauty and concomitant putrefaction and decadence, is Thomas Mann's *Der Tod in Venedig* (1912). Because their own capital, Vienna, has also been imbued throughout its existence by these polar but intertwined attributes, Austrian writers do not tend to treat Venice in the antithetical, alienated manner of Mann. Austrian writers and their characters, in my view, do not possess the ascetic North German sensibilities of a Mann or Gustav Aschenbach, and are more inured to both the shock and the seduction of Venice. Then too, it is worth remembering that Venice was part of the Austrian empire from 1797–1805, 1814–1848, and from 1849–1866. Thus, even in much later periods, Austrian authors such as those discussed here have literally felt "at home" there, and their characters evince less of a sense of alienation in Venice than those of Mann.

Because Vienna, particularly at the turn into the twentieth century, was marked by the interconnected antipodes of voluptuousness and decay, the dialectics that inform Austrian literature's engagement with Venice at both the nineteenth and twentieth century *fins de siècle* are quite different from those obtaining in *Der Tod in Venedig*. As two recent collections of essays, *Literatur und Provinz* (1986) and *Metropole und Provinz* (1994), have shown, the works of German-language authors in general and Austrian writers in particular have consistently reflected the sociopolitical and aesthetic tensions between cityscape and countryside, especially from the nineteenth century onward. What has not been elucidated, and what this essay will demonstrate, is the function in Austrian literature of Venice as a mediator between the Austrian province and Vienna at the two most recent *fins de siècle*. Drawing on works by Rainer Maria Rilke and Hugo von Hofmannsthal at the turn into the twentieth century and by Gerhard Roth (b. 1942) and Alfred Kolleritsch (b. 1931) close to its end, this essay argues that Venice's seemingly perfect blend of nature and artifice, its lack of pronounced urban and agrarian attributes, allows it to synthesize the polarities between city and province.

The relatively harmonious environment of Austria's alpine and pastoral regions is a common theme in nineteenth-century Austrian literature. It is found especially in works by writers such as Adalbert Stifter (1805–1868) and Peter Rosegger (1843–1918). As Maria Krysztofiak has shown in her essay on the tension between big city and province in Rilke's *Die Aufzeichnungen des Malte Laurids Brigge* (1910, translated as *The Notebooks of Malte Laurids Brigge*), the eponymous protagonist's deep-seated alienation in an urban milieu causes him to seek compensation in provincial images drawn from his childhood and youth, and the novel represents an artistic treatment of the traditional modernist topos of the sick city as opposed to the salubrious province (136–37). While the big city of Rilke's novel is Paris, and the province is that of the Danish countryside, it is worth nothing that the itinerant Rilke found rural environs such as Worpswede, Duino, and Sierre most to his liking, and regarded Paris as far more agreeable than Vienna, a city toward which his feelings ranged from indifference to loathing. In a letter of February 15, 1916 to his publisher Anton Kippenberg, Rilke complains that Austria's capital, with its slovenly imprecision and the shabby pleasures its residents find in it, is a personal torment.; Vienna simply causes him to suffer (*Briefe zur Politik*, 154–55). To be sure, Rilke's distaste for Vienna at this time must have been heightened by the martial atmosphere enveloping the city in the midst of the First World War, though he does not link the war to his expression of antipathy. But, writing on his late friend in 1948, the noted philosopher of culture Rudolf Kassner refers to an encounter with Rilke before the Great War, in 1907, when the Prague-born poet spoke of Vienna as a foreign city he regarded as outside his sphere of interest (328–29). While Krysztofiak shows that Malte's reveries on his youth in the Danish countryside provide a psychic counterweight to the loneliness and poverty he endures in Paris, it is Venice that Malte, late in the narrative, describes as "Das schöne Gegengewicht der Welt."[1] Although Malte's reflections on the Danish countryside sometimes assume an idyllic tone (*SM*, 6, 746), the limitations of life on Ulsgaard are underscored by his grandmother's contempt for it, a contempt stemming from the boundaries this life sets to the exercise of her talent and aptitude (*SM*, 6, 820). Malte believes Venice strikes a perfect balance between the extremes of a harmonious, spatially open but intellectually restricted rural life and the artistically stimulating but isolated and alienating life of the metropolis. What allows Venice to strike this balance, in Malte view, is the city's embodiment of the iron will that brought about its hard birth out of the sea. Physical necessity, aesthetic sensibility, and an expansive spirit have reduced Venice's size to a bare minimum, allowing its unmediated connection to its surrounding natural maritime environs, filling the city with the world's treasures and infusing even its manifold delicate adornments with latent energy (*SM*, 6, 932–33). As Richard Exner has shown in his article on Rilke's experience of Venice, the city's equipoised character — hovering between land and sea, even between life and death — is what made it so attractive for the poet, and we can add that Venice transcends the limitations of city and country by virtue of its position perfectly balanced on the narrow strip ("This strip of between-world," as Exner, citing Rilke, puts it in the title of his essay) between urbanity and naturalness. This absolute equilibrium between worlds allows Venice, in both Rilke's poems and prose, to bring into play its mirroring function. Indeed, the poems "Venezianischer Morgen" (Venetian Morning) and "Spätherbst in Venedig" turn the city into a symbol for such mirroring, a mirroring preceded in Rilke's novel by the evocation of a Venice quite different from that imagined by its hordes of tourists (Ryan, 271–72). From this milieu emerges the doppelgänger of Abelone, Malte's love in Denmark, in the form of a beautiful Dane at a Venetian party (*SW*, 6, 931–36). Like Venice itself, she appears as a perfect albeit fleeting vision not to be possessed, and her presence creates a structural counterweight to a nightmarish doppelgänger vision experienced in the Danish countryside of Malte's youth, where he must himself function as a mirror (*SW*, 6, 804–9), and an uneasy though illuminating experience of self as double brought on by Malte's feelings of isolation and claustrophobia in Paris (*SW*, 6, 777–78). Venice's ability to serve as the ideal mirror through which a double can emerge is also linked to its liminality, its situation in the space between city and nature.

Malte has a sense of being virtually quarantined in his confined and confining quarters. He feels trapped within the very "narrowness" of his own being in Paris during a night filled with a sense of carefully locked doors and a nearly opaque window (*SW*, 6, 777–78). The ambiance evoked in this passage is reminiscent of his 1903 poem "Denn, Herr, die großen Städte sind," which describes fearful people living in dark rooms, cut off from an external, natural world of which they are unaware (*SW*, 1, 345). In the poems about Venice (1907–08) contained in the important collection *Neue Gedichte*, on the contrary, human will and human presence are shown to be fully blended into the natural world; in "Spätherbst in Venedig," for example, the city's origins are evoked in the image of human will arising from the ground (*SW*, 1, 610). Bernhard Blume has shown in an essay on this poem that Rilke believed Venice's communal existence was purer than elsewhere; at its founding, natural necessity fused with powerful human determination to create achievement "aus dem puren Nichts." Venice was for Rilke the offspring of beauty emanating directly from the sea (353–54). Its embodiment of "city *as* art," to quote Tony Tanner (4), is tied to its perfect economy of form between the human and the elemental world, between an urban and a natural ambiance. Venice for Rilke was still rooted in these balance-inducing origins, as even his early poems on the city (1897), though resonant with the contrast between extremes of wealth and poverty there, suggest (*SW*, 1, 116–18). Its liminality thus prevents it from being infected with what the poet saw as the slovenly sordidness and imprecision of Vienna; in Rilke's view, Venice constituted the essence of precision and economy of form. For Rilke, Venice did not suffer from the isolation from nature he found in the big city. Thus, Malte calls Venice "das schöne Gegengewicht der Welt" in *Die Aufzeichnungen des Malte Laurids Brigge* (*SW*, 6, 933); it sublates the limitations other, less fortunate communities are unable to overcome because of their lack of perfect equilibrium.

Hofmannsthal's early tale *Das Dorf im Gebirge* (1896) juxtaposes the polarities between metropolis and province in a manner more direct than is evident in Rilke. A group of young people from the city is spending part of their summer in the alpine countryside. Their flightiness and slavish attention to evanescent fashions of the day stand in stark contrast to the constancy and rootedness of the local populace and their landscape through a plethora of concrete details. Especially suggestive is Hofmannsthal's description of the city group's tennis court construction; the courts enclose themselves within spider-web like nets, thereby distorting the surrounding land with its timeless plowing activity (*Prosa I*, 326), as though these urbanites wanted to wall themselves away from nature as they had in the city. In an article on turn of the century Viennese literature's treatment of Austria's provinces which admirably summarizes the contrapuntal technique employed in the tale, Juliane Vogel shows that although Hofmannsthal painted an idealized and artificial portrait of rural resorts seen from a distance, Hofmannsthal's experiences in the Austro-Hungarian Empire's Eastern provinces were marked by unrelieved dreariness. Therefore, he had to call on his imaginative magic to make of these places inescapable and timeless landscapes, accessible only to the dreamer (Vogel, 110). In the case of Venice, this is unnecessary, for he found this city itself *immanently* to be the most dreamlike creation in the entire world (*Aufzeichnungen*, 338). Venice became for Hofmannsthal what one critic has termed a "second home" (Bangerter, 6), and this city provided the setting for a number of his significant dramas, such as *Der Tod des Tizian* (1892), *Der Abenteurer und die Sängerin* (1899), *Das gerettete Venedig* (1905), and *Cristinas Heimreise* (1910). However, I will examine two prose works: *Erinnerung schöner Tage* (1908), and the novel fragment *Andreas* (1932). This selection is justified by the treatment of Venice as a perfect balance between urban work of art and nature in *Erinnerung schöner Tage,* and by *Andreas*'s employment of three discrete spaces: Vienna (Andreas's home), the countryside he traverses on his way to Venice, and Venice itself, which sublates the other two spheres.

In his reading of *Erinnerung schöner Tage,* Klaus Weissenberger notes that Venice, in Hofmannsthal's view, "represents a unique fusion of landscape and artisanship as a testimony to the timelessness of cultural creation" (81). The narrator of *Erinnerung schöner Tage* recollects an evening spent in the town as guide to two young siblings and in a hotel imaginatively listening to a couple in an adjoining room. While still outside in the dusk, the narrator experiences the interplay of the maritime tableaux and the city, blended both by natural and artificial light. This evening glow not only blurs the boundary between the urban milieu and its natural setting, but welds the past to the present in a manner reminiscent of Rilke's early Venice poetry.[2] The temporal synchronicity and the effacing of the separation between the human domain of the city and its vaguely chthonic insular surroundings are achieved through Hofmannsthal's painterly chiaroscuro technique, but Venice itself inspires this vision, one that stirs the narrator's creative powers before he retires to his inn. It is Venice that transcends the extreme gap between the ambiances of metropolis and province created by Hofmannsthal in *Das Dorf im Gebirge. Erinnerung schöner Tage* was written only a few years after the publication of Hofmannsthal's famous letter composed in the name of Phillip Lord Chandos (1902), so it is unsurprising that fulfillment of the creative impulse inspired by the narrator's Venetian vision always remains just out of reach; the objects he would coalesce into a coherent tale alternately resist and seem close to yielding to his efforts, as they did with Hofmannsthal's Englishman. However, *Erinne-*

rung schöner Tage closes on another harmonious note, as the narrator's "geheimnisvoll begünstigtes Auge" envisions the characters moving about in his imagination infused by the light of the sun shining behind a thunder-cloud onto a Venetian garden landscape. These characters become at once people and manifestations of the natural elements air, water, and fire (*Kritische Ausgabe* 28, 69).[3]

The harmonious vision of Venice at dusk drawn in *Erinnerung schöner Tage* should not be taken as a sign that Hofmannsthal's Venetian imagery is sanguine. In *Der Tod des Tizian*, a clear division is drawn between the ethereal realm of the painter and his apprentices who are gathered at the dying Titian's villa, and the profane hideousness of the city below it. Inspired by an Elizabethan play by Thomas Otway, Hofmannsthal's *Das gerettete Venedig* reflects the corrupt, debauched atmosphere of the city evoked in the earlier drama. Tanner suggests that it is conceivable, although not certain, that in recreating Otway's decadent and deeply corrupt milieu, Hofmannsthal "intended a comment on his own contemporary Vienna" (215). In *Andreas,* we are also presented with a degenerate Venice, that of the eighteenth century. Though this Venice is less gruesomely violent than that of *Das gerettete Venedig,* which is set in the year 1618, it is still an immoral metropolis, where the right to deflower a virgin can be sold in a lottery, and the links in this collection of fragments between the Italian city and Maria Theresia's Vienna are explicit. Though *Andreas* contains only one strand of cohesive narrative among the many notes composed in the first two decades of the twentieth century, this main strand strongly establishes three primary spatial coordinates around which the composition revolves: Vienna, the Carinthian countryside through which the protagonist Andreas von Ferschengelder must pass in traveling from his Viennese hometown to Venice, and Venice itself. Perhaps the most telling comparison between the Italian city and the hometown of Andreas and his creator is to be found in the following note: "Roman: Venedig. Die grosse Welt. Alles berührbarer als zu Haus — durch die Atmosphäre von Maskenball u. Spielbank" (*KR,* 30, 159). Venice is the "great world" in more concentrated, accessible, and seductive form than Vienna, due to its condensed topography and its masked, thereby erotic and alluring character. Although the city as described in the fragments possesses the urban sophistication necessary for such cosmopolitanism, Andreas is impressed by its tranquility, an agreeable contrast with Vienna's noisy equestrian traffic and made possible by Venice's water-based modes of transportation (*KR,* 30, 45).

Traveling through Carinthia on his journey, Andreas experiences the province and its people as elements in a rustic idyll; Hofmannsthal paints an initial picture of the simple goodness of peasants in the countryside reminiscent of traditional *Heimat* (homeland) novels (*KR*, 30, 53), and Andreas is capable of feeling at one with his temporary provincial environment, perceiving life as resonant with a harmonious totality (*KR*, 30, 76). His utopia is shattered through the depraved actions of his manservant Gotthelf, whose deeds force Andreas to confront his own dark side. Romana, the female embodiment of pastoral simplicity, naturalness, and unaffectedness whom Andreas encounters in Carinthia, quickly becomes the object of his desire, but he has a nightmarish vision of her fleeing him in a human-filled street in Vienna near his parents' home, unnaturally clothed in half-peasant, half-city clothes, with her face displaying a wooden, spoiled quality (*KR*, 30, 64). Andreas's ominous dream makes life in Vienna with Romana unpalatable, and Gotthelf's attempted murder of a servant girl in the employ of Romana's family makes a protracted stay in the Carinthian province impossible, so he moves on to Venice. In portraying this city, Hofmannsthal again blends urban and agrarian tableaux (see especially *KR*, 30, 90 and 94). Despite the malevolent corruption *Andreas* associates with Venice, Hofmannsthal envisioned his novel as enacting the overcoming of antitheses such as body and spirit, foreign world and German world (*KR*, 30, 197), and Venice is a natural site for this sublation, with its intermediary position between metropolis and province, its incorporation of ambiances otherwise divided in the novel fragment's principal narrative strand between Vienna and Carinthia. Unlike Rilke, Hofmannsthal lived in Austria's capital for most of his life. Still, in a letter to Richard Strauss dated January 31, 1914, he expressed irritation at the composer's calling him a Viennese; were that true, Hofmannsthal asserts, the city's atmosphere wouldn't go so much against his grain. Thus his "great narrative" (*Andreas*) has as its content a young Viennese's development into a human being, or German (*KR*, 30, 367). Venice, regarded by Hofmannsthal as the land of transition *par excellence* because of its spiritual and geographical situation between land and lagoon, Occident and Orient, earth and water (Alewyn, 100), and, we might add, between city and nature, would naturally facilitate Andreas's own transition as the poet envisioned it. As Tanner notes, the novel was apparently "intended to be a sort of *Bildungsroman*" (221), and given Hofmannsthal's embrace of the ideal of *Bildung* (education in the broadest sense, acculturation), even Andreas's development into a German would be enhanced, in Hofmannsthal's view, by his sojourn in a city not so foreign to a Viennese native.

Gotthart Wunberg has indicated that Austrian modernists at the turn of century, including Rilke and Hofmannsthal, found harmonious representations and a consciousness of totality to be self-understood principles, even as their work reflected an increasing awareness of fragmentation in the contemporary world (107–8). Such striving for literary "monism," as Wunberg calls it, is evident in the harmonious provincial tableaux drawn by Rilke and Hofmannsthal and in their portrayals of a Venice that bridges different kinds of antinomies. In the postmodern world of the later twentieth century, where fragmentation was so much a given that it has become a normative element in narrative technique, and where the idyllic rural world was drawn into proximity with kitsch and banality (Pott, 9), such thematic and structural monism is inconceivable. In the novels of Gerhard Roth, Austrian provincial life is resolutely stripped of all traces of sentimentality. In a number of fictional works and in the photographic collection *Im tiefen Österreich* (1990), life in the country is displayed with all its warts, limitations, and ambivalences. Roth's collection of essays entitled *Eine Reise in das Innere von Wien* (1991) is equally unsparing in bringing to light the dark side of the capital's past and present; it looks at life, for example, in an insane asylum for artists and in a homeless shelter, and reveals the past evisceration and current neglect of contemporary Vienna's Jewish presence.

Eine Reise in das Innere von Wien consists of nine essays previously published in various issues of the *Zeit-Magazin* and the *FAZ-Magazin* between 1988 and 1990. What links these essays is their clinical description of Viennese domains unfamiliar not only to Vienna's tourists, but to most of its permanent residents as well. "Das Graue Haus," for example, portrays Vienna's central prison. It opens with a depiction of the room used to execute more than one thousand prisoners, mostly political, between 1938 and 1945. Most of the subsequent essay precisely details the dismal, hope-killing circumstances under which the prison's contemporary inmates live. Roth adds a brief, Kafkaesque touch as he guides us through the building's upper floors, occupied by state judges, prosecutors, and their administrative assistants. The essay thus provides a picture of a complete, compact penal bureaucracy, replete with somewhat disorganized archival storage units. It leaves us with the impression that once an accused man sets foot in the "Gray House," he will be as completely swallowed up as K. was in Kafka's castle. Indeed, Roth notes early in the essay that "Wenn er in Das Graue Haus gebracht wird, hat der Verhaftete den Eindruck, verschluckt zu werden" (70, Roth's italics).

Roth's Vienna, in both its historical and contemporary settings, is unremittingly cheerless, a striking antithesis to the gay, carefree city which exists in the popular imagination. However, the images drawn in his delineations of Austrian provincial life are no less dismal. *Winterreise* (1978) is the tale of a schoolteacher named Nagl who inhabits the sort of drab, dreary, often alienating country village both chronicled and fictionalized with some regularity in Roth's oeuvre. As the novel opens, he has reached the point in his lonely, frustrated existence when he feels the most natural thing to do would be to give himself up (5). For Nagl, this self-surrender takes the form of a trip to Italy with his former lover, Anna, after he breaks off an affair with a policeman's wife. Before he departs, he sits in his classroom with its map of the Dual Monarchy showing Vienna as its capital. This map had struck Nagl as unusual when he entered the classroom for the first time, but now it appears to him routine (10). Roth seems to suggest that the village hasn't moved beyond the past of Austria, whose aura of monarchic pomp centered in a glorious, imperial capital has been reduced to dots and lines on an outdated map. The ambiance Roth evokes in his cursory descriptions of the village's provincial tableaux is thus utterly lacking in vibrancy, cohesion, and a sense of investment in the present day. The activities of its inhabitants are as disjointed and pointless as the general day-to-day existence of the town they live in. To cite one instance: as Nagl leaves his house for the Italian journey, his now ex-paramour's husband, the policeman, comes up to him and shoots himself in the hand (13).

Except for reminiscences of his past and that of his family, the rest of the narrative delineates the trip to and within Italy, and the reunited couple's sojourns in Naples (where the main focus is nearby Mt. Vesuvius), Rome, and, finally, Venice. The city of mystery and seduction that so enchanted Rilke and Hofmannsthal is largely emptied of these attributes in Roth's descriptions of Nagl's rambles through it. Roth published some photographs he took in Italy in preparing to compose *Winterreise* and, as is the case with his photographic and essayistic images of both Vienna and Austrian provincial life in other works, these pictures, published in *Menschen Bilder Marionetten* (1979) attempt to reveal the quotidian, gritty, alienating aspects of present day life (140–51). In the brief essay which accompanies the images, Roth stressed that creating such a feeling of alienation, largely by making people in the pictures either marginal elements or eliminating them, was his intention (138). This approach to the Venetian city- and seascape is also evident in *Winterreise*. In large measure, the Venice portrayed in both Roth's pictures and in his novel is marked by postmodern fragmentation and isolation, an ambiance enhanced rather than softened by the city's maritime milieu (*Winterreise* 126–27, 136, 153–54).

Nevertheless, *Winterreise* also provides a countervailing impression of Venice, an impression which calls to mind the Austrian modernist "monism" (Wunberg) evident in Hofmannsthal's and Rilke's holistic portraits of the city. Gerhard Melzer has elucidated Nagl's ability near the novel's conclusion to shake off the "lähmenden Allgegenwärtigkeit des Todes" which Venice symbolizes for him, an ability which allows Nagl to imagine his immortality and which stimulates thoughts eventually leading to his ultimate acts, provoking a break with Anna and flying to Alaska (390). However, despite its symbolism, Venice itself also stimulates Nagl to break free of his lethargy and take decisive action. For at times, even Roth's Venice is informed by the ambient plenitude, resonant with both the natural and human worlds, which sparked artistic inspiration in Hofmannsthal's *Erinnerung schöner Tage* and which was to have helped shape the acculturation of his Andreas. Nagl's initial image of the city stands out by virtue of the fusion of its urban and maritime domains, as the brilliant colors of the "Palazzi" seem to come from the sea (125). His intimation of immortality, with its invigoration of his thinking, follows immediately upon his contemplating a scene at St. Mark's Square, where sparrows hop among pigeons and empty gondolas gently rock in the water; this image strikes Nagl as enchanted (160). After a stroll through the city that brings forth descriptions evocative of its character as a blend of sensuous, ornate architecture and natural, maritime elements, Nagl regards a balcony on which he stands as the place built to collect all forces and fly into the universe (187). The novel's penultimate portrait of Venice evinces a complete streaming and merging at sunset of city into nature, nature into art (189–90) reminiscent of the Venetian dusk painted by Hofmannsthal at the outset of *Erinnerung schöner Tage*. Typical of postmodernist novels, *Winterreise* is divided into short, often disjointed episodes, and this lack of narrative fluidity presents an unharmonious image of Venice, unlike that of Rilke and Hofmannsthal. Because Roth relentlessly illuminates nooks and crannies in the city full of the daily, sometimes unpleasant realities of life overlooked or unseen by the tourist — the same procedure he took in examining both Vienna and Austrian provincial domains in other writing and in his photography — Roth's Venice is stripped of some of the magical aura with which it was imbued in the imaginative prose and poetry of Austrian modernism. Nevertheless, at certain key moments in *Winterreise,* the city of art becomes the city as art configured at the earlier turn of the century. These are the narrative's utopian moments, when antitheses and dissonances are overcome and the narrative and its central protagonist are invested with a certain dynamic energy.

Alfred Kolleritsch was one of the founding fathers of a celebrated cultural organization with which the young Roth was also closely linked, Graz's Forum Stadtpark. During his many years of leadership with this group, Kolleritsch battled long and hard against what he considered to be the twin evils of provincialism and *Heimat* literature, tendencies deeply rooted in the artistic milieu of the Styrian capital (see Bartsch, esp. 293 and 296). In his *Gespräche im Heilbad* (1985), a collection of essays and prose fiction, Kolleritsch describes the pastoral, agricultural world of his youth, a youth which witnessed the rise of Austrofascism and Nazism, as absolutely lacking not only in idyllic qualities, but in tradition (22). During this time, the Austrian provinces were led into the arms of a ravenous "Moloch" which brooked no opposition and which seemed to have nature on its side (79). In postwar Austria, "Heimat" becomes a term used only by nostalgic former members of the SS (72). In the novel *Die grüne Seite* (1974), Kolleritsch's characters suggest that there is little difference between cities and villages, that the distinction between country and province on the one hand, and metropolis on the other, is purely artificial (106, 138). One of the protagonists in this novel passes through the Venice of pre-war Italy during the Mussolini era, and he recalls his grandfather's assertion that Venice was a dying, sinking city. Its interplay of light and water, used by Hofmannsthal as a metonym to invoke the ideal fusion of the urban and the natural in this milieu, merges with the train departing the city in Kolleritsch's early novel, but this only creates a "paralyzing contemporaneousness" (85); this Venice is enervating rather than providing the invigoration enjoyed by Roth's Nagl in *Winterreise*.

Der letzte Österreicher (1995) evinces a change in Kolleritsch's perspective on the domains of city and country. If not quite as antithetically juxtaposed as they were at the earlier turn of the century in Austrian literature, they are evoked as highly discrete experiential spaces. To a certain degree, provincial life achieves once again in this work the positive quality traditional in earlier Austrian prose. The dying artist who is the central figure in Kolleritsch's turn of the century novel loved "die Provinz" because it ruthlessly thwarted the illusionary reassurance that one possessed generalized, superficial, overarching truth (21). The rural vineyard landscape in the countryside is comforting and reassuring (53). Jürgen Bolten has noted the emergence in recent German-language literature of a new "Heimatbewußtsein," a postmodern, regionally focused consciousness of homeland, the development of works in which the provincial and local are represented approvingly (see esp. 37–38), and while the artist of *Der letzte Österreicher* avoided the word "Heimat" when it was in vogue just before the Second World War (19), the provincial in this novel attains a guardedly affirmative status precisely because regionalism is seen to frustrate the indulgence in false totalities. In this sense, *Der letzte Österreicher* supports Bolten's thesis; the province in *Der letzte Österreicher* is embraced because it *lacks* the holistic quality ascribed to it by Hofmannsthal.

Where, then, can the artist of Kolleritsch's recent novel find plenitude? Certainly not in Paris, where he suffered "from the endless sea of modernism" (29). His life in Vienna after the fall of the Dual Monarchy was equally fruitless. His experiences in a Viennese painting school destroy his nerves, for this school embraced a style of painting informed by an "endlessness of expression," and its students paint their own prison (26). Vienna is the city of his father, before which the artist crashed (33). Venice, on the other hand, subsumes artificial divisions such as that between internal and external (9). In Venice, the artist overcomes his addiction to polarity, to extremes; he rediscovers there the sublime (27). While the Viennese school invests tons of color into painting over analyses (26), Venice brings itself forth, forbidding comparisons and frustrating metaphor. It is only itself, and its fusion of light, putrefaction, lapping waves, and sensuality make the world uniquely present and capable of being experienced. The artist himself, for whom Venice still belongs to Austria, is rendered more open to the world by the city, more devout and invested with greater sensory capacities when he resides there (71–72). In short, Venice transcends borders, the cleavages between city and nature, metropolis and province, internality and externality, thereby inspiring creation. Venice in *Der letzte Österreicher* is portrayed as a sublime, transcendent space, underscoring a trend in Austrian literature evident in both the current and previous turns of the century.

This subtly dialectic glorification of Venice is not universally evident in Austrian literature; counter examples can be seen both early and late in the twentieth century. Georg Trakl's "In Venedig" (In Venice), inspired by the poet's visit there in 1913, provides a rather disturbing image of the city, and contains little in the way of imagery suggestive of its unique space. Indeed, without one brief reference to a canal, one would not see any connection in this work between the title and the place it signifies. As is typical in Trakl's poetry, this brief verse evokes homelessness, illness, loneliness, and darkness (*Dichtungen und Briefe* 1, 131).

Closer to our own time, Peter Rosei's novel *Wer war Edgar Allan?* (1977) conveys an image of a Venice filled with illicit activity. The traditional motif of Venice as a city of conspiracy and crime is evident, but Rosei's Venice lacks the utopian, totalizing resonance with which it is invested in the previously discussed works. Although the novel's narrator occasionally perceives an artistic fusion of nature and city (for example, 56), the squalid aspects of urban Venetian life receive his predominant attention. Indeed, at one point, this drug-intoxicated first-person voice of the tale obsesses on Venice as a quintessential, apocalyptic "Metropolis" (70–77). Nevertheless, Venice's invocation as a sublated space that transcends the antithetical limitations of city and province, Vienna and countryside, is common to works of Austrian literature around 1900 and closer to 2000. The trend bridges the gap between Viennese modernist "monism" and contemporary postmodern trends toward structural and thematic fragmentation.

Notes

¹ *Sämtliche Werke* 6, 933. Henceforth referenced in text as *SW*.

² See Hofmannsthal *Kritische Ausgabe* 28, 63–65; Rilke *Sämtliche Werke* 1, 116–18.

³ Henceforth, the *Kritische Ausgabe* will be cited in text as *KA*.

Works Cited

Alewyn, Richard. *Über Hugo von Hofmannsthal.* 4th ed. Göttingen: Vandenhoeck & Ruprecht, 1967.

Bangerter, Lowell A. *Hugo von Hofmannsthal.* New York: Ungar, 1977.

Bartsch, Kurt. "*Damals vor Graz:* Die verspätete Aneignung von Moderne und Avantgarde in der Literatur aus dem Umkreis von Forum Stadtpark Graz und der Zeitschrift *manuskripte.*" *Etudes Germaniques* 50 (1995). 289–300.

Blume, Bernhard. "Rilkes 'Spätherbst in Venedig.'" *Wirkendes Wort* 10 (1960): 345–54.

Bolten, Jürgen. "Heimat im Aufwind: Anmerkungen zur Sozialgeschichte eines Bedeutungswandels." In Pott, cited below, 23–38.

Dusini, Arno, and Karl Wagner, eds. *Metropole und Provinz in der österreichischen Literatur des 19. und 20. Jahrhunderts: Beiträge des 10. Österreichisch-Polnischen Germanistentreffens Wien 1992.* Vienna: Dokumentationsstelle für neuere österreichische Literatur im Literaturhaus, 1994.

Exner, Richard. "'Dieser Streifen Zwischen-Welt' und der Wille zur Kunst: Überlegungen zu Rilke in Venedig." *Blätter der Rilke-Gesellschaft* 16 (1989): 57–68.

Hofmannsthal, Hugo von. *Gesammelte Werke in Einzelausgaben: Aufzeichnungen,* edited by Herbert Steiner. Frankfurt am Main: S. Fischer, 1959.

———. *Gesammelte Werke in Einzelausgaben: Prosa I.* Edited by Herbert Steiner. Frankfurt am Main: S. Fischer, 1950.

————. *Sämtliche Werke: Kritische Ausgabe*. Edited by Rudolf Hirsch et al. Frankfurt am Main: S. Fischer, 1975.

Kassner, Rudolf. *Sämtliche Werke*. Edited by Ernst Zinn and Klaus E. Bohnenkamp. Vol. 10. Pfullingen: Neske, 1991.

Kolleritsch, Alfred. *Gespräche im Heilbad: Verstreutes, Gesammeltes*. Salzburg: Residenz, 1985.

————. *Die grüne Seite*. Salzburg: Residenz, 1974.

————. *Der letzte Österreicher*. Salzburg: Residenz, 1995.

Krysztofiak, Maria. "Das Spannungsfeld von Großstadt und Provinz in Rilkes 'Die Aufzeichnungen des Malte Laurids Brigge.'" In Dusini, cited above, 129–38.

Melzer, Gerhard. "Dieselben Dinge täglich bringen langsam um: Die Reisemodelle in Peter Handkes *Der kurze Brief zum langen Abschied* und Gerhard Roths *Winterreise*." In *Die andere Welt: Askpekte der österreichischen Literatur des 19. und 20. Jahrhunderts. Festschrift für Hellmuth Himmel zum 60. Geburtstag*, edited by Kurt Bartsch et al. Bern: Francke, 1979: 373–93.

Pott, Hans-Georg. "Der 'neue Heimatroman'? Zum Konzept 'Heimat' in der neueren Literatur." In Pott, cited below, 7–21.

————, ed. *Literatur und Provinz: Das Konzept "Heimat" in der neueren Literatur*. Paderborn: Schöningh, 1986.

Rilke, Rainer Maria. *Briefe zur Politik*. Edited by Joachim W. Storck. Frankfurt am Main: Insel, 1992.

————. *Sämtliche Werke*. Edited by Ernst Zinn. 6 vols. Frankfurt am Main: Insel, 1955–1966.

Rosei, Peter. *Wer war Edgar Allan?* Salzburg: Residenz, 1977.

Roth, Gerhard. *Eine Reise in das Innere von Wien: Essays*. Frankfurt am Main: S. Fischer, 1991.

————. *Im tiefen Österreich: Bildtextband*. Frankfurt am Main: S. Fischer, 1990.

————. *Menschen Bilder Marionetten: Prosa Kurzromane Stücke*. Frankfurt am Main: S. Fischer, 1979.

————. *Winterreise*. Frankfurt am Main: S. Fischer, 1978.

Ryan, Judith. "'Hypothetisches Erzählen': Zur Funktion von Phantasie und Einbildung in Rilkes 'Malte Laurids Brigge.'" In *Rainer Maria Rilke*, edited by Rüdiger Görner. Darmstadt: Wissenschaftliche Buchgesellschaft, 1987. 245–84.

Tanner, Tony. *Venice Desired*. Cambridge, MA: Harvard UP, 1992.

Trakl, Georg. *Dichtungen und Briefe*. Edited by Walther Killy and Hans Szklenar. Vol. 1. Salzburg: Müller, 1969.

Vogel, Juliane. "'Unschöne kleine Städte': Provinzen der Wiener Jahrhundert-wende." In Dusini, cited above, 103–14.

Weissenberger, Klaus. "Hofmannsthal's Essays 'Erinnerung schöner Tage' and 'Augenblicke in Griechenland' — An Artistic Depiction of the Creative Process." In *Turn-of-the-Century Vienna and Its Legacy: Essays in Honor of Donald G. Daviau*, edited by Jeffrey B. Berlin et al. Vienna: Edition Atelier, 1993. 79–88.

Wunberg, Gotthart. "Österreichische Literatur und allgemeiner zeitgenössischer Monismus um die Jahrhundertwende." In *Wien um 1900: Aufbruch in die Moderne*, edited by Peter Berner et al. Munich: Oldenbourg, 1986. 104–11.

Karl Kraus

Robert Menasse

Critical Observers of Their Times: Karl Kraus and Robert Menasse

Geoffrey C. Howes

KARL KRAUS (1874–1936) AND ROBERT MENASSE (b. 1954) both oversaw an Austria in the last days of its respective form of existence, and both authors' appraisals of the Austrian condition provoked controversy among readers and critics of various political stripes. Their acerbic wit, intelligence, and literary talent place Kraus and Menasse close to the center of the Austrian public discourse of their times. Most important, in addition to their expository and polemical writings, both authors created literary works in which major cultural, political, and philosophical questions of the day assume a complex and compelling aesthetic life. This essay will illuminate the beginning and the end of the twentieth century in Vienna and Austria in light of these two important commentators, while using the historical comparison of 1900 and 2000 to elucidate their works critically as well.

Both Kraus and Menasse reveal the distance between language and reality that lies at the bottom of the political crises of their respective times, but while Kraus appeals to a conservative, utopian notion of integral culture, Menasse immerses himself in the free-for-all of postmodern civilization and explores the dialectic of social and intellectual impulses.

The dates 1900 and 2000 are more symbolic than precise, for, in Central Europe at least, the twentieth century turned out to be shorter than its allotted hundred years: it began in 1918 with the end of the First World War and the demise of the Habsburg and Hohenzollern monarchies, and ended in 1989 when the bisected map of Europe drawn at Yalta lost its ideological polarity. Within such a geopolitical approach to historical periodization, the state of Austria and the city of Vienna occupy a singular position. As has so often been noted, the treaty of St. Germain (1920), which settled the First World War between the victorious allies and Austria by separating German-speaking Austria from the hereditary Habsburg crown lands, left Austria a "rump state" that "nobody wanted." Vienna was a "hydrocephalic" former imperial capital without an empire. The new democratic state was met with ambivalence, and the first Austrian republic ("German-Austria") was German and emphatically not German at the same time. This condition was a consequence not only of the transformed geopolitical system, but also of political forces that had existed within the empire, particularly the nationalisms of the peoples subject to the Austrian crown, and the imperial and commercial ambitions of the Habsburg state itself and their handmaidens in industry and the press. These forces were among Karl Kraus's most frequent targets of criticism.

On the dissolution of the Eastern Bloc some seven decades after the end of the Habsburg monarchy, the neutrality that had given postwar Austria a good portion of its identity became largely superfluous. After the Second World War, Austria's role as a non-German German state was no longer an embarrassment; indeed, official Austria considered it a national virtue that allowed the country to distance itself from Nazism and gain the indulgence of the victorious powers (Pelinka, 16). Austria set out consciously to create a specifically Austrian identity with neutrality at its core: even the national holiday marks the adoption of the neutrality law. But with the end of the Soviet empire, the cold-war justifications for Austrian neutrality were no longer pertinent, and by the time of German unification in 1990, the antifascist justifications for neutrality were also long obsolete. After years of insisting on its nonalignment, while in fact interpreting neutrality quite flexibly, in 1995 Austria joined the EU, whose vision of a borderless economic zone with coordinated foreign and defense policies is the clearest, if not the first, practical challenge to the hypothetical yet culturally embedded principle of Austrian neutrality.

The challenge to Austria's identity after 1900 was caused by disintegration, while in 2000 the threat arose from forces of integration. European unification, economic globalization, and immigration, especially as caused by the opening of the East and the Balkan hostilities, called the Austrian status quo into question, and the uncertainty thus provoked has in part led to the most significant political change in decades: the establishment in 2000 of a coalition of the center-right People's Party (ÖVP) and Jörg Haider's far-right Freedom Party (FPÖ), ending thirty years of Social Democratic chancellorships and provoking the censure of the European Union because of the FPÖ's express anti-foreign attitudes and lack of distance from the Nazi past.

Kraus was writing at a time when the war laid bare the failings of Austria-Hungary, and the loss of the empire and the beginning of the new, truncated form of Austria deprived the country of its European and global might and its feudally grounded multinationalism. The end of aristocratic and imperial rule and the fledgling republic were part of the general Central European modernist ferment that is identified with the culture of the *fin de siècle*. Politically, modernity included not only liberal and democratic aspirations, but also nationalist ideologies that were at once progressive, because anti-imperial, and regressive in their insistence on creating identity from heritage and blood. The new democracies in Austria and Germany were shaken by the very nationalism that helped establish them, and antimodernism became a part of the ideological framework of both German and Austrian fascism in the 1930s. The complexity of Karl Kraus's attitudes stems in part from his conservatism on the one hand — he shared many antimodernist views such as distaste for technological innovations and liberal politics — and his distrust of nationalism and imperialism on the other. His biting critique of commercialism and bourgeois culture sometimes made him seem an ally of the left, yet he sniped at the middle class from an aristocratic and not a proletarian point of view.

Menasse, by contrast, is writing at a time when Austria's very inwardness is what many Austrians fear losing — smallness and detachment have become part of the Austrian identity. But so has the prosperity that resulted largely from ignoring that detachment in economic practice. The breakup of the cold-war system of Europe dovetailed with postnational and postmodern developments already underway: the transnational economy and European unification. On the one hand, these trends have led away from fascism, pernicious nationalism, and international armed conflict; on the other, they have been promoted by a class of international business interests and supranational bodies, thus threatening the economic and political autonomy of countries and individuals, to say nothing of their cultural identity. Furthermore, the influx of foreigners has provoked among many Austrians a defensive reaction of nationalist sentiment. What becomes of national and local identity in an open and uniting Europe? What becomes of national sovereignty when Brussels and multinational corporations are calling the shots? What does national identity mean when its ethnic basis is gone, and the cultural makeup of the population is diversifying? These are Austria's — and Europe's — questions in 2000 and beyond. One result of this uncertainty is the success in 1999 and 2000 of the Freedom Party, which appealed to many voters' intolerance of change and difference at the same time that it styled itself as a modern political movement willing to abolish the cronyism of the traditional partnership between the conservative People's Party and the Social Democrats (SPÖ).

Just as Kraus's malice toward the bourgeoisie did not necessarily make him a friend of the left, Menasse's opposition to the FPÖ does not necessarily make him a friend of that party's more emphatic opponents, for he regards the FPÖ's participation in a coalition with the ÖVP, which began in early 2000, not as a regression toward fascism, but as a hard though necessary step toward a democracy beyond the "social partnership" that for so long supplied a shadow government. Menasse's grudging acceptance of the new government has irritated many of his fellow intellectuals. Although often hard to place on the political spectrum, Menasse and Kraus are radical in the sense that they try to expose the intellectual roots of the Austrian predicament by discovering the prejudices and shortcomings of their contemporaries no matter where they stand politically.

Kraus and Menasse uncover fractures in Austrian culture between thought and behavior, language and reality, and intention and outcome. In approaching these quandaries, Kraus tends to align himself with absolute positions, in which integrity of language and behavior provides a standard for criticism and satire. Menasse, by contrast, tends to dwell on the dialectical potential of the quandaries themselves, not preferring one position or another, but using antithesis itself to come to grips with a complex reality.

In exploring Kraus's views of Austria, I will concentrate on the transition from the nineteenth to the twentieth century in the First World War. The actual turn of the century, to be sure, had provided Kraus with ample targets for his satire and polemics, and it was here, in the burgeoning culture based on the economic success and the political nonage of the bourgeoisie, that he developed his craft. He took aim at what Edward Timms has dubbed "the Austrian masquerade" (61) by exposing sexual hypocrisy, legal abuses, crass commercialism, artistic posturing, and the running conflict of interest between the press and its subjects. As Harry Zohn has written, Kraus "was motivated by his view of journalism as a vast switchboard that concentrated and activated the forces of corruption and corrosion" (174). He created his legendary independence from commercial and journalistic interests by establishing his own journal *Die Fackel* (The Torch, 1899–1936), to which he was eventually the sole contributor. In Kraus's writings for the *Fackel* about the war, all his favorite topics take on deadly significance, and the end of Austria-Hungary is an occasion for analyzing its fatal internal contradictions.

One of these contradictions is the use of the media and arts to appeal to the public's emotions and prejudices and mobilize support for a war whose actual purpose, Kraus claims, is to enrich commercial interests. In his famous piece "In dieser großen Zeit" (In these Great Times) at the beginning of the war, Kraus wryly notes that he understands that it is necessary from time to time to convert markets into battlefields so that they can be turned back into markets, but he wonders where the vaunted religious principles are left in all of this (*Weltgericht I*, 12). The concept of clientele replaces the concept of humanity in the religion of commerce. God created the consumer, Kraus paraphrases, but not so that he would prosper on earth, but for a higher purpose: so that the retailer would prosper (12). In condemning the reversal of means and ends, Kraus contrasts the ideas of culture and civilization: culture is the tacit agreement that aspirations (*Lebenszwecke*) are more important than commodities (*Lebensmittel*), while civilization is belief in the reverse (13).

The war, by sacrificing humanity to material gain, is the ultimate symptom of civilization and modernity, the ultimate affront to culture. Typical of Kraus's emphasis on culture is his view of war as a tool of the press, rather than the press as a tool of the warmongers. Edward Timms points out that in his disdain for the press Kraus exaggerates the role of media and commerce in the war effort, playing down the political interests of the ruling class. This allows him to view the conflict mainly as a cultural phenomenon, and the war itself as a failure of imagination (281). When the imagination is poverty-stricken, he writes in "In dieser großen Zeit," when people die of spiritual starvation without feeling spiritual hunger, when pens are dipped in blood and swords in ink, then that which is not imagined must be acted out (*Weltgericht I,* 9). Interpreting war as a cultural failure allows Kraus to combat it on his own terms: abusing language means abusing thought. The consumers of media are encouraged to think in narrow terms of self-interest and national pride, and to dehumanize the enemy.

Hence, the press, and the commercial interests it serves, is in the view of Kraus the greatest enemy of culture. This concept of culture gives Kraus a vantage point from which to criticize and satirize, and purity of language is its standard. Kraus "discerned an absolute congruity between word and world, language and life; the unworthiness of his 'language-forsaken' age was for him defined by its treatment of language, which he regarded as the moral criterion and accreditation for a writer or speaker" (Zohn, 175). On the one hand, this position affords him the opportunity to lambaste bourgeois culture, which subverts the language in order to subjugate spiritual values to material ones. On the other, Kraus's veneration of language obligates him to assume an antimodernist stance, since the degradation of language is conceivable mainly as a historical process, in which a past golden age has degenerated into the modern corrupt condition. Whether Kraus believes in an actual, historical uncorrupted state of language is questionable; the Eden of an unsullied relationship between language and reality is more the projection of a spiritual possibility than a historical reality. Kraus's term for this prelapsarian state is *Ursprung* (origin), which Zohn summarizes as representing "a kind of naive realism," a posited "unity of feeling and form from which all art, morality, and truth spring" (177).

The war seems to Kraus a culmination of the breakdown of social distinctions that maintain standards of culture. In 1916, in "Ein Wort an den Adel" (A Word to the Aristocracy), Kraus avers that one of the war's evil effects is to complement the equality of the trenches with the fraternity of the boardroom (*Weltgericht I*, 48), with the effect that entrepreneurs can rise to the aristocracy on the basis of achievements in selling canned goods and wool blankets (49). Kraus sees the indiscriminate mixing of the classes for the war effort as a step on the way to a condition in which the liberal idea of "progress" replaces the conservative idea of "development" (47). As Sigurd Paul Scheichl notes, the aristocracy represented the possibility of *Ursprung* for Kraus (422–23), and he was dismayed both by the descent of the nobility into capitalism, and by the elevation of capitalists to the nobility, especially because of their war-profiteering.

Seeing class as the organizing principle of society, shared across nations, Kraus is alarmed by the divisive power of nationalism. He rails against the abuse of nationalistic rhetoric as a motivation to war. In Austria, propaganda created identification not with the empire, but with Germanness, in order to dehumanize the British, French, and Russians with bigoted images. But for Kraus national identity without a basis in *Ursprung* is arbitrary and indiscriminate. In "Der Krieg im Schulbuch" he decries the nationalistic abuse of culture by citing bellicose and jingoistic verses in schoolchildren's required reading (*Weltgericht I*, 162–73). In "Goethes Volk" he reprints two parodies of Goethe's delicate "Wanderers Nachtlied" that appeared in newspapers in Dresden and Berlin. These poems replace Goethe's words with those of a supposed English naval captain who laments his defeat by the German U-boat fleet (*Weltgericht I*, 174–75). Kraus's principles are clear when he says that the military action celebrated by the parody is a good deed compared with the evil deed of misusing Goethe's poem. In other words, the murder of an immortal poem is worse than the destruction of mortal human beings.

Even allowing for rhetorical overstatement, this extreme position shows that Kraus's conception of humanity is based on an idea of culture that does not serve humanity but is to be served by it. Alfred Pfabigan calls this idea "aesthetic agnosticism" (23). It is the *Ursprung* that humanizes mankind in the first place, and for Kraus *Ursprung* should be the goal of politics, but every state wages war against its own culture instead of its own lack of culture (*Aphorismen*, 399). Kraus's humanitarianism is thus based on conservative principles, and rails against the timely abuse of timeless cultural values to justify the war. Evil, he writes in an aphorism, never flourishes better than when an ideal is placed in front of it (*Aphorismen*, 401).

Edward Timms locates a moderation of Kraus's hard-line conservatism in the dialogs between the figures of the "Nörgler" (Grumbler) and the "Optimist" in the massive dramatic treatment of the First World War, *Die letzten Tage der Menschheit* (The Last Days of Mankind, 1915–22). The Grumbler is Kraus's alter-ego, a pessimist who is incorrigible because reality has strayed so far from his ideals. The Optimist is not a figure of satire, but a foil for the trenchant faultfinding of the Grumbler. The Optimist is the voice of common sense that does not want to give up on the future after the war, and so finds the best possible perspective on it. The Grumbler's absolute principles are softened by his confrontations with the Optimist, and his attitude is distinguished from Kraus's own satirical voice during the war by the admission of his complicity (Timms 401). "He identifies himself with a whole generation of intellectuals who failed to bring their gifts of mind and imagination to bear on politics until it was too late" (401). This shift prepares the way for Kraus's transformation from a conservative with a weakness for the aristocracy to a supporter of the new republic.

Alfred Pfabigan has explored the paradoxes of Kraus's radical conservatism, asking the question "to whom does Karl Kraus belong?" Both the right and the left have claimed him. Pfabigan concludes (and Timms and Scheichl concur) that conservative structures of thought dominate Kraus's work throughout his life (23), but that he had to modify his stance in response to changing circumstances. The Austro-Hungarian Empire, its Habsburg rulers, and its aristocracy earned his disfavor because of their self-destructive involvement in the war. Hence Kraus greeted the republic as an end to the aristocratic state that had abused its own cultural ideals for material gain and ended in ruins. For a time, he was a strong supporter of the new republic and a strident antimonarchist. As Pfabigan notes, he explained to the readers of the *Fackel* again and again that the temporary problems that Austria was suffering from were not caused by the republic, but inherited from the empire (201). But when Austrofascism established itself in 1934, Kraus's loyalties shifted again, now to the corporate state, which seemed closest to his old ideal of a class-based cultural hierarchy.

Karl Kraus, then, was an apologist for a cultural ideal. Even if his notion that a state's purpose is to promote culture is politically unrealistic, it was an effective literary stance for exposing just how deeply destructive the war was for Europe. If Kraus exaggerated when he blamed journalists for the war, he was nonetheless correct in identifying the crucial role the media played in this first fully modern, industrial war. Using cultural ideals to win the loyalty of the people for a brutal cause inflicted damage far beyond the loss of life: it destroyed the spiritual basis for human interaction.

Kraus came to identify himself with a generation of Austrian intellectuals whose criticism of the war was too little and too late, as Timms remarked in the passage already quoted. Menasse has provoked controversy by suggesting that the criticism of the center-right coalition by his generation of Austrian intellectuals might be too early and too much. While the political successes of Jörg Haider and his Freedom Party have roused strong opposition among most of his colleagues, Menasse has suggested that putting up with the coalition is the price Austria will have to pay for gaining the democratic renewal brought about by the breakup of the old SPÖ-ÖVP political alliance.

Menasse's position after the 1999 elections is consistent with the ideas about Austria he developed in the previous decade in essays that are collected in three books on the Austrian condition: *Die sozialpartnerschaftliche Ästhetik* (1990, The Aesthetics of Social Partnership); *Das Land ohne Eigenschaften* (1992, The Land without Qualities); and *Dummheit ist machbar* (1999, Stupidity Can Be Achieved). To these books one should add *Hysterien und andere historische Irrtümer* (1996, Hysterias and other historical errors), which is shorter than the other collections but significant as a document of Menasse's thinking in 1995, when Austria was the center of attention at the Frankfurt Book Fair, and Menasse was the keynote speaker.

The subtitles of the three main books of essays give an idea of the range and purpose of Menasse's observations: they promise, respectively, essays on the Austrian mind (*Geist*), essays on Austrian identity, and essays to accompany the "standstill" of the republic. While many of his fellow writers have spent their energies uncovering the Austrian Nazi past and its lingering manifestations in the present, Menasse has concentrated more on criticizing the establishment than the far right. He is less worried about the Freedom Party's threat than about what the Social Democrats did to deserve losing power to them. The possibility that fascism might again come to life does not worry him as much as the possibility that the social partnership might continue.

He accuses his fellow intellectuals and journalists of overreacting, mixing up categories, and defending business as usual in Austrian politics as long as it means opposition to Haider. In an interview on the occasion of the 1995 Frankfurt Book Fair, Menasse concedes that Haider employs unacceptable methods to defame Austrian artists, but states that the artists who call Haider a Nazi are also using such methods. He cannot agree with stupid statements just because they attack Haider (*Hysterien*, 41). Like Kraus, Menasse is concerned about accurate use of language, and for him, calling Haider a Nazi demonizes him, makes the political climate hysterical, and contributes to downplaying Nazism (*Hysterien*, 40). Menasse implies that by overdramatizing their opponents, the professed antifascists overdramatize themselves and the importance of their mission.

Haider, says Menasse, is systematically trying to destroy all of the constitutive taboos and legends of the Second Republic: the social partnership, the "first-victim" lie, and the neutrality myth (*Hysterien*, 42). This means that Haider is attacking everything that the intelligentsia of Austria has also been against all along, but which it now defends on the principle that my enemy's enemies are my friends. While not advocating Haider's means or goals, Menasse is willing to admit the interest he shares with him: the Second Republic as it has existed must end.

Menasse's critique of the Second Republic began well before the elections of 1999, around 1986, the year that marked the ascendancy of Haider within the Freedom Party and Kurt Waldheim's election to the federal presidency. Unlike some other commentators, Menasse sees these two events not primarily as the rise of a dangerous right wing and the excusing of Austria's participation in the Nazi state, but as a natural and ultimately salutary development in response to the Austrian government's persistence in its pseudodemocratic politics of proportionately divided spoils and back-room deals. Employing broad irony, Menasse attributes the gradual normalizing of Austria to the "classical enlightenment figure" Waldheim and the "new leftist" Haider. Menasse is less interested in persons as purveyors of ideas and agents of historical change than as casualties of ideas and objects of change. In spite of Waldheim's self-serving obscuring of the past, Menasse asserts that everything he said or did led to a deeper and broader social awareness of what Austria had become (*Hysterien*, 9). Whatever his intentions, Waldheim's social role contributed to enlightenment by arousing public doubt about Austria's dubious past, and by bringing anti-Semitism, nationalism, and xenophobia out of the woodwork. When such sentiments are overt political programs rather than privately held resentments, Menasse suggests, they can be dealt with in rational, structural ways (10). Menasse similarly refers to Jörg Haider's political function rather than his political intentions when he ironically calls him a member of the "new left." When the left wing has become the establishment — Menasse cites the Soviet Union as an example — the "right" (conservatives) are the hard-line socialists, while "left" becomes a synonym for "oppositional" and "antisocialist" (*Hysterien*, 11). In Austria, where opposition has been stifled by the Social Partnership, and where for thirty years the federal chancellors were Social Democrats, Haider has precisely this function: oppositional and antisocialist. According to Menasse, like Waldheim, Haider acts inadvertently as a force in favor of democratic renewal and critical public thinking in Austria.

Menasse resembles Kraus to the extent that he roots out discrepancies between language and practice, not only with the right, but even more so with the left-of-center Social Democratic Party of Austria and its perennial coalition partner, the People's Party. By portraying itself as a guardian of progressive values while in fact acting mainly as a guardian of its own interest in staying in power, the Social Democratic Party has debased the language of its own party program and created conditions in which the Freedom Party is attractive. Before the elections of 1999, the coalition of SPÖ and ÖVP was in a bind, according to an essay entitled "Österreich-Liebe in Zeiten der Cholera" (Love for Austria in the Time of Cholera; *Dummheit*, 152–59). They could either maintain their political marriage of convenience, and thus continue the situation that the Freedom Party — with some justification — was criticizing; or they could emphasize their ideological differences, and thus induce the rupture with tradition that the Freedom Party was trying to provoke anyway (*Dummheit*, 153). Maintaining continuity would mean perpetuating the distance between language and practice, while emphasizing difference would narrow that distance. But it would take a political courage that seems lacking, and so the FPÖ, ironically, is left to bring about democratic renewal in Austria.

The discrepancy between language and practice, the cause and result of defective thinking, is what Menasse means when he uses the word *Dummheit* (stupidity). *Dummheit ist machbar* is the title of his collection of essays in reaction to the events of late 1999, and of an essay that appeared in the rearranged and expanded German edition of that book, *Erklär mir Österreich* (Explain Austria to me). Austria, he writes, is facing two crises: the political crisis and the crisis of its interpretation. It will work through the first crisis, because it has objective causes, but Menasse doubts whether the second crisis can be overcome. The interpreters, the vehement critics of the new government, are in an enviably comfortable position, Menasse asserts mockingly: they have moral integrity, which means they are not defined by their intellectual curiosity; and they are educated, which means everything they have learned was right — yesterday (*Erklär mir Österreich*, 148). This cutting assessment overgeneralizes and oversimplifies — he mentions no names — but it brings out one of Menasse's central ideas: that intellectual curiosity should supersede political tendentiousness.

This idea is seen in Menasse's view of the political situation as a clash of interests, a dialectical confrontation of antitheses. He sees himself in the position of an intellectual synthesizer who trusts in change because it mediates between ideological positions, and possibly even moderates stupidity. Even if the new government in Austria is undesirable, it will provoke opposition and lead to a new synthesis. Since the social partnership monopolized politics and was not about to create its own antithesis, the main hope for political change in Austria came, perversely, from the far right. Menasse's impatience with what he regards as a hysterical reaction to Austria's crisis stems from his confidence that the antithesis of the new government — a revitalized left wing — will result in a new synthesis, one that is healthier for Austrian democracy (*Erklär mir Österreich*, 151).

Menasse's tolerance of Haider and the FPÖ is not shared by many of his fellow intellectuals, who have taken measures to protest against the administration, in the press, in public forums, and on the street in the form of the Thursday demonstrations organized by Doron Rabinovici and others. A sometimes harsh debate has arisen between the protest faction and those who have come to be known as *Wendephilosophen*. There is no neat English translation for this phrase, which means "those who take the rightward shift philosophically." In the pages of the newspapers *Der Standard* and *Die Presse*, the battle is fought between those who think that the outrageous FPÖ can be combated only with outrage, and those who counsel patience and perspective.

In one of the most prominent skirmishes in this battle, Karl-Markus Gauss, the Salzburg essayist and editor of *Literatur und Kritik*, and Elfriede Jelinek, the noted dramatist and novelist, took each other to task in the *Standard* in late 2000 and early 2001. Gauss has long maintained that the left-wing intellectual opposition in Austria has a false sense of its own historical position because the tradition of critical opposition in Austria has been forgotten. He accuses the anti-Haider opposition of creating the specter of Nazism so that it can act out antifascism. In an essay published on New Year's Eve 2000, he reviews the "topsy-turvy" year 2000 and questions the political motivation of the extraparliamentary opposition, calling it a new conformism with attitudes but not convictions, a dupe of media hype. This antifascism is cut off from the genuine humanistic Austrian tradition of intellectual opposition, which was admired even by those who were forced into exile.

In her brilliant and even more polemical response a few days later, Jelinek has a hard time discovering in her own experience the humanistic, patriotic opposition that Gauss invokes. She brings up the generational difference of those who grew up immediately after the war (she was born in 1946, Gauss in 1954), saying her "antifascist hysteria" was incubated in a world in which the guilty were set free and the innocent were accused. To show that this past is not past, she cites recent controversies over reparations for forced labor and stolen art. Merely reciting the contents of Jelinek's polemic cannot do justice to its rhetorical fire: she excels in blending argument with a seemingly barely controlled emotion, conveying her conviction that the problem is not too much, but too little hysteria in the face of repression, oppression, and bigotry.

Gauss and Jelinek became the rallying points for those who defend zealous opposition (like Armin Thurnher, Isolde Charim and Doron Rabinovici, to name some main examples) or those who call for a differentiated, patient response. There is no doubt that Robert Menasse is among the latter, the *Wendephilosophen,* which opens him to the criticism of not taking the threat to Austrian democracy seriously enough. It may be that the public discussion that has resulted from this controversy is more productive for Austria's political and intellectual culture than a fully united opposition would be. This speculation itself, however, is indebted to Menasse's concept of intellectual curiosity. Since one's own position is only one element in the dialectical interplay of social and intellectual forces, it is less important than critically watching where things are going, and what social and linguistic mechanisms are taking them there.

This combination of philosophical detachment and literary passion is not unlike what Alfred Pfabigan called Kraus's "aesthetic agnosticism." Kraus and Menasse both try to create as independent a position as possible, to rise above the fray, not out of disinterest, but to supply their interest the greatest possible range of targets. This detachment perhaps helps explain why both Kraus and Menasse, while they reflect on the position of the Jews in Austrian society, do not make a public issue of their own Jewishness or identify expressly with a Jewish perspective. Both place a sort of humanism — conservative and liberal, respectively — above such alignments. If for Kraus intellectual independence is based on the conservative cultural concept of *Ursprung,* Menasse defends the independence itself. The function of *Ursprung* in Kraus is assumed in

Menasse by the basic liberal idea of freedom of expression and inquiry. Chiefly responsible for the interruption of productive discourse is *Dummheit* — stupidity — which, as we have seen, is the gap between the use and meaning of language.

With this we would be at the end of our comparison of Kraus and Menasse, except that we have not yet addressed Menasse's fiction. I will conclude by briefly considering Menasse's novels in light of this comparison. Again, Kraus himself is a good point of departure: referring to his own anticommercialism, he writes in an aphorism that he would still rather live among the business rabble (*Geschäftspöbel*) than the emotional rabble (*Gesinnungspöbel*) (*Aphorismen*, 367). In other words, as distasteful as grubby commerce may be, it is still preferable to pretending to be pursuing things of the mind while merely spouting attitudes. Menasse devotes his novels to the "emotional rabble" (though he would be quicker than Kraus to include himself among them). As in his essays, where he criticizes the criticizers more than the objects of their criticism, in his fiction Menasse is fascinated by the rift between the intellectual (and linguistic) structures his characters create or adopt and the world they purport to represent. The middle-class intellectuals that people Menasse's fictitious world talk, think, and write endlessly, and their talking, thinking, and writing makes up the stuff of Menasse's narrative.

Menasse's contribution to fiction consists of the three novels of the "Trilogie der Entgeisterung" (Trilogy of Despiritualization). (The novel *Die Vertreibung aus der Hölle* [The Expulsion from Hell] came out in 2001, too late to be considered here.) The first of the trilogy, *Sinnliche Gewißheit* (Sensual Certainty), appeared in 1988; the second, *Selige Zeiten, brüchige Welt* (translated as *Wings of Stone*), followed in 1991; and *Schubumkehr* (Reverse Thrust) came out in 1995. These novels share a cast of characters, chiefly the German teacher Roman Gilanian, the literature student Judith Katz, and the would-be philosophy professor Leo Singer. They also share a connection between Austria and Brazil (where Menasse himself spent time as a university lecturer in German), although the exotic is not experienced for its own sake, but as part of a general subjective sense of detachment (Beckermann, 80).

Sinnliche Gewißheit is a first-person narrative by Roman Gilanian set in São Paulo. It explores the weird noninvolvement of the Austrian protagonist in his own life. Living abroad only underscores his detachment, and he becomes lost in an ever-growing self-reflection that destroys any spontaneity (Braun, 77); the book is a sort of "Bildungsroman in reverse" (Braun, 78).

Selige Zeiten, brüchige Welt is a third-person novel that moves from Vienna to Brazil. The protagonist Leo Singer is a would-be philosopher who is able to dazzle his audiences in public but who cannot manage to write down the treatise that is his life's goal. His life dissolves in failed attempts to produce the life he thinks he wants, and he ends up murdering his former companion Judith Katz so he can get her notes from his spontaneous lectures and publish them. At the end he is alone, as Erich Hackl writes, having perceived the world at the cost of life — his own and Judith's. He has pursued an intellectual error until it becomes reality, producing absolute mindlessness, the eternity of stupidity (110).

Schubumkehr returns Roman Gilanian to Austria — this time in the third person — just at the time of the great political shifts in 1989 and 1990. He witnesses his mother's failed attempt to return to a natural, simple life in her adopted small border town, and he sees the community's inability to deal with its past, much less the breaking present. The quarry, once the economic heart of the village, is to become a quarry museum, a desperate attempt to rescue both the past and the present through a commercial scheme. Menasse's fragmentary narrative dismantles the idea of *Heimat* (homeland) both socially and personally until there is no hope of simple identification and identity (Posthofen, 259).

Menasse's protagonists are fanatical narrators, as Andrea Gerk notes. They must create through talking that which cannot be had, and which they cannot live without: a context for their lives, meaningful self-images, comprehensive knowledge (41). Meaning is counterfeit and can only be produced by mediation of or translation into language (41). If Kraus tries to appeal to uncorrupted language as an intimation of the utopia of *Ursprung,* language is for Menasse's characters a false utopia, not an origin but a refuge. Instead of the "sensual certainty" that Leo Singer believes is the modern condition, a regression from the absolute apperception of Hegel, there is nothing but uncertainty, kept at bay by constant discourse.

It is significant that Karl Kraus's preferred mode of belletristic expression is the drama, whereas Menasse writes novels. Kraus was a satirist, less concerned with reflecting actual social conditions than with placing a distorting mirror before his contemporaries (Scheichl, 419). Kraus furthermore resisted the modish tendency to psychoanalyze the world. He did not want to make subjectivity, and pathological subjectivity at that, the principle by which the world is interpreted. The uttered word, and by extension, the dialogue, are the building blocks of reality for Kraus. He is of course the farthest thing from a proto-deconstructionist one can imagine: language is not a superficial phenomenon for him, but a source and path of profundity, but the psyche, as analyzed by oversimplifying science, is not deep as long as the words used to describe it are shallow. Psychology, he wrote, is the omnibus that accompanies an airship (*Aphorismen,* 349).

Menasse makes no claims about the airship, but the bus ride fascinates him, not as psychology alone, but as the variety of attempts to explain the world. The novel, the genre in which the self confronts the world, is well suited for describing this bus ride. In Menasse's novels the self is presented not for its psychological interest, but as the site of that dialogue between inside and outside. While Menasse is not primarily a satirist, satire is one of the genres he weaves into his multigeneric novels (Posthofen, 257–58), and its main mechanism is the discrepancy between what characters tell themselves and what they actually do or have happen to them. In other words, in both his fiction and his essays Menasse exposes stupidity, understood, as we have seen, as the disparity between language and reality. One of Kraus's principles of life and thought, according to Sigurd Paul Scheichl, is maintaining clean polarities, as opposed to mediating and blurring opposites (422). The postmodernist Menasse worries less about polarities than about the edge where opposites collide or intermingle. In other words, he treats the ways in which the "emotional rabble" mediate and blur the opposing forces that make up their lives.

Roman Gilanian in *Sinnliche Gewißheit,* for example, repeatedly makes spur-of-the-moment decisions, seemingly unmotivated, but with significant consequences. His mind and his life seem divorced. He says in a conversation that everything particular that he experiences disappears, either because he forgets it, or in the generalizations of words (67). Leo Singer responds that this is the general state of development today: we have lost our mental command of the world. Our only certainty is immediate, sensual certainty. This is the result of the "despiritualization" that has proceeded since Hegel's time, according to Singer, in which experience is less and less mediated by intellect, and increasingly a matter of direct, but ungeneralizable and hence meaningless sensory perception. In *Selige Zeiten, brüchige Welt,* when Singer murders Judith to gain possession of his "own" philosophical treatise, he destroys in one act the ethical basis for his philosophical authority. In *Schubumkehr,* Roman experiences the tumultuous events of 1989, but mainly as a silent witness bearing a video camera. In these and many other plots and subplots, Menasse's characters try to bridge the gap between the world they encounter and their main medium for interpreting it: language. But the gap remains, unaffected by the volumes of writing and hours of talking.

This chasm between language and experience is of course Karl Kraus's theme, but in Menasse it comes without the assurance that a solution lies in the conscientious maintenance of language itself. Reading Menasse in the light of Kraus shows us that in spite of his ideological superstructure, Kraus's literary achievement was not creating unity, but uncovering the gap, and so in practice he is closer to Menasse than one might think. We see that Kraus's modernity, his continued relevance, derives not from his ideas, but his method. He tried to remove himself to a place where he would have an intellectual Archimedes' point for moving the universe, by putting out the *Fackel* outside of the main-stream literary and journalistic world. But his aloofness did not ultimately give him the power to attain the *Ursprung*. The *Ursprung* was only a philosophical construct with which to betray the unoriginality of virtually all human expression.

Similarly, Menasse's fundamental concepts of sensual certainty and the phenomenology of despiritualization (the loss of intellectual meaning in favor of disjoined sensations) are literary-philosophical constructs that betray the distance between language and reality. The problem in Menasse is trying to decide how seriously to take the constructs (Schuh, 75). The implicit (and sometimes explicit) answer is: take them seriously by not taking them seriously. This paradox is embodied in Menasse by the fact that his "trilogy" actually consists of four books. Menasse brought out *Phänomenologie der Entgeisterung,* the book that Leo Singer published from the murdered Judith Katz's notes, as an actual separate book, under his own name. Does this mean that Leo Singer's ideas are actually Robert Menasse's? That Menasse wants us to take the ideas of a blowhard and murderer seriously? Is the *Phänomenologie* "only" fiction or "really" philosophy? However we sort this out, one thing is clear: Menasse takes no stock in an idea's deriving validity from the stature of the person professing it. But he also takes no stock in ideas isolated from experience, which is why he relativizes the *Phänomenologie* by showing its origins in the author's rather bizarre life. This suggests that we should not look to Menasse's "nonfiction" for guidance to understanding his fiction any more than we look to his fiction to understand his nonfiction. The distinction is formal, not ontological. For, as the end of the *Phäno-menologie* states: consciousness no longer knows anything, but it has sublimated everything that it has forgotten as a collection of quotes and paraphrases. In the beginning is the copy (86–87).

Kraus's method was to reproduce others' texts, and by their very ap-pearance as copies in the *Fackel* their unoriginality became their central theme. Menasse does this, in effect, not only to the texts around him, but to himself. He quotes Leo Singer (who is merely assembling quotes) and then quotes his quotation by publishing the fictional treatise of a fictional character as a separate book. Menasse-as-Leo-Singer writes in the *Phänomenologie der Entgeisterung* that the anonymous domination of the market and its apparent autonomy have suspended and replaced the dependence of artists on personified domination and the autonomy of free-lance artists (26).

This autonomy is precisely the position that Karl Kraus still insisted on holding. His resignation from the *Neue Freie Presse* and the establishment of *Die Fackel* were the attempt to maintain freelance status in a world that he already recognized as dominated by the market. Menasse no longer even pretends to maintain freelance status. He does not try to resist the world of copies, but plunges into it to see what it produces. While Kraus resorts to "culture" as a principle superior to "civilization," Menasse does not celebrate the superiority of one explanation of the world over another. Rather, he sees the dialectical confrontation of ideas as the necessary function of civilization, and he distrusts any ideology or scheme that tries to impede this. As it did for Karl Kraus, this aloofness opens Menasse to justified criticism. Yet precisely because of their scrupulous intelligence and mastery of the imperfect instrument of language, there are few more valuable sources than these two for understanding Austria at the beginning and the end of the twentieth century.

Works Cited

Beckermann, Thomas. "Versuch, die Auslöschung eines Bildes zu beschreiben. Robert Menasses erste Romane." In *Die Welt scheint unverbesserlich: Zu Robert Menasses "Trilogie der Entgeisterung,"* edited by Dieter Stolz. Frankfurt am Main: Suhrkamp, 1997. 79–102.

Braun, Michael. "Bar jeder Hoffnung. Robert Menasses Rückentwicklungsroman 'Sinnliche Gewißheit.'" In Stolz, *Die Welt scheint unverbesserlich.* 76–78.

Gauss, Karl-Markus. "Mein verkehrtes Jahr 2000. So kann man sich täuschen — gesammelte Merkwürdigkeiten aus der 'Wende'-Republik." *Der Standard* [Vienna], 30 Dec. 2000.

Gerk, Andrea. "Eine Geschichte des erinnerten Vergessens — Robert Menasses 'Trilogie der Entgeisterung.'" In Stolz, *Die Welt scheint unverbesserlich.* 37–49.

Hackl, Erich. "Weltgeist zu Besuch." In Stolz, *Die Welt scheint unverbesserlich.* 105–10.

Jelinek, Elfriede. "Rote Wangen, stramme Waden. Erwiderung auf Karl-Markus Gauß' Wendejahr-Bilanz." *Der Standard* [Vienna], 5 Jan 2001.

Kraus, Karl. *Aphorismen. Sprüche und Widersprüche. Pro domo et mundo. Nachts. Schriften,* vol. 8, edited by Christian Wagenknecht. Frankfurt am Main: Suhrkamp, 1986.

———. *Die letzten Tage der Menschheit: Tragödie in fünf Akten mit Vorspiel und Epilog. Schriften,* vol. 10, edited by Christian Wagenknecht. Frankfurt am Main: Suhrkamp, 1986.

———. *Weltgericht. I. Band. Schriften,* vol. 5, edited by Christian Wagenknecht. Frankfurt am Main: Suhrkamp, 1988.

Menasse, Robert. *Dummheit ist machbar: Begleitende Essays zum Stillstand der Republik.* Vienna: Sonderzahl, 1999.

———. *Erklär mir Österreich: Essays zur österreichischen Geschichte.* Frankfurt am Main: Suhrkamp, 2000.

———. *Hysterien und andere historische Irrtümer.* Mit einem Nachwort von Rüdiger Wischenbart. Vienna: Sonderzahl, 1996.

———. *Das Land ohne Eigenschaften: Essays zur österreichischen Identität.* Vienna: Sonderzahl, 1992.

———. *Phänomenologie der Entgeisterung: Geschichte des verschwindenden Wissens.* Frankfurt am Main: Suhrkamp, 1995.

———. *Schubumkehr.* Roman (1995). Frankfurt am Main: Suhrkamp, 1997.

———. *Selige Zeiten, brüchige Welt.* Roman (1991). Frankfurt am Main: Suhrkamp, 1994.

———. *Sinnliche Gewißheit.* Roman (1988). Frankfurt am Main: Suhrkamp, 1996.

———. *Die sozialpartnerschaftliche Ästhetik: Essays zum österreichischen Geist.* Vienna: Sonderzahl, 1990.

Pelinka, Anton. *Zur österreichischen Identität: Zwischen deutscher Vereinigung und Mitteleuropa.* Vienna: Ueberreuter, 1990.

Pfabigan, Alfred. *Karl Kraus und der Sozialismus: Eine politische Biographie.* Vienna: Europa-Verlag, 1976.

Posthofen, Renate. "Menasse verstehen: Analyse und Deutung von Robert Menasses Schubumkehr (1995)." In *Towards the Millennium. Interpreting the Austrian Novel 1971–1996. Zur Interpretation des österreichischen Romans 1971–1996,* edited by Gerald Chapple. Tübingen: Stauffenburg Verlag, 2000. 241–59.

Scheichl, Sigurd Paul. "Die Historischen und die Vordringenden. Karl Kraus' 'Fackel' als (Zerr-)Spiegel der Wiener Gesellschaft." In *Die Wiener Jahrhundertwende: Einflüsse, Umwelt, Wirkungen,* edited by Jürgen Nautz and Richard Vahrenkamp. Vienna/Cologne/Graz: Böhlau, 1996. 419–34.

Schuh, Franz. "Robert Menasse und unsere Liebe zu Hegel." In Stolz, *Die Welt scheint unverbesserlich.* 71–75.

Stolz, Dieter, ed. *Die Welt scheint unverbesserlich: Zu Robert Menasses "Trilogie der Entgeisterung."* Frankfurt am Main: Suhrkamp, 1997.

Timms, Edward. *Karl Kraus, Apocalyptic Satirist.* New Haven/London: Yale UP, 1986.

Zohn, Harry. "Karl Kraus and *Die Fackel.*" In *Vienna: The World of Yesterday, 1889–1914,* edited by Stephen Eric Bronner and F. Peter Wagner. Atlantic Highlands, NJ: Humanities Press, 1997. 168–86.

II. Arts and Culture

Wiener Secession.
Photo by Ernst Grabovszki.

Art and Architecture 1900 and 2000

Douglas Crow

1900–1918

"Hüllt unser Volk in eine österreichische Schönheit ein!"

WITH THESE WORDS, Hermann Bahr (1863–1934), writer, critic, playwright and journalistic provocateur, invoked Vienna's artists at the end of the nineteenth century. Bahr foresaw the rise of a new ideal of beauty, which he proclaimed in apocalyptic terms: "Die Gerechtigkeit wankte und die Sitte ward erschüttert und der Glaube brach. Und alles ward neu. Und eine neue Schönheit ging mit jeder neuen Sonne auf, mit fremdem Namen und mit fremdem Antlitz und befremdsam geschmückt."[1]

Though seemingly novel, the "neue Schönheit" had theoretical underpinnings in Kant's eighteenth-century doctrine of the autonomy of aesthetic standards. Over time, Kant's theories were given form in England by the Romanticists, the Pre-Raphaelites and the aestheticists. By the beginning of the twentieth century the preciosity, symbolism and decorative use of organic forms of the New Beauty were internationally dominant. In France and America it was called Art Nouveau, in Spain Modernismo, in Italy Stile Floreale and in Germany Jugendstil, after the Munich periodical *Die Jugend,* which featured art nouveau designs.

Although Vienna was a relative late-comer to Jugendstil, its coffeehouse culture quickly made up for lost time. Bahr's table in the downtown Café Central became the frequent meeting place of "Jung-Wien" writers Arthur Schnitzler (1862–1931), Hugo von Hofmannsthal (1874–1929), and Felix Salten (1869–1945); leading artists and architects Gustav Klimt (1862–1918), Alfred Roller (1864–1935) and Otto Wagner (1841–1918), among others, held their lively discussions at the Café Museum, within view of the Academy of Fine Arts, while the composers Gustav Mahler, Alban Berg, Arnold Schönberg and Anton von Webern contemplated musical innovations over *Einspänner* at the Café Imperial, located near the court opera house.

Bahr recognized the ambivalence of Jugendstil beauty, which arose from its combined symbolism of existence and essence. The symbol "is" — hence the typical titles of Jugendstil art: "Youth," "Hope," "Death and Life" — signaling eternal, irreducible meaning, while its artistic representations were clear manifestations of the temporal and physical world. He knew also that artistic beauty defied critical analysis: "Schönheit läßt sich nicht beweisen, mit dem Verstande werden wir ja der Kunst nicht nachkommen."[2] However, Bahr was more analytical in discussing Jugendstil's literary version, Symbolism, and his comments on Jugendstil literature illuminate Jugendstil art: "Die alte Technik nimmt das Gefühl selbst oder seinen äußeren Grund und Gegenstand zu ihrem Vorwurfe — die Technik der Symbolisten nimmt einen anderen und entlegenen Gegenstand, aber der von dem nämlichen Gefühle begleitet sein müßte."[3] For illustration, he cited Hugo von Hofmannsthal's "Mein Garten," which begins:[4]

> Schön ist mein Garten mit den goldnen Bäumen,
> Den Blättern, die mit Silbersäuseln zittern,
> Dem Diamantenthau, den Wappengittern,
> Dem Klang des Gong, bei dem die Löwen träumen

Bahr might easily have quoted from a score of other symbolist works to the same effect, for Symbolism had a marked stylistic cohesion, as is evident in Hofmannsthal's "Prolog zu dem Buch Anatol":

> Grüne, braune stille Teiche,
> Glatt und marmorweiß umrandet,
> In dem Spiegelbild der Nixen
> Spielen Gold- und Silberfische
> Auf dem glattgeschornen Rasen
> Liegen zierlich gleiche Schatten
> Schlanker Oleanderstämme;
> Zweige wölben sich zur Kuppel,
> Zweige neigen sich zur Nische
> Für die steifen Liebespaare,
> Heroinen und Heroen[5]

The visual artists of Jugendstil employed elements of expression identical to those of literary Symbolism: the colors gold and silver, Japonisme (the gong and bronze lions), preciosity (Diamantenthau), decorative plants ("Oleanderstämme") setting off human forms which symbolize a larger identity (Heroinen und Heroen), and the overarching garden setting (Bahr's "entlegener Gegenstand"), a metaphor for the formal order brought to nature by art.

Jugendstil art can be understood as a visual expression of symbolist poetry. Like Symbolism, it is formalist, sacral, solemn and Dionysian. It is sharply drawn, for, as the Symbolist Rainer Maria Rilke (1875–1926) stipulated: "Das Ding ist bestimmt, das Kunstding muß noch bestimmter sein; von allem Zufall fortgenommen, jeder Unklarheit entrückt, der Zeit enthoben und dem Raum gegeben, ist es dauernd geworden, fähig zur Ewigkeit."[6]

The sacral aspect of Viennese Jugendstil is revealed in the phrase "Ver Sacrum" (Sacred Spring), which was the title of Viennese Jugendstil's literary journal. The concept of sanctified art originates with English Romanticism and finds expression especially in the poetry of William Blake and John Keats:

> Beauty is truth, truth beauty, — that is all
> Ye know on earth, and all ye need to know.[7]

Ultimate truth through beauty, the Romanticists believed, was achieved by the agency of "holde Kunst,"[8] (Franz von Schober [1798–1882], poet and librettist) which in their view penetrated the existential wall between contemplator and contemplated, thereby effecting a "holy union" of the two.

Viennese Jugendstil was named "Secession Style" for a group of nineteen artists who seceded in 1897 from the Künstlerhaus, the representative Austrian organization of painters, sculptors, and architects, to break with an establishment dominated by Realism and Historicism. The "Vereinigung bildender Künstler Österreichs — Secession" was a phenomenon of its time. Munich had a secession in 1892, Berlin in 1899. All were motivated by the desire to establish a new and original concept of beauty, hence the designation "Jugend" (youth), used in the title of the Munich Secession's periodical, *Die Jugend*. Otto Wagner explained: "Jede Kunstepoche hat sich ablehnend gegen die früheren verhalten und einem anderen Schönheitsideale gehuldigt. Künstlerisch neugeborenes Schönes reißt uns zur Bewunderung hin und erhebt sich bergehoch über alles Kopierte."[9]

The Viennese Secession distinguished itself from other secessionist movements by an exceptional virtuosity, an early expression of which was the Secession, its exhibition hall built in 1898 on the Karlsplatz across from the Künstlerhaus. Based on a drawing by the painter Gustav Klimt, The Secession was designed by architect Joseph Olbrich (1867–1908) as a collation of finely proportioned stereometric forms crowned by a wrought iron globe of gilded laurel leaves and blossoms. Above the building's entrance stood the motto: "Der Zeit ihre Kunst, der Kunst ihre Freiheit."

Unlike other artistic insurgencies, such as French impressionism, Viennese Secessionism emanated from within the artistic establishment. Its leaders, the architects Wagner and Olbrich, the painters Klimt, Alfred Roller, Karl Moll (1861–1945), Josef Hoffmann (1870–1956) and the sculptors Edmund Hellmer (1850–1935) and Anton Hanak (1875–1934), were established artists, most linked to the Vienna Academy of Fine Arts and thus to a uniquely Viennese institution called the Master School. Each artistic discipline at the Academy had a Master School, and all were organized along essentially the same lines. Ferdinand Welz (b. 1914) described his experience in the Master School for Sculpture:

> Wir konnten frei arbeiten. Wir konnten immer arbeiten, was wir wollten — nur mit dem Unterschied, daß wir 4 Jahre sogenannte allgemeine Bildhauerei machen mußten, und dann konnte man ein Zeugnis verlangen und war akademischer Bildhauer. Aber nun gab es eine Spezialeinrichtung, die Meisterschule. Die dauerte wieder vier Jahre. Und somit war das das längste Studium in Europa — acht Jahre. [. . .] Der Professor wollte keine Schüler haben, die ihn imitieren, in seiner Arbeit, in seiner Auffassung, das wollte er nicht. Er wollte eigenschöpferische Künstler heranbilden. [. . .] Man mußte, wenn man's nicht konnte, Steinbearbeitung lernen, man mußte Holzschnitzen lernen, und so weiter. Wir hatten vier Jahre Zeit, um alle Prüfungen zu machen, denn ohne Prüfungen konnten wir keinen Diplom erreichen. [. . .] Nach dem vierten Jahr, wenn der Professor eingewilligt hat, daß der Student in die Meisterschule weiter aufsteigt, hat er ein eigenes Atelier bekommen und konnte auch Aufträge annehmen und hatte das Recht, den Professor zu konsultieren. Also, er war trotzdem die vier Jahre noch unter der Aufsicht des Professors. Ich meine, höher geht es für niemanden. Das war das bestmögliche Studium, das ein Künstler überhaupt haben könnte . . . (From an unpublished video interview owned by the author, 1989)[10]

The eight years of training with one professor were the foundation not only of an exceptional virtuosity, but of a special bond between students and professors. Hellmer's class was described by a contemporary observer: "Seinen Schülern war und ist er nicht ein pedantischer Meister und Herr, sondern ein rathender Freund; frei und ungehindert kann sich jedes Einzelnen Talent entfalten, frei und ungefesselt Jeder seinen stylistischen Neigungen folgen."[11] The atmosphere in the Master Schools tended to banish the generation gap. Professor of Architecture Otto

Wagner, at the age of 58, joined his students in founding the Secession (Bahr was to write in his obituary of Wagner: "Die Jungen von Wien waren seine Kinder, ehe er ihr Kamerad wurde."[12]) Similarly, the naturalistic sculptors Hellmer and Hans Bitterlich (1860–1949), at the turn of the century 50 and 40, respectively, embraced "die neue Schönheit." Hellmer's Youth (1900) for the Dumba monument and Bitterlich's memorial to the Empress Elizabeth (1904) are examples of Jugendstil sculpture at its best.

The Secession's first president, Gustav Klimt, however, was shut out of the Academy, despite unanimous recommendation by the faculty. The opposition came "von höchster Instanz," Crown Prince Franz Ferdinand, passionately involved in Viennese artistic matters. He considered Klimt's frank depictions of nudity "krankhaft." His mural for the Aula of the University of Vienna, "Philosophy" (1900), caused a major scandal, with eighty-seven University professors signing a letter of protest. One wrote to a Viennese daily, "Eher lege ich meine Professur zurück, als daß ich zugebe, daß nackte Frauenzimmer in der Universität aufgehängt werden." Klimt's earlier, "Nude Veritas" (1899), had been prophetic, for on it he had painted Schiller's words: "Kannst du nicht allen gefallen durch deine That und ein Kunstwerk, mach es wenigen recht. Vielen gefallen ist schlimm." In the end it was Bahr who pronounced posterity's judgment of Klimt: "Klimt spricht aus, was wir mit unseren elenden Worten nicht sagen können, aber wir können nicht leben, wenn es uns nicht gezeigt wird, deshalb ist den Menschen die Kunst gegeben. [. . .] Erzählen wir, was sie uns geschenkt hat, und lasset uns dankbar sein."[13]

Of extreme importance for Viennese Jugendstil was the concept of the "Gesamtkunstwerk," art combining various media for a unified aesthetic effect. Three examples stand out: the collaboration at the Vienna Court Opera between set designer Alfred Roller and musical director Gustav Mahler, Otto Wagner's Vienna Transportation System, and the "Wiener Werkstätte." During the 1903–1909 seasons, Roller and Mahler coordinated set designs, texts, music and lighting to create performances of seamless effect. Roller's set models may be viewed today as independent masterpieces in Vienna's Museum of the Theater. Wagner's system of transportation, the "Stadtbahn," was an embodiment of his assertion, "ohne Zweifel kann und muß es so weit kommen, daß nichts dem Auge Sichtbares entsteht, ohne die künstlerische Weihe zu empfangen"[14] This is seen in every aspect of the gigantic commuter system: the geometry of design, the harmony of ornamentation, the comfortable rise of platform stairs. Wagner's greatest achievement was his adaptation of the transportation experience to the passenger's perception. Hermann Czech commented,

> Es ist kein Zufall, daß sich in Wien das Zeitunglesen in öffentlichen Verkehrsmitteln nicht eingebürgert hat. Der Wiener schaut hinaus, auch in den Tunnels. Das hügelige Terrain zwang dazu, zwischen Hoch- und Tiefbahn zu wechseln, und auch die Tiefbahn wurde womöglich im offenen Einschnitt oder, wie am Donaukanal, in Galerien geführt. Welchen Eindruck der völlig neue Maßstab der Stadt auf die Zeitgenossen machte, können wir daran ermessen, daß die Stadtbahn jahrelang hauptsächlich für Vergnügungsfahrten benützt wurde.[15]

The mission of the "Wiener Werkstätte," the organization of Jugendstil craftsmen and artists, was summed up in the words of art critic Frantisek Xaver Salda:

> Zweck ist, an der Verschönerung des Lebens zu arbeiten, am Ganzen zu wirken und dem Ganzen zu dienen. [. . .] Einheit von Kunst und Leben, wird Gegenstand unseres Hoffens. [. . .] Wir wollen [. . .] eine neue Ehe zwischen Kunst und Leben, eine neue Weihe des Alltags, eine neue Einheit von Schönheit und Arbeit, von Schönheit und Wirklichkeit, eine neue Religion der Menschlichkeit [. . .], die dauernd auch in den kleinsten unserer Häuser und in den unruhigsten unserer Gassen, in unseren Gärten, in unseren Uferstraßen, an unseren niederen Schulen und Hochschulen, in unseren Werkstätten und in unseren Krankenhäusern Wohnung nehme.[16]

The workshops of "Wiener Werkstätte," staffed by artisans trained at the Vienna Academy of Applied Arts, designed jewelry, silverware, dishes, fabrics, menus, labels for bottles, even a cabaret, Die Fledermaus. The Palais Stoclet, designed and built in Vienna under the supervision of architect Josef Hoffmann and erected in Brussels in 1911, was their most completely realized "Gesamtkunstwerk."

While Viennese artists pursued the beautification of daily life, the Habsburg monarchy inexorably sleepwalked toward the abyss of the World War. Viennese *Gemütlichkeit* was disturbed by fractious labor demonstrations and nationalistic uproar in Parliament. The works of Sigmund Freud (1856–1939) taught that leapfrogging the rational mind attained more fertile and true depths in the subconscious. A miasma of unease invaded Viennese cultural life. In *Der Brief des Lord Chandos* (1902, translated as *The Lord Chandos Letter*), Hofmannsthal expressed his sense that the current poetic vocabulary could no longer adequately represent reality:

Mein Innres aber muß ich Ihnen darlegen, eine Sonderbarkeit, eine Unart, wenn Sie wollen eine Krankheit meines Geistes, wenn Sie begreifen sollen, daß mich ein ebensolcher brückenloser Abgrund von den scheinbar vor mir liegenden literarischen Arbeiten trennt, als von denen, die hinter mir sind und die ich, so fremd sprechen sie mich an, mein Eigentum zu nennen zögere.[17]

Hofmannsthal was eventually to abandon the writing of lyric poetry.

In architecture Adolf Loos began a revolution in Vienna with his buildings shorn of external adornment. Loos opposed the idea of architecture as art and identified ornament as a sign of degeneracy.[18] A harbinger of the Bauhaus, Loos was called by Walther Gropius (1883–1969) "ein Prophet." He also performed the role of midwife to Vienna's Expressionist movement, supporting its painters in newspaper articles and with funds. In his 1910 essay "Architecture"[19] he postulated new creative premises for artists and architects:

The house has to please everyone, contrary to the work of art, which does not. The work of art is a private matter for the artist. The house is not. The work of art is brought into the world without there being a need for it. The house satisfies a requirement. The work of art is responsible to none; the house is responsible to everyone. The work of art wants to draw people out of their state of comfort. The house has to serve comfort. The work of art is revolutionary; the house is conservative. The work of art shows people new directions and thinks of the future. The house thinks of the present. Man loves everything that satisfies his comfort. He hates everything that wants to draw him out of his acquired and secured position and that disturbs him. Thus, he loves the house and hates art. Does it follow that the house has nothing in common with art, and is architecture not to be included in the arts? That is so. Only a very small part of architecture belongs to art: the tomb and the monument. Everything else that fulfills a function is to be excluded from the domain of art.[20]

The advent of expressionism, initiated in Vienna by break-away Klimt followers Egon Schiele (1890–1918) and Oskar Kokoschka (1886–1980), was a decisive event in art history. It marked the displacement of Illusionism, the dominant artistic vision since the Renaissance, in favor of a subjective depiction of passions and emotions. By 1908, Schiele and Kokoschka were producing pictures which displayed characteristic expressionistic primitivism, exaggerated lines, vivid, unnatural colors, and themes of mortality, violence and sickness. Classic Illusionism receded into what art-critic and curator Lawrence Alloway has termed the "invisible art world,"[21] continuing with its own tastes and markets, but dropping from the radar screens of those concerned with the traditions of fine art.

Loos's theories dissolved the ancient bond between sculpture and architecture, which had been the sculptors' bread and butter. Sculpture was banished to the salon, the tomb or the monument. As to the monument, Siegfried Charoux's "Lessing" on Vienna's Morzinplatz demonstrates the incompatibility of Expressionism with the monumental function.

Literary Expressionism flourished in Vienna at this time, encouraged by Karl Kraus (1874–1936) and represented, among others, by Albert Ehrenstein (1886–1950), Franz Werfel (1890–1945) and Max Brod (1884–1968). The thematic kinship between expressionistic visual art and expressionistic literature is seen in a 1914 poem by Ehrenstein:

Leid

Wie bin ich vorgespannt
Dem Kohlenwagen meiner Trauer!
Widrig wie eine Spinne
Bekriecht mich die Zeit.
Fällt mein Haar,
Ergraut mein Haupt zum Feld,
Darüber der letzte
Schnitter sichelt.
Schlaf umdunkelt mein Gebein.
Im Traum schon starb ich,
Gras schoß aus meinem Schädel,
Aus schwarzer Erde war mein Kopf.[22]

Kokoschka contributed works of expressionistic drama, narrative and poetry which showed stylistic links to his paintings, as in this lyric from his book of fairy tales, *Die träumenden Knaben* (1908, The Dreaming Boys).

rot fischlein
fischlein rot
stech dich mit dem dreischneidigen messer tot
reiss dich mit meinen fingern entzwei
dass dem stummen kreisen ein ende sei
rot fischlein
fischlein rot
mein messerlein ist rot
meine fingerlein sind rot
in der schale sinkt ein fischlein tot [23]

1918–1938

The "Volkskomiker" Hans Moser (1880–1964) summed up Vienna's economic situation between the World Wars in the words of Seiberl, the grocer in the 1930 play *Essig und Öl — ein Märchen von heute* (Vinegar and Oil — a Modern Fairytale):

> Es waren Zeiten, da hab ich zwei, drei Prager
> Schinken verkauft, an einem Tag —
> Jetzt schneid ich in der Woche zwei — und auch
> diese zwei waren nie in Prag.
>
> Es waren Zeiten, da war für das Personal
> der Frau Baronin nichts zu fein —
> Jetzt kauft die Frau Baronin selbst nur mehr
> hie und da ein Paar Würsteln ein.[24]

If the Frau Baronin could not afford a "Schinken," neither was she in the market for painting or sculpture. The arts joined the Viennese economy in severe crisis. Major figures disappeared from the scene. The year 1918, alone, saw the deaths of Schiele, Klimt, Kolomann Moser (1868–1918) and Otto Wagner. Bahr summed up the loss of Wagner: "Ohne Wagner hätten wir keine Sezession, keine Klimt-Gruppe, kein Wiener Kunstgewerbe, keinen Alfred Roller, und keinen Adolf Loos. Denn Otto Wagner stellte die Atmosphäre her, in der dies alles erst möglich wurde."[25]

The most notable new development in Viennese painting following the First World War was "New Objectivity" (Neue Sachlichkeit), an unidealized, solid, static, simplified, unsentimental illusionism, rendered with thinly painted surfaces and scarcely perceptible brush strokes. Its representatives were Franz Sedlacek (1891–1945), Sergius Pauser (1896–1970) and Albin Egger-Lienz (1868–1926). A literary corollary was the contemporary emphasis on the historical novel and the documentary. Robert Musil captured the pervasive sense of anxious cultural nostalgia in his metaphorical description of a journey by rail in *Der Mann ohne Eigenschaften* (1930–43, translated as *The Man Without Qualities*):

> . . . es kommt vor, wenn man nach längerer Pause hinaussieht, daß sich die Landschaft geändert hat; was da vorbeifliegt, fliegt vorbei, weil es nicht anders sein kann, aber bei aller Ergebenheit gewinnt ein unangenehmes Gefühl immer mehr Gewalt, als ob man über das Ziel hinausgefahren oder auf eine falsche Strecke geraten wäre. Und eines Tages ist das stürmische Bedürfnis da: Aussteigen! Abspringen! Ein Heimweh

nach Aufgehaltenwerden, Nichtsichentwickeln, Steckenbleiben, Zu-
rückkehren zu einem Punkt, der vor der falschen Abzweigung liegt!
Und in der guten alten Zeit, als es das Kaisertum Österreich noch gab,
konnte man in einem solchen Falle den Zug der Zeit verlassen, sich in
einen gewöhnlichen Zug einer gewöhnlichen Eisenbahn setzen und in
die Heimat zurückfahren.[26]

Between the world wars the artistic avant-garde felt out of place in
Vienna. Kokoschka moved restlessly from Dresden (1919) to Munich
(1924) to Paris (1932), and, with the advent of the Nazis in Vienna, to
London (1939), from where he wrote:

What am I to do in this hole? I must invent new subjects for my paintings. I am quite starved for something to see. When the spring comes
I feel how it stirs in me as in a migrant bird, and I become quite nervous: I must leave town and paint something real — a grasshopper or
something. When I come back to town the landscapes turn into political pictures. My heart aches, but I cannot help it. I cannot just paint
landscapes without taking any notice of what happens.[27]

The foremost expressionist painter in Vienna was Herbert Boeckl
(1894–1966), who stayed on due to his large family. Forced to withdraw
from a professorship of painting at the Academy during the Nazi period,
he worked in isolation, developing a strongly colorful impasto style in
oils and painting bright, loose yet controlled landscape watercolors.
Boeckl briefly came into contact with the Nötscher Circle, a group of
landscapists which included Anton Kolig, Gerhart Frankl, Sebastian Isepp
and Franz Wiegele, but Frankl emigrated to England, Pauser to Germany, and Wiegele to Switzerland. The dispersal of Viennese artists
explains why, as art critic Bénédicte Ramade wrote:

"Jamais il n'exista de véritable groupe expressionniste autrichien à
l'instar des 'Blaue Reiter' ou 'Die Brücke' allemands. Sous ce label
étaient regroupées de fortes personnalités, toutes indépendantes et in-
dividualistes, sans qu'il y soit développé une unité stylistique ou une
quelconque invention formelle ou théorique."[28]

The Academy's Master Schools were another casualty of the Third
Reich. Welz recalls:

Und dann kam Hitler, hat uns ja annektiert, hat uns überrannt im
neununddreißiger Jahr. [. . .] Wie ich schon gesagt habe, hat das Studi-
um vier beziehungsweise acht Jahre gedauert. In Deutschland waren es
vier Jahre, und damit hatte es sich. Das wurde in Österreich leider
Gottes durch Hitler eingeführt. Und das geht bis heute. Es ist mir un-

verständlich, daß man nicht zurückgegriffen hat auf die Meisterschule. Heute ist das eine Augenauswischerei, wenn das heute Meisterschule heißt! [. . .] Aber das war damals die unterste Ausbildung, diese vier Jahre, dann kam erst die Meisterschule! Heute heißt das alles Meister-schule, und das soll schon genügen. (From an unpublished video inter-view, 1989)[29]

The economic situation was even more difficult for sculptors than for painters, due to the relatively greater outlay for materials, but Welz, with his Master School background, could adjust: "So hatten wir unsere Weltwirtschaftskrise und waren arm. Und so habe ich mich eben in das kleine Format geflüchtet, weil ich mir teures Material als Bildhauer nicht leisten konnte, Steine, und so weiter. So habe ich mich in die Medaille geflüchtet." In 1940 Welz found employment with the Austrian Mint. His achievements in the field of medallic art eventually gained him world recognition.

1945–2000

"You cannot retreat from the present, there is no way back into the past, and ahead there are dim, vague shapes, stange, unfamiliar — the future — and that is just where you have to go, step by step, carry-ing your light."

Ernst Jandl, 1971.[30]

Before the Second World War, when one spoke of Modernism in Vienna, it referred to the Klimt-Schiele school. In the interim between the world wars the city had been isolated from contemporary international art currents. Now, in 1945 with the occupation, the speed limits on Vi-enna's streets were raised literally and figuratively, and its artists, thor-oughly in the spirit of the legendary Augustine, awakened to new ideas from Paris and New York.

The early postwar years saw a flurry of groupings and re-groupings in clubs and associations, as artists reacted to wave upon wave of interna-tional influence. The Art Club, advocating autonomy in the arts, was organized in 1947. It attracted artists, writers and composers to its membership. Led by painters of the school of Fantastic Realism, Albert Paris Gütersloh (1887–1973), Rudolf Hausner (b. 1914), Anton Lehmden (b. 1929), Ernst Fuchs (b. 1930) and Arik Brauer (b. 1929), with their center at the Academy of Fine Arts, it dominated the art scene in the late 1940s and early 1950s. Fantastic Realist dreamscapes drew on Surrealism, depicting bizarre, hermetic, Breughelian images with a tech-nical expertise reminiscent of the Flemish Masters.

The leading postwar figure of avant-garde sculpture was Hanak disciple Fritz Wotruba (1907–1975). His cubistic stone sculptures influenced a host of young sculptors, among them Josef Pillhofer (b. 1921), Joannis Avramidis (b. 1922), Andreas Urteil (1933–1963) and Alfred Hrdlicka (b. 1928), the last mentioned noted for his realistic-expressionistic memorial against war and fascism on the Albertinaplatz. Wotruba also designed architecture. His church of the Trinity at Mauer is a paradigm of abstract design. Other Viennese sculptors who combined abstractionism with realism were Wander Bertoni (b. 1925), Hans Knesl (1905–1971), Rudolf Hoflehner (1916–1995) and Franz Xaver Ölzant (b. 1934).

In 1950 a group of younger artists influenced by Informalism established the "Hundsgruppe," an offshoot of the Art Club. Membership included Arnulf Rainer (b. 1928), Ernst Fuchs, Anton Lehmden, Arik Brauer, Wolfgang Hollegha (b. 1929), Josef Mikl (b. 1929), Markus Prachensky (b. 1932), Hans Staudacher (b. 1923) and Maria Lassnig (b. 1919). Their works were marked by the instinctual, dynamic, non-formal approaches of abstract expressionism and action painting. The Informalists gathered under the patronage of Monsignor Otto Mauer (1907–1973) and his "Gallery next to St. Stephan," where yet another offshoot was founded in 1959 by Rainer, Fuchs and Friedensreich Hundertwasser (1928–2000), called the "Pintorarium, a crematorium to incinerate the Academy." It was a declaration of war against the Fantastic Realists. In the years immediately following, Rainer attracted international attention with his formulation of "Malerei, um die Malerei zu verlassen."

A corollary development in literature was the Wiener Gruppe, another spinoff of the Art Club. Its members rejected conventional literary forms and drew the attention of the press with their "poetic parlor games" (poetische Gesellschaftsspiele). These literary cabarets featured readings, songs and theatrical sketches. Among the participants were Oswald Wiener (b. 1935), Hans Carl Artmann (1921–2000), Gerhard Rühm (b. 1930), Konrad Bayer (1932–1964), Ernst Jandl (1925–2000) and the architect Friedrich Achleitner (b. 1930). Wiener Gruppe writings frequently relied on rhythms or sound patterns more than on sense, echoing Gertrude Stein and the heightened linguistic consciousness of Ludwig Wittgenstein (1889–1950). An example is Rühm's "glaubensbekenntnis":

> der text wird in ableierndem sprechgesang auf einem ton vorgetragen;
> nur das "ja" im zwanzigsten satz ist um einen ganzton höher, und das
> "ko-" des vorletzten wortes um einen ganzton tiefer zu intonieren.

ich glaube an ein kalb.
ich glaube auch an zwei kälber.
ich glaube, dass jedes kalb ein hirn hat.
ich bin überzeugt, dass man kälber schlachten kann.
ich glaube an eine henne.
ich glaube auch an zwei hennen.
ich glaube, dass jede henne aus einem ei geschlüpft ist.
ich glaube fest, dass hennen eier legen.
ich glaube auch, dass eine henne zwei eier legen kann.[31]

The whimsical, provocative, and sometimes macabre literary productions of the Wiener Gruppe directly influenced the development of artistic Actionism, Austrian performance art inspired by American art's happenings. Actionism, primarily a phenomenon of the 1960s and early 1970s, combined elements from the visual arts, music and literature to extend art beyond object to experience. Foremost among the actionists were Günther Brus (b. 1938), Rudolf Schwarzkogler (1940–1969), Otto Mühl (b. 1925) and Hermann Nitsch (b. 1938). They demanded absolute freedom from traditional artistic forms. The performances, which were documented with photography or film, featured ritualistic nakedness, self-mutilation, sado-masochism, defecation, urination, the manipulation of blood and entrails from animal cadavers, especially those of lambs, and political-social diatribe. Actionist readings identified Austrian society as dystopian, and during the performances Austrian national symbols were sometimes degraded. Spectators were encouraged to take part by undressing and performing socially taboo behavior to express self-liberation. The stated aim of literary Actionism was to shock Austrian society into debating about the world's political and social injustices, but the Actionists' behavior impressed the public rather as a form of fascistic hooliganism and understandably aroused hostilities, making reasonable dialogue impossible.

The literary component of Actionism is illustrated in Oswald Wiener's text to "The Zock Exercises," a Viennese happening of 1967: "nicht wir sind entfremdet, sondern die welt. die institutionen ersticken uns. die kommunikation ist fremd. wir brauchen chaos. nur das zerbröseln von institutionen schafft luft, nur der affront, die verfremdung bezeichnet die entfremdung."[32]

Literature also played a major role in Conceptual Art, which arrived on the Viennese scene in the 1970s. Conceptualism is an international movement in which the idea and description of a work of art matter more than its physical representation. It thus demonstrates the central importance art criticism had begun to have in twentieth century art.

Sculptors Walter Pichler (b. 1936), Bruno Gironcoli (b. 1936) and
Edelbert Köb (b. 1942) have been major forces in Viennese Conceptualism. Köb demonstrated the conceptual approach to sculpture in
a discussion of the genesis of his monument to eighteenth-century painter Angelika Kaufmann:

> Ich habe mir lange überlegt, wie ich ein Denkmal für sie mache. Dann
> habe ich gedacht, ich kann für sie kein Denkmal machen, sondern eine
> Skulptur über das Thema des Denkmals. Was ist ein Denkmal heute?
> Und da ist mir eingefallen, daß ich die Trennung von Mensch und At-
> tributen des Fotografierens im letzten Jahrhundert immer lustig gefun-
> den habe, wo die Fotografen Interieurs gehabt haben, mit einem
> Vorhang, einer Marmorsäule und eben einem Stuhl dazwischen. Und
> dann ist eben der berühmte Mann hineingegangen, hat sich hingesetzt,
> fotografieren lassen. Dann ist ein Offizier gekommen, hat sich foto-
> grafieren lassen, etcetera. Die Personen sind auswechselbar. Und dann
> hat mich auch ein anderer Aspekt beim Denkmal interessiert, nämlich
> die Auswechselbarkeit des Menschen in der Geschichte. Weil die Rö-
> mer sparsame Menschen waren, haben sie nach dem Tod eines Kaisers
> einfach nur die Köpfe ihrer Denkmäler ausgetauscht. Bei den großen
> Kolossalfiguren, wenn ein Kaiser gestorben war und ein neuer kam, ha-
> ben sie nur den Kopf ausgewechselt, auch auf Büsten. Die Köpfe waren
> also zum Abnehmen. Und dieser Aspekt hat mir auch gefallen: daß
> Köpfe und Menschen austauschbar sind, daß sie herunterkullern und
> die Nasen abgeschlagen haben, daß sie respektlos behandelt wurden,
> daß wir von vielen Denkmälern, die in der Stadt sind, keine Ahnung
> mehr haben, wer das war. Oder daß wir viele Menschen, die da auf
> Pferden sitzen, irgendwelche Feldherren, heute mit unseren Maßstäben
> als Kriegsverbrecher bezeichnen würden. Alle diese Dinge haben mich
> interessiert. Und deshalb habe ich für Angelika Kaufmann ein Proto-
> typdenkmal gemacht. Das heißt, ich habe eine typisch klassizistische
> Kulisse aus Marmor aufgestellt, ein Stück Wand mit einem Vorhang
> und eine Säule. Diese Kulisse habe ich aus einem Selbstporträt ent-
> nommen. Sie hat sehr viele Porträts gemacht, und sie hat, wie es damals
> üblich war, fast immer den gleichen Hintergrund verwendet. Seit der
> Renaissance kennen wir das: ein Stück Vorhang, ein Stück Wand und
> ein Stück Säule. Das findet man bei unzähligen Porträts. Das ist das
> Klischee. Und das habe ich genau nachgebaut nach einem Selbstporträt
> von ihr, wo sie vor dieser Kulisse, mit Pinsel und Palette und einer
> Mappe mit Zeichnungen sitzt. Also, ich habe eine Fläche gemacht, eine
> Wand, eine Säule, einen Hocker, sie aber habe ich weggehen lassen. Sie
> ist nicht auf dem Bild, sondern nur das, was wichtig von ihr ist. Nicht
> ihr Gesicht, das man nicht mehr konstruieren kann, sondern die Insi-
> gnien ihrer Kunst: eben die Palette, die Mappe und die Pinsel. Die sind
> in Bronze gegossen, und sie sind da hingelegt. Die Personen sind aus-

wechselbar, die geistern durch die Geschichte, die tauchen kurz auf in einer Momentaufnahme und sind wieder weg. Ich verschleiere meine Neigung, meine Leidenschaft, kann man fast sagen, oder meine Liebe für die Antike oder für Dinge, die ich liebe, indem ich sie ironisch behandle. Ich mache mich nicht lustig über sie, aber ich versuche Distanz zu haben, weil ich mir bewußt bin, daß es nicht in die Zeit paßt, daß meine Neigung eigenartig ist. Es hat eben Gründe, wie ich gesagt habe, warum die modernen Menschen für naive Verehrung nicht mehr fähig sind. (From an unpublished video interview, 1989)[33]

Arguably the most celebrated Viennese artist of the last half of the century was Friedensreich Hundertwasser. Starting in the early 1950s under the influence of French Tachism and Informel, he later took part in Actionism. In the late 1950s he depicted cityscapes and landscapes in a naively colorful spiral style. His precepts, such as "The straight line is godless," reminded some of Jugendstil. As an architect, Hundertwasser designed and built world-famous structures full of playful fantasy, sloping floors, random windows, gold onion domes and a surfeit of ornamental baubles. His structures included the Bad Blumenau spa complex in Styria, the Hundertwasser House in Vienna, the garbage incinerator at Spittelau, service stations, schools, and churches. Hundertwasser had trees planted on the roofs to follow his own rule that no building should be higher than a tree. Although his architecture was denounced by academics and the architectural establishment as kitsch, ordinary citizens loved it.

The last quarter of the twentieth century saw a diminution in the importance of artistic associations, with a simultaneous rise in the application of electronic media and modern reproduction methods in the creation of art. The trend of art as experience as well as object continued, opening the way to installation and digital art. Former actionists Valie Export (b. 1940), Adolf Frohner (b. 1934) and Peter Weibel (b. 1944) worked in genres as varied as conceptual photography, electronic media, and abstract painting. Others, like Heiko Bressnik (b. 1961), Brigitte Kowanz (b. 1957) and Flora Neuwirth (b. 1971) employed electronic media to create pop-techno computer-generated images, collages, and room installations.

In the 1980s there was a resurgence of easel painters, such as the "Vienna Naturalists" and the "New Wild Ones," including Siegfried Anzinger (b. 1953), Christian Ludwig Attersee (b. 1940), Erwin Bohatsch (b. 1951) and Kurt Kocherscheidt (b. 1943). The "Realities" (Peter Pongratz [b. 1940], Franz Ringel [b. 1940], Martha Jungwirth [b. 1940], Kocherscheidt, et al.) drew inspiration from the paintings of children and the insane. Pongratz summed up his purpose in self-description: "Bildnarren wie ich gehen nicht von existierenden Bildern aus. Sie erfinden neue, die es noch nie zuvor gegeben hat."[34]

At the end of the century, postmodernism, which challenges the basic ideas of originality and cultural progression in modern art, was represented in the works of sculptor Heimo Zobernig (b. 1958) and the painter Arnulf Rainer. Zobernig addressed the question of what a work of art is and what it is not with his museum installations of packing crates, while Rainer, by then Vienna's internationally most famous artist, overpainted photographs in his continued quest for "Malerei, um die Malerei zu verlassen."

Beginning with expressionism, Viennese art had taken a path leading from cohesion to dispersal. If the artists of 1900 aimed at ideals and standards of beauty consistent with conceptions of art as handed down from the past, the tendencies from the time of expressionism were in the interest of unfettered self-expression. The twentieth century was mostly characterized by experimentation and uncertainty, as the above quotation from Jandl indicates. Artists sought in the subconscious the totality which was disintegrating more and more in the outer world. But since this quest originated in the subconscious and required that the individual plumb the depths of his own psyche, it primarily yielded narcissism. This is seen in the frantic efforts to create something new, "die es noch nie zuvor gegeben hat," "Malerei, um die Malerei zu verlassen," etc. Similar tendencies were also to be seen in literature (the writings of the Wiener Gruppe come to mind), where their influence was limited, due to the requirement of coherency in language, and in music, where the inventor of the twelve-tone row, Arnold Schönberg, asserted: "For in art, only that which is new and unspoken [*das Neue, Ungesagte*] is worth saying."[35] In no previous century had novelty in artistic expression been pursued with such avidity.

Was the path taken by art in twentieth-century Vienna ascendant or descendant? The answer, of course, is a matter of taste. Friedensreich Hundertwasser's appraisal, however, was unambiguous. In his last years (he died at the beginning of 2000) he clashed with the artistic establishment by insisting that art and architecture be in harmony with nature and with human nature. In a 1989 discussion, Hundertwasser mused on Vienna's artistic past and future:

> (Jugendstil) war der letzte Rest von Menschentum und Menschenwürde. Mit Loos 1908 wurde dann alles nivelliert. Dann hatten wir die Bescherung. Es ging alles in die Leere. Die Umwelt, die wir haben, für die

sind wir verantwortlich. Und noch im größerem Maß sind Architekten und Maler und Kunstschaffende für die Häßlichkeit unserer Umwelt verantwortlich. Und wenn sie Verantwortung ablehnen, dann sind es Fahnenflüchtige, Feiglinge, denn der Mensch hat ein Anrecht auf Schönheit, auf Romantik und auf Freude. Man kann nicht ganz einfach diese Sehnsüchte des Menschen als niedrige Instinkte abtun. Das ist ein Verrat an den Gefühlen des Menschen. Das Buch der Natur ist kein Buch mit sieben Siegeln. Das Buch bleibt verschlossen für den, der böse ist und der bösen Willens ist. Der hat da keinen Zugang. Es ist nur zugänglich für den, der eben aufgehen will in der Natur und in der Kreativität. Wenn die Kreativität des Menschen und die Kreativität der Natur Hand in Hand gehen, dann haben wir so viele, so viele Probleme gelöst. (From a published video interview)[36]

Notes

[1] Hermann Bahr, *Zur Überwindung des Naturalismus* (Stuttgart: Kohlhammer Verlag, 1968), 25.

[2] Fred Hennings, *Solange er lebt: Aus dem Wien der Jahrhundertwende.* (Vienna: Herold, 1968), 57.

[3] Hermann Bahr, *Zur Überwindung des Naturalismus,* 113.

[4] Hermann Bahr, *Zur Überwindung des Naturalismus,* 115.

[5] Hugo von Hofmannsthal, *Gesammelte Werke in Zehn Einzelbänden.* Vol. 1 (Frankfurt am Main: S. Fischer, 1958), 59.

[6] Pausenhof.de, "Rainer Maria Rilke," in *Gegenströmungen des Naturalismus.* Accessed 25 July 2001; available from http://schulhilfen.com/referate/refdeu/refdeun 001.asp

[7] John Keats, "Ode on a Grecian Urn," in *John Keats and Percy Bysshe Shelley: Complete Poetical Works* (New York: The Modern Library), 186.

[8] Richard Capell, *Schubert's Songs* (New York: E. P. Dutton and Company, 1924), 142.

[9] Otto Wagner, *Die Baukunst unserer Zeit* (Vienna: Löcker, 1979), 8–9.

[10] We could work freely. We could always do what we wanted — but you had to do 4 years of so-called general sculpture and then you could apply for a certificate and become a certified sculptor. But then there was a special institution, the Master School. It was another 4 years. This was thus the longest course of study in Europe — eight years. The professor did not want students who imitated him. He wanted to train independent artists. We were required, if we could not already, to learn stone carving, woodcarving, and so on. We were given four years to complete all the tests, because without all the tests you could not get diploma. After the fourth year, with the permission of the professor, the student might then enter the Master School, have his own studio, accept sculptural commissions, and have the right to consult with the professor. That is to say, after four years he still had access to the

professor's guidance. In my opinion it could not be any better. This was the best possible education for a sculptor.

[11] A. Martinez, *Wiener Ateliers,* I. Band (Vienna: Plant & Co., 1893), 39.

[12] Fred Hennings, *Solange er lebt: Aus dem Wien der Jahrhundertwende* (Vienna: Herold, 1968), 15.

[13] Fred Hennings, *Solange er lebt,* 56–57.

[14] Otto Wagner, *Die Baukunst unserer Zeit* (Vienna: Löcker, 1979), 96–97.

[15] Fred Hennings, *Solange er lebt,* 17–18.

[16] Helmut Weiss, *"Was ist Jugendstil?" Schwarz auf Weiss. Das Reisemagazin aus Bremen* [journal online]. Accessed 6 July, 2001. Available from http://www.schwarzaufweiss.de/Prag/was_ist_jugendstil.htm

[17] Hugo von Hofmannsthal, *Gesammelte Werke in Zehn Einzelbänden.* Vol. 1 (Frankfurt am Main: S. Fischer, 1958), 59.

[18] *Adolf Loos: Das Werk des Architekten,* edited by Heinrich Kulka (Vienna: Löcker, 1979), 20.

[19] Adolf Loos, "Architecture," 1910. Quoted by Roberto Schezen, *Adolf Loos: Architecture 1903–1932* (New York: The Monacelli Press, 1996), 15.

[20] *Adolf Loos: Das Werk des Architekten,* 15.

[21] Sylvia Yount, *Maxfield Parrish* (New York: Harry N. Abrams, Inc., 1999), 16.

[22] Conrady, Karl Otto (ed.). *Das Große deutsche Gedichtbook.* Zürich/Düsseldorf 1997. Available from http://www.geocities.com/~aristipp/texte/ehrenstein1.htm

[23] Oskar Kokoschka HomePages. Available from http://www.btinternet.com/~j.p1/kokoschka/kokoschka.html.

[24] Georg Markus. *Hans Moser: Ich trag im Herzen drin . . .* (Vienna: Tosa, 1994), 133–34.

[25] Fred Hennings, *Solange er lebt,* 15.

[26] Robert Musil, *Der Mann ohne Eigenschaften* (Hamburg: Rowohlt, 1970), 32.

[27] Edward Lucie-Smith, *Lives of the Great 20th-Century Artists. The Artchive* [journal online] accessed 25 July, 2001. Available from http://www.artchive.com/artchive/K/kokoschka.html

[28] Bénédicte Ramade, *La Vérité Nue — L'Expressionisme autrichien. NART Magazine* [journal online]. Accessed 14 July 2001. Available from http://www.nart.com/events

[29] And then came Hitler, annexed us, overran us in '39. [. . .] As I said, the course of study lasted four or, as the case might be, eight years. In Germany it was four years, and that was it. This was unfortunately introduced into Austria by Hitler. And so it continues today. It is incomprehensible to me that we have not gone back to the Master School concept. It is eyewash to call it Master School today. Four years was the primary training in those days, and only then came the Master School! Today it is all called Master School and that is supposed to suffice.

[30] Ernst Jandl Obituary. *The London Daily Telegraph,* 21 July 2000.

[31] Rühm, Gerhard. Frauenfelder Lyriktage: Gedichte von Gerhard Rühm.

http://www.swbv.uni-konstanz.de/eu/lyriktage/vier-ruehm.html

[32] Kurz, Horst. Der Wiener Aktionismus.
http://www2.gasou.edu/facstaff/hkurz/wiener/ow-c-3.htm

[33] I considered for a long time how to make a monument for her. Then I thought, I cannot make monument for her, but I can create a sculpture on the theme of the monument. What is a monument today? And then it occurred to me that I always found comical the separation of personality and attributes in the photography of the last century, where the photographers had interiors with a curtain, a marble column, and in between a chair. Then the famous man would come in, sit down and be photographed. Then came perhaps an officer, was photographed using the same props, etc. The people are interchangeable. And an aspect of the monument interested me. It was the interchangeability of persons in history. Because they were a thrifty people, the ancient Romans simply substituted the heads on colossal monuments when an emperor died. They also did this with busts. The heads were detachable. And this aspect appealed to me: that sculptures and people are interchangeable. They are pulled down, they are treated disrespectfully, the noses and ears are broken off busts of famous people, and with many monuments in the city we have no idea whom they represent. Some general or other, who sits high above on a horse would be considered a war criminal by our present-day standards. All these things interested me. And for this reason I made a prototype monument for Angelika Kaufmann. That is, I set up a classical marble backdrop, a bit of wall with a curtain and a column. This backdrop I took from her self-portrait. She painted many portraits using almost always the same background. We are familiar with this from countless portraits of the Renaissance: a bit of curtain, a wall, a column. It is a cliché. This I imitated precisely from her self-portrait, where she sits in front of a backdrop with brush and palette and a portfolio of drawings. So I made a space: a wall, a column, a stool, but her I left out. It was very carefully reconstructed, but she was not present, only what is important about her. Not her face, which we cannot reconstruct any more, but the insignias of her art, that is, the palette, the portfolio and the brush. They were cast in bronze and placed there. I made a mock-up and placed the them on the empty stool. People are interchangeable. They float through history like ghosts, materialize like snapshots and then disappear again. I veil my affection, one could almost say, my passion or my love for antiquity, or for things which I love, by dealing with them ironically. I do not ridicule them but try to create distance because I am aware that my affection is odd, that it no longer suits the times. There are reasons, as I said before, why modern man is no longer capable of naive veneration.

[34] Peter Pongratz soulpainting 1962–1997. Historisches Museum der Stadt Wien. http://www.museum.vienna.at/dynamicPage.asp?MenuID=1841

[35] Matthew Gurewitsch, "A Maudlin Farewell From a King of Grandiosity," *The Wall Street Journal,* 4 October 2001.

[36] (Jugendstil) was the last remnant of humanity and of human dignity. Then came Loos in 1908 and everything was flattened out . . . Then we had the results. It was the end of everything. We are responsible for our environment, and to an even greater extent architects and painters and those who create art are responsible for the ugliness of our environment. When they deny responsibility they are deserters and cowards; for people have a right to beauty, to romanticism and to joy. One cannot

simply dismiss these yearnings as low instincts. That is a betrayal of human feelings . . . The book of nature is not a book with seven seals. It is closed to him who is evil and of evil intent. He has no access . . . (It is) accessible only to him who would be absorbed into nature and creativity . . . When human creativity and the creativity of nature go hand in hand, then we have solved so many, so many problems.

Works Cited

Anonymous. "Ernst Jandl." Obituaries. *The Daily Telegraph,* 21 July 2000.

Bahr, Hermann. *Zur Überwindung des Naturalismus.* Stuttgart: Kohlhammer, 1968.

Capell, Richard. *Schubert's Songs.* New York: E. P. Dutton and Company, 1924.

Gurewitsch, Matthew. "A Maudlin Farewell From a King of Grandiosity." *Wall Street Journal,* 4 October 2001.

Hennings, Fred. *Solange er lebt: Aus dem Wien der Jahrhundertwende.* Vienna: Verlag Herold, 1968.

Hofmannsthal, Hugo von. *Gesammelte Werke in Zehn Einzelbänden.* Vol. 1. Frankfurt am Main: S. Fischer, 1958.

Keats, John. "Ode on a Grecian Urn." In *John Keats and Percy Bysshe Shelley: Complete Poetical Works.* New York: The Modern Library.

Kulka, Heinrich, ed., *Adolf Loos: Das Werk des Architekten.* Vienna: Löcker, 1979.

Loos, Adolf. "Architecture" (1910), in Roberto Scherzen, *Adolf Loos: Architecture 1903–1932.* New York: The Monacelli Press, 1996.

Edward Lucie-Smith. *Lives of the Great 20th-Century Artists,* in *The Artchive* [journal online] accessed 25 July, 2001. Available from http://www.artchive.com/artchive/K/kokoschka.html

Markus, Georg. *Hans Moser: Ich trag im Herzen drin . . .* Vienna: Tosa, 1994.

Martinez, A. *Wiener Ateliers,* I. Band. Vienna: Plant & Co., 1893.

Musil, Robert. *Der Mann ohne Eigenschaften* Hamburg: Rowohlt Verlag, 1970.

Pausenhof.de, "Rainer Maria Rilke." *Gegenströmungen des Naturalismus* http://schulhilfen.com/referate/refdeu/refdeun001.asp

Ramade, Bénédicte. *La Vérité Nue — L'Expressionisme autrichien. NART Magazine.* http://www.nart.com/events.

Wagner, Otto. *Die Baukunst unserer Zeit.* Vienna: Löcker Verlag, 1979.

Weiss, Helmut. *"Was ist Jugendstil?" Schwarz auf Weiss. Das Reisemagazin aus Bremen.* http:/ /www.schwarzaufweiss.de/Prag/was_ist_jugendstil.htm.

Yount, Sylvia. *Maxfield Parrish.* New York: Harry N. Abrams, Inc., 1999.

Café Central in Herrengasse.
Photograph courtesy of Ernst Grabovszki.

Jugendstil-Stadtbahnstation designed by Otto Wagner. Today used as a showroom. Photograph by Ernst Graborszki.

A view of the "Hundertwasserhaus" in the Löwengasse,
an apartment house designed by Friedensreich Hundertwasser.
Photograph by Ernst Grabovszki.

Literature and Austrian Cinema Culture at the Turn of the Centuries

Willy Riemer

A USTRIAN FILM HAS HAD SOME remarkable accomplishments in recent years. At the 2001 film festival in Cannes Michael Haneke's *Die Klavierspielerin* (The Piano Teacher, 2001) received three major awards: the Grand Prix of the Jury, as well as the awards for best actress (Isabelle Huppert) and best actor (Benoît Magimel); Jessica Hausner's feature debut *Lovely Rita* (2001) was accepted for screening at Cannes, as was Ruth Mader's short *Nulldefizit* (Zero Deficit, 2001). At the 1999 festival in Venice Nina Proll received the Mastroianni award for her superb performance in Barbara Albert's *Nordrand* (Northern Skirts), and in 2000 at Locarno the best acting award was given to the trio of Josef Hader, Joachim Bissmeier and Roland Düringer in Florian Flicker's *Der Überfall* (Holdup). Cabaret artist Düringer also starred in Harald Sicheritz's *Hinterholz 8* (1998) which set an attendance record for Austrian film. Austrian film as cultural artifact and commodity thus seems to be thriving. However, for all these achievements at prestigious international film festivals and occasionally at the box-office, Austrian cinema culture and its film industry are at a precarious juncture where continued film production and traditional modes of exhibition face severe difficulties.

More than any other art form, film is big business and risky venture. Right from its diffuse beginnings in the late nineteenth century, business considerations have shaped the multiple steps from conception to screening, and thus the "look" of a film itself. The boundaries between production, distribution and exhibition continue to be contested with each innovation, organizational realignment and demographic shift. While the details have changed in the past hundred years, the underlying issues have persisted.

Just three months after its public introduction in Paris, the cinématographe of the Lumière brothers was demonstrated in Vienna on March 27, 1896. For all the technical deficiencies of this first screening and the very modest program of short films, the event was a resounding success and led to daily showings. Within three weeks Emperor Franz Joseph attended a performance and formed an enthusiastic opinion of the new medium. Indeed, over the years he frequently presented himself to the camera.

Film was fascinating because, unlike photography, it could represent motion in an age that had become enamored with movement and speed. As Hilmar Hoffmann points out, it is not the illusion of reality that leaves a strong impression, but the depiction of motion (27). However, once seen, the novelty effect quickly fades so that this new medium in its first decade soon found its place in transient entertainments, at fairgrounds, amusement parks and vaudeville shows. Exhibitors traveled the provinces in search of new audiences and a formula for programming their small stock of short films so that it would appeal to the mostly uneducated mass audience. Film as spectacle and attraction was strictly business. It was cheap entertainment manufactured in an assembly line fashion in film factories and sold outright to the exhibitors.

The running time of a few minutes did not allow early film to develop narrative structure or extensive coverage; it focused on representing motion and "actuality" as spectacle. Usually in static long shot, trains arrive, people leave factories, carriages and streetcars move along, and skits show episodes acted out in shallow theatrical space. Some films pander to curiosity by putting on display the unusual and inaccessible, the exoticism of royalty as well as that of far away places. However, this is also the "golden age" of erotic film (Caneppele, 26); it was a staple of itinerant exhibitors (Kieninger, 43). Racy images tantalizing the edges of propriety no doubt assured good attendance. Because of their questionable legitimacy, such films were usually restricted to designated "Herrenabende," that is, performances reserved for male adults, often on the last evening of a gig to avoid police action.

The attitude toward sexuality reveals certain incongruities of turn-of-century Vienna. Gustav Klimt's (1862–1918) portraits, for example, show women exquisitely attired, their body covered with richly ornamented fabrics. These flat surfaces are contrasted with an elusive sensuality of posture and facial contour. Similarly the bourgeoisie cultivated decorum and ritual to sustain its social ambitions and concern for status, while also finding ways to accommodate its desires. High culture and the theatricality of daily life thus served to stabilize class structure while, for men at least, sexual gratification was transacted in a gray zone of morality. The pictures of this time show women of polite society elegantly shrouded from head to toe, from fanciful hat to fashionable footwear. Little is revealed of the body, and Sigmund Freud's (1856–1939) successful practice suggests that even less was admitted of the workings of their mind. Men of means could indulge their desires by engaging in "aesthetic dalliance" (Johnston, 117) with obliging young women from the outlying districts of Vienna, the "süße Mädel" given literary currency by Arthur Schnitzler among others. Newspapers at once denounced prostitution and in the same issue carried advertisements for brothels.

In this climate of sexual repression and moral duplicity an industry for producing simulacra of sex and nudity flourished. Pornographic novels did a brisk business. In 1906 John Cleland's *Memoirs of Fanny Hill* appeared in German translation, with illustrations by Franz Bayros that in their explicitness make the film offerings at "Herrenabende" look innocuous. *Josefine Mutzenbacher,* an anonymous and supposedly auto-biographical novel of a prostitute, includes detailed descriptions of licentious practices, but also documents the degrading conditions in the poor neighborhoods. It has been speculated that the book was written by Felix Salten (1869–1945), a respected author, theater and art critic (Fischer, 54). Nude photographs were readily available, ostensibly for artists who could not afford real models and also for scientific purposes. Indeed, Vienna was a major center for producing nude photography (Seemann and Lunzer, 9). However, as the occasional police actions and confiscations indicate, the boundary between nude photography and pornography is a matter of interpretation; neither was acceptable in polite society.

Paolo Caneppele suggests that erotic film derives from a long tradition of desire and its representation; with photography its beginnings predate the first showing of the Lumière cinématographe (10). But while texts in the print media are designed for private consumption, film is presented as a public event. The communal viewing of an erotic film involves a sense of illicit complicity as well as a tacit approval of questionable morality. Quite apart from satisfying the curiosity about the female body and what this means in terms of gender politics, such soft porn tantalizes by a contents that is mildly subversive of sexual repression and social morality. It is then not surprising that various formats of censorship were tried out. In 1907 the police in Vienna decreed that an official would preview each new movie program (*KR* 20 [1907], 6).[1] By 1910 the police regularly published its findings in a trade magazine and approved film descriptions to be used for promotion (*KR* 101 [1910], 4). It is of interest to note that as often as erotic contents, the depiction of excessive violence was prohibited (*KR* 15 [1907], 1).

The advertisements in trade magazines suggest that there was a considerable market for erotic films. Max Rády-Maller was one of the first to establish a film exchange in Vienna. In an advertisement of 1907 he offers new and used films, including a large selection of "pikante Films," the designation for films showing nudity (*KR* 5 [1907], 6). Some entrepreneurs offered exclusively erotic films (Caneppele, 26). Reporting on a court case, an editorial defends its customer and points to the legal duplicity of tolerating prostitution while prosecuting cinema operators who screen erotic films (*KR* 10 [1907], 1). A later editorial asks, who is to blame for the increased popularity of erotic films and concludes that it is a matter of supply and demand. Responsibility therefore lies with the public who prefers and supports such entertainment fare (*KR* 27 [1908], 1).

The French company Pathé Frères, the dominant force in European film production, distributed most of the erotic films. In 1906 the first advertisement for Johann Schwarzer's Saturn-Film appears (reproduced in Achenbach, 76). In its directory of 1907 two entries for film fabrication appear in *KR:* Pathé Frères and Saturn-Film (*KR* 7 [1907], 7). Schwarzer can thus be regarded as the first Austrian producer of fiction film, if only for a narrow genre.

Schwarzer started his career as a photographer, but soon branched out into erotic film. The 1907 catalog of Saturn-Film (reproduced in Achenbach, Caneppele and Kieninger) describes films that were mostly shot outdoors. One may assume that the success of Schwarzer's early products allowed him to establish the studio that then provided the location for later films. Schwarzer was well aware of the problematic status of erotic films. The catalog includes the assertion that the films are purely artistic in intention; as condition of purchase, exhibitors are required to restrict screenings to adult audiences only. In spite of these precautions, there were court cases at home and abroad. In 1911 most of his films were banned and the catalogs destroyed. For a time he tried to salvage his enterprise, but to no avail. Schwarzer was killed in action early in the First World War (Achenbach, 93).

A compilation made available by the Austrian Film Archive gives an impression of style and contents of erotic films produced by Saturn-Film. As Caneppele (16) has observed, four themes recur: dance, voyeurism, disrobing, and artist and model scenes. In other words, the films develop around a pretext for displaying the nude female body. None of the films show sexual action. Erotic scenes are sometimes given a humorous tone, perhaps to placate the censors (Caneppele, 22). Two films in particular, "Beim Fotografen" (1908–1910, At the Photographer's) and "Eine aufregende Jagd" (1906–1907, An Exciting Hunt) reveal a creative use of cinematography.

"Eine aufregende Jagd" begins on the wooded banks of a pond, with a woman first reading a book and then disrobing to go for a swim. The anticipative camera positions the spectator as a voyeur, a witness to illicit pleasures. However, the entire film is photographed in a long shot. The whole nude body is therefore seen, not just some fetishized part of it. The film experiments with editing rhythm: long calm scenes alternate with hectic activity. As happens often in such films, the nude woman is confronted by a male authority figure, which then leads to chase scenes. The opposition of dour propriety and libertine joy occurs often in Schwarzer's films. In this case, the inept policeman is the target of laughter. But polite society too is satirized. In a grove, a picnic in the style depicted by French impressionist painters is in progress when the nude woman runs through the halcyon little group. There is outrage by the women and eager pursuit by the men, and intended laughter for the spectators. Apart from an occasional pan, perhaps the most innovative aspect of this film is the use of the chase to produce cinematographic depth. By comparison to the theatrical stagings of typical films of the time, the effective use of spatial depth explores an important aspect of film art. Finally, the matter of gaze needs to be addressed. While the camera does not use close-ups to fragment the nude body, and no specifically male point of view is established, the woman in her run along the wooded paths does present herself in a way designed to appeal to the male eye. Her primary purpose is to gratify the desires of the male spectators attending an adult show.

The principal model in "Beim Fotografen" is presented in a more assertive way. The film is a delightful spoof of what can be imagined to be going on at a session of nude photography. In this later film two qualities in particular stand out: the greater independence of the model and the self-reflexivity of the film. A sleazy photographer and his efficient assistant are all business trying to take erotic pictures of a prim model who is soon replaced by another, a woman more compliant and professional in disrobing. In quick change of props that indicates routine, a number of poses are photographed. At the end some male customers congregate in the studio to purchase the pictures, only to be dispersed by an umbrella-wielding woman representing the moralist position.

It is important to distinguish the erotic studio pictures from the film about the making of them. The samples of pictures that are shown and the poses are indeed the expected images for consumption by the male gaze: nude women with various props leaning against a wall, languorously draped on a couch, or reclining in a chair. The film, however, does not adopt this strategy of representation. The model does her job in a very practical way: she strips, but not teasingly; she creatively improves poses by using props, and the session ends with a handshake. This is not a woman exploited and abused: she is a partner in the problematic business of producing simulacra of her body for the erotic market. This effect of self-consciousness is heightened by the self-reflexive cinematography. Repeatedly the photographer gestures to the back wall of the studio, the location of the movie camera, and directs the gaze of the model in this direction — but it is not by any means a "come on" look. By drawing attention to the cinematographic apparatus, the photographer makes the spectator aware that this is not an illusion in which desire is gratified, but business executed efficiently and with a sense of humor.

Schwarzer worked innovatively with the medium, exploring the possibilities of editing and cinematographic depth in his outdoor productions and the relationship of spectator to apparatus in his studio work. His subject matter and the intended sector of the film market, however, precluded a pioneering role that would influence the development of Austrian film. Although erotic films were deemed suitable entertainment for the military, exhibitors fearing the loss of their license and struggling to attain cultural respectability distanced themselves from this genre; indeed, by 1910 adult showings were prohibited (Achenbach, 99).

After the first decade since the demonstration of the Lumière cinématographe, Austrian cinema culture evolved rapidly in a complex interaction of developments in production, distribution, and exhibition. Traveling exhibitors began to encounter spectator fatigue: their stock of short mass-produced films lacked originality. With their seasonal market, they could not afford the new films that had longer running times and better production values. Innovations thus favored permanent urban theaters with changing programs and a system of film distribution that reallocated cost and profit. In the cities, film began to find acceptance as an alternative mode of entertainment. Since some of the theaters opened only intermittently or were part of vaudeville productions, the statistics are not always consistent; they all, however, show a steady growth of the permanent theater base. In 1903 there were three theaters in Vienna; by 1907 the number had grown to ten (Fritz, 18). The statistics of 1909 list seventy-six movie theaters, most of them with 100 to 300 seats for a total of 11,616; it was estimated that every adult saw a movie four or five times a year (*KR* 67 [1909], 2).

Film had evolved into a viable industry with its own infrastructure and discourse. The various sources of revenue were fiercely contested and catalyzed new organizational structures. An association of theater operators was formed in part because of the alleged plan by Pathé Frères to acquire theaters as a step towards vertical integration (*KR* 20 [1907], 1). At the first convention of Austrian theater operators the *Kinematographische Rundschau* was selected as the official trade publication (*KR* 20 [1907], 1). Pathé Frères, the largest producer of films with subsidiaries in many countries, by 1909 claimed a daily production of 80,000 meters of film (*ÖK* 31 [1909], 10). In the preceding year Pathé Frères had commenced to rent films, rather than selling them outright, which further favored the programming style of large theater enterprises (*KR* 39 [1908], 1). Distributors consolidated the market by representing the numerous foreign film producers. For example, Hans Christensen, one of the largest, offered 4,000 meters of new film each week (*ÖK* 24 [1909], 3).

Cinema had developed into the "theater of the small towns" (*KR* 19 [1907], 1) and began to make inroads into the cultural market of large cities. Programming and format were explored for attracting more of a middle-class audience; one theater operator planned to include an up-scale restaurant (*ÖK* 12 [1909], 6). In this competitive context film not unexpectedly faced the hostility of the established high culture and the press (*KR* 23 [1908], 1).

While the organization and structures for the new medium were soon in place, its cultural role continued to be debated. For the permanent theaters in the cities, the cinema of attractions needed to be modified to broaden the base of spectators and to counter the stigma of film as corruptor of public morals. The potential of film as art is thus repeatedly advocated, as are its didactic possibilities, especially for the youth (*KR* 15 [1907], 1). One educator, for example, succeeded in obtaining subsidies for training teachers in the use of film equipment for instructional purposes (*FW* 25 [1913], 14). Films were produced to illustrate, for example, the work of different professions. The tedious approach of these films was to characterize didactic documentaries for generations to come. Unlike literature, however, film never became part of the school curriculum; audiences to this day are thus left to develop their own film literacy.

The rallying call for the film industry was art (Hoffmann, 23). To achieve the transformation from entertainment commodity to respectable art, longer films patterned on bourgeois stage drama replaced the program of short attractions. The future, according to one editor, belongs to the dramatic film and its social mission of making the enjoyment of theatrical performance accessible to the public at a moderate admission charge (*ÖK* 4 [1908], 1). A short report entitled "Le Film Esthétique" described a projected series of art films by the Gaumont company on themes such as mythology and religion and with sets designed by artists to rival the best of paintings (*KR* 117 [1910], 4). In a full-page advertisement, Gaumont then promoted these films as marvels of cinematography created by top stage artists and painters (*KR* 118 [1910], 2). Where art and culture in bourgeois Vienna had at first promised to facilitate assimilation to the aristocracy, by the turn-of-century it had become a vehicle for self-expression. With its turn to art, the film industry hoped to tap into this lucrative pool of well-off customers.

By comparison to other countries, Austria was slow in developing its own film production industry. Undoubtedly theater operators all along made short documentaries of local interest for their own use; as I have mentioned, as early as 1907 Saturn-Film exploited a lucrative market niche to establish a presence abroad as well as in Austria. With companies founded in 1910 Anton and Luise Kolm, and Jakob Fleck produced a range of successful short documentaries and adaptations. They can thus be taken as the pioneers of commercial Austrian film. In 1911 they established the "Wiener Kunstfilm," the first Austrian production company of narrative films committed to the *film d'art* movement.

The extraordinary success of multi-reel films from Italy, France and Denmark soon thereafter brought about a second upheaval in the Austrian cinema culture. The longer running times made it possible to have screen plays with more elaborately constructed narratives. Whereas the shorts modeled on the Lumière films had given inadequate representations of reality, the new features opened the doors to the imaginary and the use of cinematographic space and time. The earliest extant Austrian narrative film is the second version of *Der Müller und sein Kind* (The Miller and his Child) produced by the Österreichisch-Ungarische Kinoindustrie in 1911 just before Kolm and his associates left to found the Wiener Kunstfilm.

In terms of cinematography, *Der Müller und sein Kind* is very similar to *Szenen und Typen aus dem Wiener Volksleben* (1911, Types and Scenes from Viennese Public Life), a compilation of short documentaries produced at about the same time. Documentary and narrative fiction are thus not differentiated for the camera. The images are usually in long shot. The open frame has people walking in and off. Kolm started as photographer; the compositions not unexpectedly therefore have the appearance dictated by the aesthetics of photography. Apart from an occasional hesitant pan, there is no camera movement. In other words, the productive potential of the camera was not yet realized: space and time retained the constraints of a theater production. *Der Müller und sein Kind* is based on a popular play by Ernst Raupach; the art aspect of the film thus refers to its literary antecedent, not to its cinematographic aesthetics. The individual shots are edited not for filmic effect, but to correspond to the scenes of a theatrical production; continuity is therefore choppy. With theater as model, the acting style could not be expected to be appropriate for film. For example, there is a great deal of dialog and some flute music that appear to be important and that therefore irritate by drawing attention to the lack of sound. As Markus Nepf notes, *Der Müller und sein Kind* is by no means a significant work of art; it is important as a starting point for considering the subsequent growth of the film discourse (20). A comparison with *Der Millionenonkel* (1913), produced just two years later by the charismatic Alexander Joseph Count Kolowrat-Krakowsky's (1886–1927) Sascha-Film, strikingly illustrates the rapid development of film art.

In 1913 the trade weekly *Die Filmwoche* began publishing lists and descriptions of new films as well as reports and commentaries on the film industry. A series of editorials provides a sometimes nostalgic critique of developments in the film industry. The good old days when theater operators had some editorial control of their medley of program shorts were fading fast as competition for the audience brought new ways of doing business. The novelty of the medium had been replaced by the appeal of each film on its own terms. The practice of first-run booking of culturally respectable long films with good production values favored large theaters and well-capitalized producers. Indeed, producers and distributors started to carve up territories into potential audience pools for offering exclusive first-run rights. Such monopolistic tactics in the marketing of films with screen plays by well-known writers ("Autorenfilm") pressured theater operators into ruinous competition. Films had to be hits and hits were expensive. In a commentary on "Die Filmfabrikation in Österreich" (The Manufacture of Film in Austria) the editor notes that none of the Austrian films can be regarded as quality commodities for the market. To be sure, there is ample creative potential and a sufficient infrastructure in Austria. The Wiener Kunstfilm, however, is undercapitalized; while Sascha-Film has the resources, it lacks artistic direction (*FW* 23 [1913], 6–7). With regard to the "Autorenfilm" the editor suggests that film develop in two distinct directions: literary film as art intended for the intelligentsia, and film as didactic entertainment for the masses (*FW* 24 [1913], 9–10). Kolowrat, however, well understood that the future of popular film belonged to entertainment plain and pure, and he had the resources to realize this vision.

The flamboyant count was obsessed with the technical innovations relating to speed and perception. A racing car driver, pilot and balloonist,

Kolowrat experimented with film and in 1912 produced his first commercial success, a conventional documentary on a mining and smelting operation. Kolowrat's Sascha-Film continued to make documentaries, but soon ventured into narrative film designed to amuse and entertain. His breakthrough came with *Der Millionenonkel,* which tapped into the popular operetta market.

Count Kolowrat as racing enthusiast and charismatic producer.
Courtesy of Filmarchiv Austria.

By the late nineteenth century the operetta had attained a cultural status that put it on a par with theater and opera; in Vienna it was by far the most popular of the three. Between 1905 and 1915 as many as forty productions were put on annually (Brusatti, 81). Ranging from comedy to satire, its lighthearted music and dance rhythms were just right for an age given to hedonistic pleasures. However, with the commercialization of the genre its artistic niveau declined. Beginning with Heinrich Reinhardt's *Das süße Mädel,* the themes were given over to sweet and hypocritical distortion of reality (Deutschmann, 142). Operetta came to be disdained by the other arts, but continued to be popular. And one of its most popular stars was Alexander Girardi (1850–1918), whom Kolowrat signed up for the lead role in *Der Millionenonkel.*

An advertisement for its premiere promotes *Der Millionenonkel* as the first film operetta (Gottlein, 13). The ingenious plot involving affairs in aristocratic circles was designed as a retrospective of Girardi's numerous stage successes, allowing him to reenact a great many of his best known operetta roles. In his accomplished performance Girardi gives the best of stage technique. However, *Der Millionenonkel* is particularly significant for exploring the possibilities of cinematography. The film is no longer based on depicting set scenes; space and perspective are cut loose from theatrical antecedents. The point of view is mobile and the framing ranges from long shot to close up. On several occasions crosscutting is used to indicate concurrent actions in different places. Shots of telephone conversations, for example, alternate between the two participants. The film attempts to establish narrative continuity by showing segmented actions. But the selection of shots do not always make sense visually. In one instance a car drives off and disappears on the left of the frame; its arrival in the subsequent shot, however, is shown from a position to suggest that the motion had been to the right. Nonetheless, *Der Millionenonkel* introduces techniques that acknowledge film as an art form with its own possibilities. Fast paced, full of fun and with reminders of familiar songs in the intertexts, the film was a great success.

With his considerable inheritance, Kolowrat was not hampered in his ambitious projects by financial accountability; as Günter Krenn points out, this in no small measure was the key to his success as producer (Krenn, 46). A great many internationally celebrated directors, cinematographers and actors had their start at Sascha-Film, Michael Kertész (Michael Curtiz), Alexander Korda, and Marlene Dietrich to name just a few from a long list (Krenn, 45–46). After exploratory visits to the American film market, Kolowrat produced *Sodom und Gomorrah* (1922) and *Die Sklavenkönigin* (The Slave Queen, 1924), monumental silent films that put Austrian film on the map internationally. In addition to these two films, Kertész also directed the film adaptation of Arthur Schnitzler's *Der junge Medardus* (Young Medardus, 1923), in which the screen could provide the epic battle scenes that the stage could not. After the premiere of this film Ladislaus Vajda, the chief screenwriter at Sascha-Film, reflected on the guiding principles for his profession and offered the following advice: "Das Publikum sei dein Gott! Lebe nur, um ihm zu gefallen" (Let the audience be your god! Live only to please it, 16). The complex narrative structure of *Der junge Medardus,* however, suggests that his tongue in cheek remark is not so much a practical guideline as an ironic reference to the filmmaker's high wire act between art and commerce. From its beginnings, the imperative for commercial success and thus the need to cater to the whims of a mass audience has been a

constant ingredient in the changing parameters determining the mainstream film experience, its productions, and its venues. The transformations of venue illustrate this aspect of Austrian film history.

The principals of Der Millionenonkel *in discussion:*
Alexander Girardi, Hubert Marischka and Count Kolowrat.
Courtesy of Filmarchiv Austria.

The Multiplex Phenomenon

With today's multiplex centers, film has returned to its roots. The provi-
sional tent theater at the turn-of-century fairground provided one of
many diversions clustered in a compact location. The spectacle of film,
games of skill and chance, food, astounding displays, side shows, and
stalls for selling trinkets or produce all contributed to an exciting, somewhat unstructured ambience. All of these activities were accessible in the
same time frame; people could in different ways satisfy their needs and
desires. This all changed with the development of the urban film culture.
Resembling stage and concert performances in decorum, and sharing in
their aspiration for cultural recognition, film screenings in the 1920s
became focal activities centered at film palaces. An evening at the movies
might be combined with dining but, with stores closed, there was no
shopping or browsing. In time, sound and color, the star system, and the
magic of special effects gave film a lucrative place in the world of enter-

tainment. At least until the advent of television and video. By once again situating movies in a carnivalesque environment as a kind of urban fair, the multiplex of the current turn-of-century broadens the appeal of its entertainment with a variety of leisure time activities for its customers. Restaurants, bars, stores and boutiques, discothèques and fitness centers promise pleasures for all. Multiplex ventures, however, are instruments for maximizing return on investment and are managed accordingly.

In the mid-1990s a building boom for multiplexes began in Vienna. By 2001 there are nine multiplex centers in Vienna, most of them in shopping malls at the periphery of the city and typically with a dozen screens and more than two thousand seats. Comfortable stadium seating, digital sound, and a coordinated haven of shops and food courts pander to lifestyle preferences of the mostly young consumers. The selection of films, often premieres, favors mainstream high-concept productions with staggered starting times. Studies show that people make enthusiastic use of these extended facilities; they often spend as much time shopping and dining as they do watching a movie. Indeed, as often as not they don't bother to find out in advance what is playing (Everschor, 40). The consumers do not so much go out to see a specific film as to enjoy an evening of diversions which may include a film at the multiplex. The unaccustomed convenience of Sunday afternoon shopping at the mall further enhances the experience (Oczko).

A comparison of the statistics of 1995 and 1999 suggests that with the introduction of multiplex centers, film culture in Austria is undergoing a major change. In this time period both the number of seats and the number of admissions increased by some 25%, while gross receipts rose 37% (Schweighofer, 6). It would therefore seem that film in general is enjoying a resurgence of audience interest. The number of screens, however, provides a more telling indicator. In 1995 there were 379 screens in use, by 1999 the number had increased to 524 (Schweighofer, 6), an increase of 38%. More recent data for Vienna cites 93 screens for 1998 and 150 for 2000 (*Der Standard online*, 16 Oct. 2001), an increase of more than 60%.

The statistics provide optimistic overall numbers; however, they do not reveal how the audience has been segmented between traditional cinemas and the new multiplex centers. In a compelling way the frequent announcements of cinema closings do just that. In the issue of 23 Oct. 2001, for example, *Der Standard online* reports on the large crowds at the opening weekend of the UCI *Kinowelt Millenium City,* a multiplex with 21 screens and 3,514 seats. The manager anticipated that within three years this facility for "Rundumfreizeitvergnügen" (unlimited leisure fun) would be out of the red. The same report describes the attempts at salvaging the financially strapped *City Cinemas,* a company that had been formed to save a chain of traditional inner city cinemas from being closed (Waldbrunner). Three reasons are suggested for the difficulties: increased rent, outdated facilities, and competition from the multiplex centers.

Actually, all three reasons are related to the introduction of multiplex centers. Using shared facilities, multiplex centers can break even at as low as 15 to 30% of attendance capacity (Volger); they are thus not as vulnerable to fluctuations in operating cost. However, the rich offering of other cultural events in the city, the nearly two thousand feature films shown on TV every year, and the ready availability of videos for viewing in home theaters equipped with Dolby and surround-sound make for a very competitive market. Indeed, Viennese on average take in only two movies a year. The adventure of going to a multiplex center constitutes a distinct draw, not least because of the excellent projection technology and the selection of popular films. As in the outings to country fairs, consumers are ever in search for novelty and spectacle; to remain competitive, cinemas are thus pressured into regularly upgrading the technical standards of their facility, something that the small traditional movie house is not in a position to do. However important efficiency and projection technology may be, it is overscreening (the proliferation of movie screens in cinemas) and the monopolistic practices of film distribution that have the greatest effect on Austrian film culture.

With the profit motive as imperative and Vajda's professed devotion to the audience, multiplex operators compete for market share by programming a selection of films that are thought to have mass appeal. A glance at the list of movie hits for the weekend of 2 Nov. 2001 reveals public preference and marketing strategies. Topping the list was the American action thriller *Swordfish* starring John Travolta (Dir. Dominic Sena). The film was released with sixty copies. In Vienna it played in eight multiplexes and four other venues. The runner-up was the German comedy *Der Schuh des Manitu* (Dir. Michael Herbig), with ninety-eight copies. *Lovely Rita* (Dir. Jessica Hausner), which had just received the Vienna Film Award and in the following week would be nominated for the Fassbinder Prize of the European Film Awards, placed seventeenth. The film was released with just eight copies, four of them in Vienna. On 12 Nov. 2001 a total of sixty-four films were screened in Vienna, thirty-two of which were American productions. Typically the newer American films had multiple showings in most of the multiplexes. Apart from *Lovely Rita,* two other Austrian films were shown on this day, both with only one screening each in a small traditional cinema.

Cinemas are businesses; they attempt to provide film commodities that will sell well. Overscreening and consolidation of distributor control, however, saturates the Austrian market with imported mainstream productions. Consumers going to the movies but twice a year in turn are likely to be attracted by expensively promoted blockbusters with glamorous stars presented in the stimulating context of a multiplex rather than by a low-budget Austrian production playing in a small traditional cinema. Thus, while statistics indeed show increasing overall attendance and revenue, Austrian film culture is slipping into commercialization, to the detriment of both traditional cinemas and the Austrian film industry. In the past few years on average only fifteen feature films were made each year (Schweighofer, 6). Even if producers and filmmakers can secure funding for a film, the prospects of having their work presented locally, let alone internationally, are unpromising.

For the past three years traditional cinemas qualified for subsidies for improving their infrastructure and programming. The representative of Constantin, the major distributor and cinema operator in Austria, objected that such subsidies put the multiplex centers at a competitive disadvantage as if to punish them for their success in catering to the wishes of the public (*Der Standard online*, 16 Oct. 2001). After all, in a market economy the forces of supply and demand, and the bottom line should reign supreme. Quite apart from the oversimplification of such argument, the much-discussed success of multiplex centers may soon require a boost. In Germany, where multiplex centers were introduced earlier, at the beginning of the 1990s, their novelty appears to have worn off and attendance is once again stagnating (Riemer). The overscreening in Vienna will no doubt have multiplex operators exploring ways of increasing market share. Full digitization, though not of immediate technical advantage, may be used as a novelty for strengthening their competitive position. Various aspects of film production have been carried out with digital equipment for some time, but with recent developments in digital cinematography, standards based on the 1080/24p specifications are evolving that will resolve technical incompatibilities and especially change the way films are made and distributed. The film industry is in the midst of adopting an innovation that in its impact will be comparable to the introduction of sound and color; it will no doubt affect Austrian film in the near future and should therefore be briefly considered.

The weakest link in digital film production has been the camera. After a much-publicized comparative study of a conventional camera and the new Sony HDW-F900 digital high-definition camera, George Lucas decided to use the digital camera for most of the live-action scenes of *Star Wars — Episode II: Attack of the Clones*. Working with this camera has many advantages. Cost reductions in large productions and distribution provide strong incentives for the film industry, but the cinematographer benefits as well. Images can be seen in real-time, pictures can be altered on the set, and special effects can be more spectacular than ever. There is no degradation of image from repeated playing: every spectator gets to see the same film. The colors are excellent, the details crisp and grainless; only contrast, highlights and textures in dark areas tend to be less satisfactory than film. For Lucas the image produced by the digital tape had enough of the elusive "film look." When *Star Wars* has its well-orchestrated worldwide premiere on 16 May 2002, it will not only once again demonstrate the synergies of global release — no doubt, every multiplex will try to feature this film — but also set a benchmark for digitization.

In a commentary on digitization Rob Sabin suggests that "digital projection could open avenues for the exhibition of less commercial films, creating more choices for consumers" (cf. Sabin). However, fully digitized production is too expensive for low-budget projects. If anything, this development will widen the box office gap between small productions and the big budget Hollywood films, especially if one recalls that in Austria the pool of potential spectators is very limited in an entertainment environment already crowded with diversions. Digitization is best suited for multiplex centers, where the large initial outlay is more easily absorbed.

The long-standing quest for film as art seems lost in economic terms at least: most of the revenue from the exhibition of films goes to imported mainstream productions. Film, however, is not only popular entertainment but in its various creative modes also an expression of cultural substance. Everyday concerns, desires and fears, legacies and visions are refracted in their diversity. Filmmakers and producers understand this well. Veit Heiduschka, for example, subscribes to this approach from a producer's point of view, "we make films that reflect life in Austria today"(64). Slick mainstream productions designed for a global market blur such distinctions. Subsidies for traditional cinemas and especially for the production of films have been thus justified on cultural grounds (e.g. Schedl, 177). Indeed, as elsewhere in Europe, it would be difficult to sustain a film industry without substantial subsidies.

In 1912 Edmund Porges, the editor of the *Kritische Rundschau*, organized an international congress and exhibition on cinema. The detailed description of the event indicates that cinema had by then achieved critical mass. High officials, though not the heads of the ministries, attended the grand opening; some shorts of Emperor Franz Josef were shown. A series of speakers explained the importance of the film industry, indeed a section head of the interior ministry stated that the government was persuaded of the great economic significance of the film industry and that it regarded its aims and ambitions with sympathy (*KR* 241 [1912], 2–5). By the current turn of century nearly a hundred years later, Austrian film has matured and taken its place in world cinema.

The Austrian Film Commission (AFC) has been instrumental in developing Austrian participation in international film festivals. Indeed, given the limited commercial access to Austrian films, the festivals provide a forum at which these films can be seen by a critical audience and be placed in an international context. Much of what is known abroad about Austrian film comes from the experiences and reviews at festivals. Apart from serving as the gateway to film festivals, the AFC functions as a clearing house for information on the Austrian film industry, publishing for example the journal *Austrian Film News* and an annual catalog on film productions. There are a number of annual film festivals in Austria. The two most prominent are the *Diagonale,* which provides an overview of Austrian productions, and the *Viennale,* a respected international event. The infrastructure includes professional associations, institutional organizations and resources such as the Filmarchiv Austria. A complex network of people and facilities thus provide the support for the making of films.

The films that receive awards and publicity at prestigious festivals are absorbed into world cinema and enhance the reputation of Austrian film as a whole. For example, the films of Michael Haneke, Austria's most accomplished director, are well known in America. In recognition of his success, a retrospective devoted to his major films is planned by the American Cinematheque in Los Angeles. Haneke's *Die Klavierspielerin* was nominated as the Austrian entry for the Academy Awards 2002 and for the European Film Prize. Haneke is not alone, however; there are a good many creative Austrian filmmakers, some established and others just out with their debut work, who have gained international recognition. In this article I will give a brief overview of a sampling of their films.

Some of the films are in dialect and with recognizable context; they specifically target a part of the domestic market. Films associated with stars from the cabaret culture, for example, in this way have found a ready audience. Paul Harather's *Indien* (1993) stars Josef Hader and Alfred Dorfer in a cabaret adaptation that in its satire of Austrian country life and story of a friendship provides clever entertainment. The excellent reception of *Indien* led to a series of films cast with cabaret celebrities and adapted from stage productions. Of these, Harald Sicheritz's *Hinterholz 8* has been commercially most successful by far. In addition to Alfred Dorfer and Nina Proll, this film features Roland Düringer, a one-man entertainment phenomenon that in his draw could be compared to Girardi who had moved his operetta fans to see *Der Millionenonkel*. In the most recent variant of the cabaret constellation, Düringer and Hader again engage in a riotous combination of biting satire and urban blues; Florian Flicker, however, nudges his film *Der Überfall* towards a more general audience.

The link to the minor literary art of the cabaret scene has given renewed vitality to one sector of Austrian cinema culture; the connection to literature, traditionally strong, has primarily benefited film productions intended for television. Michael Haneke has made a number of adaptations of literary works by authors such as Joseph Roth (1894–1939), Peter Rosei (b. 1946) and Ingeborg Bachmann (1926–1973). In 1997 he created an adaptation of Kafka's *Das Schloß*.

The discourse on film adaptation is dominated by a concern for the fidelity of the film in letter and spirit to its literary source, with the printed text usually taken to be the superior work. This bias reflects the cultural position of film as popular culture, whereas the novel belongs to high culture. It seems to me, however, that the question of fidelity is not particularly illuminating. As the Russian director Andrej Tarkowskij (1933–1986) claims for *auteur* filmmakers, texts, even film scripts ultimately have to be shaped through the director's own creative conceptions (21).

A novel consists of an array of signifiers that gradually develop an atmosphere, actions, characters, and ideas. Rules of syntax and markers for tense and person regulate this reading scan. Film differs in several important ways from the verbal text. Most obviously, it is highly iconic and its sound can be heard. It thus leaves little scope for the imaginative activity of the viewer; the images have a compelling presence, but not the potential of meaning found in the vocabulary of literary texts. Perhaps of even greater consequence is the spatial perception of film, where the literary text is linear. Within each frame, the gaze of the viewer needs to be guided by the complex conventions of mise-en-scène, lighting, or movement. In this artificial reality there is little room for a nondiegetic narrator, that is, a narrator off-screen who plays no role in the film itself, and that is the third significant difference. Conventional film does not offer the instant commentary on unfolding action that is common in novels. The cinematic code of an adaptation necessarily gives a mediated rendering of its source; it unavoidably favors some details over others.

Thus, ultimately, Haneke too cannot escape interpretation in his adaptations. Although Haneke's *Das Schloß* follows Kafka's text quite closely, it constructs the castle as an allegory for the futility of a depraved and empty rationality.

The central device of the film is the tracking shot following the surveyor K. as he paces along, always in a straight line, as if to put the territory in order. He makes his way through the deep snow on the outskirts of the village; he repeatedly walks along against the background of unfriendly walls. The tracking shots convey the sense of unrelieved and endless searching: K. always has a destination in mind, but even when he meets someone, it is a motion that leads nowhere.

Kafka's strategy of ambiguity involves the subtle manipulation of narrative perspective; this certainly applies to Haneke's film as well. There are two main narrators, one of them in voice-over faithfully reads from the novel, mostly providing continuity and locating of action, sometimes expressing feelings and on a few occasions doubling the voice of a character. In each frame the camera as narrator guides the gaze of K. and of the viewer, in its setup sometimes assuming an omniscient position. What the narrator of the voice-over says, however, does not always accord with the image. The best example of this is the sequence shot at the end of the film.

Just as K. is beginning to weaken under the entreaties and temptation of Pepi to come and live with her, Gerstäcker blusters in and cajoles K. to come along. He offers the alternative of an untroubled, if not comfortable life, working for him in the stables. K. protests that he knows nothing of stable skills or horses. No matter. He did not, in the entire narrative, give the least indication that he knew anything about surveying either. The voice-over narrator embellishes this offer by reading the last paragraph of the novel to the point where it breaks off in mid-sentence. But by the sheer power of the image, this source narrator is discredited, since the camera-narrator once again in a tracking shot has K. and Gerstäcker not in a cozy cottage, as the novel indicates, but struggling through a snow storm in the dark of the night. That then in the film is the implied pessimistic open-ended continuation, K.'s fate and intimated meaning of the narrative. Kafka ends the novel in mid-sentence; with this last sequence Haneke would seem to suggest that this occurred not for want of vigor.

Facing realities. Arno Frisch in Michael Haneke's Benny's Video.
Courtesy of Wega-Film.

Haneke's most recent film, *Die Klavierspielerin,* is based on Elfriede Jelinek's (b. 1946) novel by the same title (1983). Haneke narrows the focus to the central conflict and thematically develops, among others, the theme of sexuality. As was the case in Schwarzer's time at the beginning of Austrian film, sexuality within and beyond the limits of propriety continues to attract film audiences. However, after decades of debate, the perception of sexuality now includes a political dimension that involves the specters of Freud and Jacques Lacan (1901–1981).

With her analysis of Douglas Sirk's films Laura Mulvey has argued that mainstream cinema uses the cinematographic apparatus in a way that produces a voyeuristic male gaze: the point-of-view shot, for example, is manipulated so that women on screen are fetishized and seen as erotic objects. Pornography further caters to the male spectator by having women on screen behave in a way that gratifies male scopophilia.

One short set of images in the video booth of *Die Klavierspielerin* is hardcore. The screen presents the woman protagonist with a menu illustrating various formulaic options. She inserts a coin and selects fellatio, thus alluding to the American pornographic film *Deep Throat* (1972), one of the biggest box office hits of its time. The image on the monitor displays in a mechanistic way body parts in this kind of activity.

The sound track for the video is repetitive and muted. The body is thus depicted as machine and presented as a spectacle.

Ruby Rich in her review of *Not a Love Story* (1982–83) questions whether a cinematic critique of porn can use the very same techniques of representation. The answer is all in the context. The images in *Die Klavierspielerin* are distanced and they appear only for a few moments. More important, it seems to me, is the gaze in Haneke's film. The camera has the protagonist's face in close-up for a long time; there is no expression on this face, no "come-on" look. It is not designed for a male spectator: the protagonist is in her own fantasies.

Except for the short inserts in the video booth, Haneke constructs his sexual images with long takes, in one instance with a complex sequence shot. This allows him to suggestively express desire without showing explicit sexuality. In his controversial film *Nachtfalter* (2001, Butterflies of the Night) Franz Novotny, a creatively most provocative filmmaker, takes a very different approach. The film explodes in a fireworks of creative energy, ripping along at a frenetic pace as it critiques the commercialization of sexuality. There are numerous intertextual references, allusions, and revelations. But here too, in a film that is steeped in images of nudity and decadence, the point of view is predominantly that of the woman protagonist. In the end, she decides what to do with her life.

Although a great deal more explicit sexuality can now be seen in public screenings than could in the "Herrenabende" at the turn of century, a significant reorientation has taken place: the depicted nude female body is no longer there as object to be fetishized and enjoyed with a male gaze. One other development becomes significant by such a comparison: the representation of violence, it seems, has become acceptable entertainment. Mainstream film and television programming, ever in search of entertainment products for success at the box office, exploit shocking action and violence for visual effect. In tandem with developing hi-tech action spectacles, the expectations of viewers are conditioned to prefer such media commodities.

Especially younger Austrian filmmakers are addressing the issues of cultural identity in a time of migration and globalization. The Habsburg Empire comprised numerous nationalities, religions, and languages. In the early documentaries foreigners were given no special attention; the matter of identity was contested in other ways. However, with the First World War on the horizon, the longer feature films, such as *Der Millionenonkel*, in their linear stories mostly excluded foreigners, except as stereotypes. Recent films take a very different approach. Barbara Albert's

Nordrand, for example, no longer highlights the predictable monuments and narrative rituals of the dominant culture. The attempts at inscribing national identity in streets and revered places are deflected. Her young people come from very different backgrounds; they make their way in urban settings that can be difficult, impersonal, and sometimes wonderfully exhilarating. Albert's images explore the possibilities of film art in today's complex reality.

The reports in early trade magazines reveal a striking similarity in the commercial aspects of film discussed then and now. Given the great significance of cinema for public entertainment and didactic purpose, the enterprise should receive support (*ÖK* 1 [1908], 2); people are too agitated, so that they come to the cinema for diversion (*ÖK* 5 [1908], 1); there are repeatedly references to overproduction and competition. One contributor, who refers to himself as an old expert, suggests that cinema programming take the customer into account (*KR* 2 [1907], 1). Film is a commodity (*FW* 23 [1913], 1), nothing more. Today, this commercial aspect is prominent as well and headed for more control than could have been imagined a hundred years ago. But the filmmakers of today also create exquisite works of art that reflect and shape our various constructions of reality. Austrian film has a significant part in this project. As one cineaste remarks after considering the effects of digitization, "I don't expect to abandon film any time soon" (Bailey).[2]

Perversions of discipline and desire.
Isabelle Huppert and Benoît Magimel in Michael Haneke's
Die Klavierspielerin. *Courtesy of Wega-Film.*

Notes

[1] The following abbreviations will be used: *KR* for *Kinematographische Rundschau,* *ÖK* for *Österreichischer Komet,* and *FW* for *Die Filmwoche.*

[2] Some of my research on the early history of Austrian film was done at the Filmarchiv Austria. In this work I was generously supported by Elisabeth Streit and collegially advised by Günter Krenn. My wholehearted thanks to them both.

Works Cited

Achenbach, Michael. "Die Geschichte der Firma Saturn und ihre Auswirkungen auf die österreichische Filmzensur." In *Projektionen der Sehnsucht. Saturn. Die erotischen Anfänge der österreichischen Kinematografie,* edited by Michael Achenbach, Paolo Caneppele and Ernst Kieninger. Vienna: Filmarchiv Austria, 1999. 75–102.

Bailey, John. "Film or Digital? Don't Fight. Coexist." *New York Times,* 18 Feb. 2001, sec. 2: 9+.

Bono, Francesco. "Bemerkungen zur Österreichischen Filmwirtschaft und Produktion zur Zeit des Stummfilms." In *Elektrische Schatten: Beiträge zur Österreichischen Stummfilmgeschichte,* edited by Francesco Bono, Paolo Caneppele and Günter Krenn. Vienna: Filmarchiv Austria, 1999. 47–75.

Brusatti, Otto. "*Die Fledermaus* — ihre Vorläufer und ihre Folgen oder: Vom wirklichen Traum zur erträumten Wirklichkeit." In *Traum und Wirklichkeit: Wien 1870–1930.* Catalog to the exhibition, Vienna, 28 March–6 October 1985. Vienna: Museen der Stadt Wien, 1985. 78–83.

Caneppele, Paolo. "Projektionen der Sehnsucht. Die erotischen Anfänge der Kinematografie." In *Projektionen der Sehnsucht. Saturn. Die erotischen Anfänge der österreichischen Kinematografie.* With a video compilation, edited by Michael Achenbach, Paolo Caneppele and Ernst Kieninger. Vienna: Filmarchiv Austria, 1999. 7–41.

Cook, David A. *A History of Narrative Film.* 3rd ed. New York: Norton, 1996.

Deutschmann, Wilhelm. "Die Wiener Operette zwischen dem goldenen und silbernen Zeitalter." In *Anatols Jahre: Beispiele aus der Zeit vor der Jahrhundertwende. Katalog zur Ausstellung in der Hermesvilla.* Vienna: Museen der Stadt Wien, 1982. 139–43.

Everschor, Franz. "Vom Multiplex zum Megaplex." *Film-Dienst* 13/1997: 40–41.

Fischer, Jens Malte. *Fin de Siècle: Kommentar zu einer Epoche.* Munich: Winkler 1978.

Fritz, Walter. *Kino in Österreich 1896–1930: Der Stummfilm.* Vienna: Öster-reichischer Bundesverlag, 1981.

———. Reconstruction of *Der Müller und sein Kind.* Vienna: Österreichische Gesellschaft für Filmwissenschaft, Kommunikations- und Medienforschung, 1982.

Gesek, Ludwig. *Filmzauber aus Wien: Notizblätter zu einer Geschichte des öster-reichischen Films.* Vienna: Österreichische Gesellschaft für Filmwissenschaft, 1965/66.

Gomery, Douglas. *Shared Pleasures: A History of Movie Presentation in the United States.* Madison: U of Wisconsin P, 1992.

Gottlein, Arthur. *Der österreichische Film: Ein Bilderbuch.* Vienna: Österreich-ische Gesellschaft für Filmwissenschaft, Kommunikations- und Medienfor-schung, 1976.

Heiduschka, Veit. "Producer's Challenge: Art and Commerce." Interview. In *After Postmodernism: Austrian Literature and Film in Transition,* edited by Willy Riemer. Riverside, CA: Ariadne, 2000. 62–67.

Hinterholz 8. Dir. Harald Sicheritz. Perf. Roland Düringer, Nina Proll, and Alfred Dorfer. Dor Film, 1999.

Hoffmann, Hilmar. *100 Jahre Film: Von Lumière bis Spielberg, 1894–1994.* Düsseldorf: Econ 1995.

Indien. Dir. Paul Harather. Perf. Josef Hader and Alfred Dorfer. Dor Film, 1993.

Jacobsen, Wolfgang. "Frühgeschichte des deutschen Films." In *Geschichte des deutschen Films,* edited by Wolfgang Jacobsen, Anton Kaes, and Hans Helmut Prinzler. Stuttgart: Metzler, 1993. 13–37.

Janik, Allan, and Stephen Toulmin. *Wittgenstein's Vienna.* New York: Simon and Schuster, 1973.

Johnston, William M. *The Austrian Mind: An Intellectual and Social History, 1848–1938.* Berkeley: U of California P, 1972.

Der junge Medardus. Dir. Michael Kertész. Perf. Michael Varkonyi, Agnes d'Ester, Mihael Xantho. Sascha-Film, 1923.

Kieninger, Ernst. "'Herrenabende' — Erotik im Wanderkino." In *Projektionen der Sehnsucht. Saturn. Die erotischen Anfänge der österreichischen Kinemato-grafie,* edited by Michael Achenbach, Paolo Caneppele and Ernst Kieninger. Vienna: Filmarchiv Austria, 1999. 43–73.

Die Klavierspielerin. Dir. Michael Haneke. Perf. Isabelle Huppert and Benoît Magimel. Wega-Film, 1997.

Krenn, Günter. "Der bewegte Mensch — Sascha Kolowrat." In *Elektrische Schatten: Beiträge zur Österreichischen Stummfilmgeschichte,* edited by Francesco Bono, Paolo Caneppele and Günter Krenn. Vienna: Filmarchiv Austria, 1999. 37–46.

Kuchenbuch, Thomas. *Die Welt um 1900: Unterhaltungs- und Technikkultur.* Stuttgart: Metzler, 1992.

Lovely Rita. Dir. Jessica Hausner. Perf. Barbara Osika. Coop '99 and Prisma Film.

Der Millionenonkel. Dir. Hubert Marischka. Perf. Alexander Girardi. Sascha-Film, 1913.

Der Müller und sein Kind Dir. Walter Friedmann. Österreichisch-Ungarische Kinoindustrie, 1911.

Mulvey, Laura. "Visual Pleasure and Narrative Cinema." In *Film and Theory: An Anthology,* edited by Robert Stam and Toby Miller. Oxford: Blackwell, 2000. 483–94.

Nachtfalter. Dir. Franz Novotny. Perf. Eva Lorenzo and Maria Schuster. Novotny & Novotny Film, 2001.

Nepf, Markus. "Die ersten Filmpioniere in Österreich. Die Aufbauarbeit von Anton Kolm, Louise Veltée/Kolm/Fleck und Jakob Fleck bis zu Beginn des Ersten Weltkriegs." In *Elektrische Schatten: Beiträge zur Österreichischen Stummfilmgeschichte,* edited by Francesco Bono, Paolo Caneppele and Günter Krenn. Vienna: Filmarchiv Austria, 1999. 11–36.

Nordrand. Dir. Barbara Albert. Perf. Nina Proll. Lotus-Film, 1999.

Nulldefizit. Dir. Ruth Mader. Filmakademie Wien, 2001.

Obermaier, Walter. "Aus Anatols geheimer Bibliothek." In *Anatols Jahre: Beispiele aus der Zeit vor der Jahrhundertwende. Katalog zur Ausstellung in der Hermesvilla.* Vienna: Museen der Stadt Wien, 1982. 162–69.

Oczko, Birgit. "Sonntageinkauf: Zur Premiere voll." *Der Standard online,* 17 Nov. 1997.

Pochlatko, Dieter. "Tolerance for a Complex World." Interview. In *After Postmodernism: Austrian Literature and Film in Transition,* edited by Willy Riemer. Riverside, CA: Ariadne, 2000. 68–72.

Sabin, Rob. "The Movies' Digital Future Is in Sight and It Works." *The New York Times* 26 Nov. 2000, sec. 2: 1+.

Schedl, Gerhard. "Die österreichische Filmförderung." In *Nahaufnahmen: Zur Situation des österreichischen Kinofilms,* edited by Gustav Ernst and Gerhard Schedl. Vienna: Europa-Verlag, 1992.

Das Schloß. Dir. Michael Haneke. Perf. Ulrich Mühe and Susanne Lothar. Wega-Film, 1997.

Schorske, Carl E. *Fin-de-siècle Vienna: Politics and Culture.* New York: Knopf, 1980.

Schweighofer, Martin. "Austrian Film between Festival Success and Market Constraints." Interview. In *After Postmodernism: Austrian Literature and Film in Transition,* edited by Willy Riemer. Riverside, CA: Ariadne, 2000. 55–61.

———. *Austrian Film Guide 2001.* Vienna: Austrian Film Commission, 2001.

Seemann, Helfried, and Christian Lunzer, eds. *Das süße Mädel und die erotische Photographie im Wien der Jahrhundertwende.* Vienna: Album Verlag, 1994.

Der Standard online. "Wiener Innenstadtkinos fürchten das Aus." 16 Oct. 2001.

Szenen und Typen aus dem Wiener Volksleben. Österreichisch-Ungarische Kinoindustrie, 1911.

Tarkowskij, Andrej. *Die versiegelte Zeit: Gedanken zur Kunst, zur Ästhetik und Poetik des Films.* Berlin: Ullstein, 1996.

Der Überfall. Dir. Florian Flicker. Perf. Roland Düringer, Josef Hader, Joachim Bissmeier. Allegro Film, 2000.

Vajda, Ladislaus. "Die zehn Gebote der Filmdramaturgie." *Komödie* 4/41 (1923): 16–17.

Volger, Gernot. "Die kritische Masse ist bald erreicht." *Süddeutsche Zeitung online,* 22 May 1999.

Waldbrunner, Andrea. "Gesellschafter entschulden City Cinemas, UCI-Kino eröffnet." *Der Standard online,* 23 Oct. 2001.

Riemer, Willy. "Multiplex-Crash." *epd Film* 2 (2000): 2.

"Wien bleibt Wien": Austrian-Jewish Culture at Two *Fins de Siècle*

Hillary Hope Herzog and Todd Herzog

WIEN IST ANDERS." This was the bold proclamation at the center of a recent advertising campaign to promote tourism in the city of Vienna. The motto appeared on posters and brochures juxtaposed with the familiar images of the city marketed to tourists: the golden Johann Strauss statue, the Lippizaner horses, the Hofburg, St. Stephen's Cathedral. The effect of the images is to transport the viewer back to the days of Habsburg rule, to conjure up the image of the city that is most familiar — Vienna at the turn of the last century. Clearly the slogan is at odds with the images, invoking the question: if Vienna has changed so little, from what, exactly, is it different? The very same images also accompany a second, more successful ad campaign by the city, anchored by the motto: "Wien bleibt Wien." *Wien ist anders — Wien bleibt Wien.* It seems that the tourist office wishes to have it both ways, portraying Vienna at once as a dynamic, cosmopolitan, modern city while also promising to deliver to the tourist the Vienna of a hundred years ago. In complicated ways, both slogans ring true, and as we will argue in this essay, this apparent contradiction at the heart of the city's self-understanding is indicative of the complexity that underlies Vienna as a cultural space.

It should not be surprising that Viennese cultural identity is marked by contradictions. Austrian national identity is still an unstable enterprise, its reconstruction after the world wars undermined by the substitution of powerful cultural myths for a thorough process of self-examination and evaluation. It is therefore not surprising that contemporary Austrian literature includes a strong contingent of important critical voices reflecting on the complexity and limitations of Austrian self-understanding. Some of the most interesting and profound reflections have emanated from Austrian-Jewish writers in Vienna, intellectuals who occupy a unique position that is at once at the center and on the margins of Austrian culture, and who are the subjects of this essay.

Vienna is the center of Austrian-Jewish life, home to the majority of Austria's Jewish population. It is also significant as the chief site of spatial identification, as a cultural center, as a city connecting the nation to the rest of the world, and as a reservoir of memory, linking today's Jewish community with Austrian-Jewish life of the past. When Austrian-Jewish writers discuss Vienna, their depictions call forth a complex and, again, contradictory image of the city. In a 1995 essay responding to the advertising campaign mentioned above, Doron Rabinovici (b. 1961) wrote: "'Wien bleibt Wien,' das ist die [...] gefährlichste Drohung, die eine Stadt je ausgesprochen hat."[1] In Robert Menasse's (b. 1954) novel, *Selige Zeiten, brüchige Welt* (1991, translated as *Wings of Stone*), the central character bitterly characterizes Vienna as a city "die so besonders erstarrt erschien in ihrem Sein, daß der Satz, 'Wien bleibt Wien' nur deshalb als Lüge empfinden wurde, weil er zu euphemistisch klang: das Verbum 'bleiben' war schon viel zu dynamisch."[2] And yet, both Menasse and Rabinovici, who have both spent considerable time in and have ties to other nations, choose to continue to live and work in Vienna.

For Viennese Jews, the motto "Wien bleibt Wien" is an impossibility, as prewar Vienna is sharply divided from the present by the Shoah and by a generation of Jews who left Austria for exile and, for the most part, did not return. Seen in the context of relations between Jewish and non-Jewish Austrians, the motto evokes the decades of avoidance of a real national dialogue about Austria's recent history. At the same time, with Austrian-Jewish writers having assumed a vital presence on the German-language literary scene, the phrase might also suggest the rich cultural legacy of Viennese Jews at the last *fin de siècle* as Vienna again emerges as a center of Jewish culture.

In what follows, our aim is to examine the complex relationships of significant Austrian-Jewish writers to the contemporary Austrian cultural sphere and to the cultural legacy of pre-Shoah Jewish Vienna.

The process of negotiating an Austrian-Jewish identity at the beginning of the twenty-first century is extraordinary in its complexity, requiring a thorough investigation of both terms "Austrian" and "Jewish," as well as the challenging task of reflecting on their relationship to each other. The notion of an Austrian identity is itself problematic, highly unstable after a century that required numerous re-constructions and re-definitions of the nation. For Jews and non-Jews alike, identity formation departs from an examination of the past, complicated by official Austria's poor record of dealing with its history during the Nazi period, as well as by the break in communication and interaction between Jewish communities from before and after the war. Additionally, the Jewish population of Vienna is, and has always been, remarkably and consciously heterogeneous. Just as Vienna's Jews around 1900 were sharply divided between assimilated and largely secular Jews and orthodox immigrants from the East, recent waves of immigration from Eastern and Southeastern Europe in the wake of the collapse of communism have increased the size of the Jewish community, augmenting the small and shrinking population of German-Austrian Jews in Vienna. This expansion has brought not only increased visibility and diversity, but also a degree of fragmentation. Jewish identity in Austria thus rests on a host of complex issues involving not only national, ethnic, religious, and cultural identifications, but issues related to politics, generation, gender, and language as well.

This process has always entailed a kind of balancing act for Austrian Jews. In the multi-national Habsburg empire, all imperial subjects maintained a variety of allegiances, affiliations, and identifications. After emancipation in 1867, the Jews of the empire developed what Marsha Rozenblit has characterized as a "comfortable tripartite identity," by which they defined themselves as Austrian according to political loyalty, German, Czech, or Polish by cultural identity, and Jewish by ethnic attachment.[3] These multiple identifications were open to Jews because of the dynastic structure of Austria, in which nation and state were not coterminous and eleven different nationalities were officially recognized. In the absence of an Austrian national identity, the Jews, while not an officially recognized nation, constituted a distinct group within the empire. To a greater extent than was possible in the nation states of Germany or France, Jews in Austria identified themselves in terms of ethnicity.

The experience of the First World War and the dissolution of the monarchy further strengthened this reliance on multiple identifications. Although the imperial structure supporting this position had disappeared, Jews clung to an ethnic identity in the face of the turmoil and crises of the inter-war period. The rise of virulent anti-Semitism had solidified by the turn of the century, effectively isolating the Jews politically. Anti-Semitism strengthened Jewish identification as a group, as Jews turned their attention inward to the Jewish community in response to the popularity of overtly anti-Semitic political groups and then to the increasing acceptability of anti-Semitism across the public sphere.

Postwar turmoil intensified anti-Semitic hostility in Vienna, prompting Jewish groups including Liberals, Zionists, Socialists, and the Orthodox to continue this tendency of withdrawal into the Jewish community. As Harriet Freidenreich has argued, anti-Semitism strengthened rather than precipitated this tendency, which had its roots in the legacy of Habsburg Jewish identity.[4]

Anti-Semitism permeated the Jewish experience throughout all levels of society. Jewish intellectuals at the turn of the century, even those steeped in the traditions of German culture, were not immune to anti-Semitic hostility. Rather, generations of students at the University of Vienna from Sigmund Freud (who entered the university in 1873) to Arthur Schnitzler (who entered the medical school in 1879), to Karl Kraus (who began his studies in 1892), were subject to virulent anti-Semitism that went largely unchecked because the university was outside the jurisdiction of city police.

Freud's autobiography reflects his shock and disappointment at the hostile climate he encountered as a Jew as the university. For Freud, Schnitzler, Kraus, and Theodor Herzl (1860–1904), as for many Jewish students of the era, the experience of anti-Semitism at the university unleashed a crisis of identity as prevailing attitudes foreclosed the possibility of a positive identification as an assimilated Jew. Arthur Schnitzler had grown up without close ties to traditional Judaism; his parents belonged to the assimilated professional class in Vienna. Yet the erosion of liberalism and the rise of anti-Semitism in the late nineteenth century had undermined the liberal assimilationist path chosen by Schnitzler's father, who identified chiefly with his chosen profession of medicine and for whom any concerns of confession or race were incidental. Schnitzler's memoirs reveal that in the Vienna of his youth, these latter designations were the only ones that mattered:

> Es war nicht möglich, insbesondere für einen Juden, der in der Öffent-
> lichkeit stand, davon abzusehen, daß er Jude war, da die andern es
> nicht taten, die Christen nicht und die Juden noch weniger. Man hatte
> die Wahl, für unempfindlich, zudringlich, frech oder für empfindlich,
> schüchtern, verfolgungswahnsinning zu gelten. Und auch wenn man
> seine innere und äußere Haltung so weit bewahrte, daß man weder das
> eine noch das andere zeigte, ganz unberührt zu bleiben war so unmög-
> lich, als etwa ein Mensch gleichgültig bleiben könnte, der sich zwar die
> Haut anaesthesieren ließ, aber mit wachen und offenen Augen zusehen
> muß, wie unreine Messer sie ritzen, ja schneiden, bis das Blut kommt.[5]

The vehemence of anti-Semitism in Vienna thus affected all Austrian Jews — of all classes, nationalities, and levels of assimilation — forcing them to re-define their Jewish identity. The responses to this crisis, though, varied tremendously. Some Jews held fast to the liberal tenets developed over the nineteenth century. Moriz Benedikt (1849–1920), the editor of the *Neue Freie Presse,* championed this position, for which he became the favorite target of the satirist Karl Kraus. In the pages of his journal *Die Fackel* and in numerous pamphlets from the 1890s into the 1930s, Kraus railed against the Jewish liberal press and other elements of Jewish society he identified as the scourge of modern civilization and source of the Jews' problems. While Kraus chose the solitary path of the critic, other Jews favored a collective solution to the "Jewish Question," joining the Zionists or Socialists. The response of Sigmund Freud was nearly as radical as that of Theodor Herzl, as Freud undertook a thorough redefinition of Judaism in his final treatment of Jewish identity, *Der Mann Moses und die monotheistische Religion* (1939, translated as *Moses and Monotheism*), purging the Jewish tradition of those elements that made the Jews degenerate and effeminate in the eyes of the anti-Semites. Arthur Schnitzler took a decidedly less radical approach, following the trajectory of many of his peers in what Carl Schorske has famously characterized as the bourgeois retreat into aesthetics. Yet Schnitzler did not take up writing as a form of escape, but rather thematized the issues of Jewish identity and the problem of anti-Semitism in his writing. Richard Beer-Hofmann (1866–1954) differed sharply from all of these figures in responding to the pressures brought to bear on Jewish identity with a rediscovery of and deeper commitment to his Jewish heritage.

As we find ourselves at another *fin de siècle,* a new group of Austrian-Jewish writers is once again engaged in the complex project of negotiating Austrian and Jewish identities, an exceptionally difficult task in the wake of the Shoah. This post-Shoah generation, which now largely consists not of survivors, but of the children of survivors, has inherited both the catastrophe of the Shoah and the legacy of the Austrian-Jewish writers of the last turn of the century. The responses of contemporary Austrian-Jewish writers to questions of identity, like those of the previous generation, reflect a multiplicity of strategies and experiments. In this essay, we will concentrate on three contemporary Austrian-Jewish writers who are united in their combination of fictional works with more directly politically-engaged essays, yet represent three divergent positions in their negotiations of their place in today's Austria.

Doron Rabinovici first emerged in the political arena in the wake of the 1986 election in which Kurt Waldheim was elected to the office of *Bundespräsident.* In the debates that followed the election, Rabinovici came forward as a representative of the Jewish students' organization from the University of Vienna, joining a chorus of critical voices that at last came to challenge one of the founding myths of the Second Republic — the notion of Austria as the first victim of fascism. Rabinovici's literary work is marked by his political engagement, and he has also

continued to be a presence in the public arena, contributing essays and public addresses on current political and cultural issues in Austria.

Rabinovici was born in 1961 in Tel Aviv. At the age of three, he moved to Vienna with his family, and has maintained both Israeli and Austrian citizenship throughout his lifetime. For Rabinovici, these two poles of his existence combine to compose his identity. The various components of his self-identification — as Austrian, Israeli, writer, and Jew — do not always share a harmonious relationship. On October 18, 1999, in the wake of the startling success of Jörg Haider's Freedom Party in the federal elections, Rabinovici published an essay in the newspaper *Der Standard*. In the essay, which ran with the title, "Der nationale Doppler," Rabinovici imagines himself as a cultural hybrid, split into two halves, Israeli and Austrian. These two identities, however, seem irreconcilable; each side is pitted against the other in a heated debate:

> Vor einigen Tagen drohte der in Tel Aviv geborene Doron R. dem in Wien lebenden D. Rabinovici damit, die Beziehungen zu ihm zu über-denken. Seitdem geht es auch in mir rum. Die beiden können nicht mehr voneinander lassen, streiten und urteilen hart über die Medien, aber bloß über jene des jeweils anderen Landes.[6]

Rabinovici constructs a dialogue in which his Israeli self threatens to cut off relations with his Austrian self, which in turn bristles at international pressures being brought to bear on the internal matter of national elections. The conflict deepens: "So gehe ich als nationaler Doppler, als hochprozentiges Gemisch, durch die Straßen, in denen eben noch flammengelb der Hass gegen die Fremden geschürt wurde, und fühle mich so eigen und ganz fremd."[7]

In his fantasy, the Israeli self, which he refers to as "mein innerer Orientale," gains the upper hand, exerting a sense of moral superiority over his Austrian self: "Ihr Diasporajuden feiert den israelischen Unabhängig-keitstag, lasst es Euch gut gehen, weil Ihr wisst, dass Ihr jederzeit bei uns Unterschlupf finden könntet. Was machst Du überhaupt noch in Wien, Du Überfremdling?"[8] The two halves of the term "Austrian-Jewish" seem irreconcilably split by the hyphen that is supposed to join them.

Evoking the term *Überfremdung,* which was resurrected from the Nazi era in the Freedom Party's 1999 campaign, Rabinovici signals the extent of the divide between his two selves. Employing this loaded term, the Israeli in him calls upon his Austrian counterpart to be mindful of the historical parallels between the present and Austria's repressed past; implicit is the notion that remembering this history renders life in Austria untenable for Jews. The debate continues, although the dialogue breaks down before reaching any sort of resolution as each side merely stakes out its position. Rabinovici's Austrian self argues that a global, multicultural diasporic life is a universal feature of the modern world. Yet this position is undermined as he suggests that while common issues and concerns may exist in different parts of the world, the responses are always contingent and divergent. He illustrates the extent of the cultural gap on such issues by highlighting the limits of language. What constitutes a Neo-Nazi, for example, is very different in Austria and Israel. Given the very different valences of language in these two contexts, even a discussion of problems of racism or Haider's populist politics is difficult.

Rabinovici's two selves seem to be speaking to each other across an unbridgeable divide; his identity is fractured. He writes:

> Einig sind sich meine beiden bloß, dass sie in einer schizoiden Situation leben. In einer Welt, die mit der Eindeutigkeit ethnischer Zugehörigkeit populistische Erfolge feiert, summt in mir das Stimmengewirr verschiedener Identitäten. Auch horche ich dem, was gesagt wird, in mehreren Klangwelten zu. Ich höre räumlich und lebe im Widerhall vieler Kulturen.[9]

The space that Rabinovici occupies as a Jewish writer living in Vienna is thus a conflicted one. The fragmentation of his identity is not overcome at the close of the essay. Yet ultimately, this position is depicted in positive terms. Exposed to the "Stimmengewirr verschiedener Identitäten," Rabinovici is open to multiple voices and cultures. Giving voice to both parts of his own identity, Rabinovici has found a productive position from which to work.

In 1995, Rabinovici was asked in an interview if he would leave Austria if Haider were elected chancellor. The question subsequently became an occasion for him to reflect on the current political climate and his relationship to it as a Jew. For Rabinovici, the question may be motivated by sensitivity to the problematic relationship of Jews to Austria, but is based in a fundamental misunderstanding: "Die Erkundigungen nach jüdischen Exilgedanken unterstellt, daß Juden, kraft einer abgestammten Ohnmacht, immerzu Opfer wären. Traumatisierte, eine verängstigte Schar, die seit 1945 auf gepackten Koffern säße. Schlichtweg der 'ewige Jude.'"[10] Rabinovici rejects such an identification as victim, insisting instead on his rights as a citizen of the Austrian Republic. While he resists being read strictly as a Jewish writer, he also openly proclaims his Jewish identity and suggests that it plays an important role in defining his critique. Reflecting on the interview, he notes, "So gesehen sind meine Texte vielleicht, wenn ich recht bedenke, auch eine jüdische Artikulation

gegen die Wirklichkeit dieser Republik, aber sie sind andererseits ein
Beharren auf Eigenständigkeit."[11] This assessment allows for the possibility of recognizing in his works the ways in which his Jewish identity
informs his perspective. As a writer who embraces the often dissenting
and contradictory elements of his own identity, Rabinovici's texts under-
score the instability of cultural identity and serve to illuminate and critique the harmonizing tendency of Austrian culture that seeks to exclude
difference and dissent.[12]

Robert Menasse occupies a space not unlike that of Rabinovici, living
and working in Austria but with strong ties to another place. Menasse
was born in 1954 in Vienna, to which his Jewish parents had returned
after living in exile in Great Britain. Menasse lived and taught for eight
years in Brazil, and, like his parents, returned to Vienna in 1988. Yet,
while Rabinovici's writing is clearly informed by his position as a Jew in
Austrian society, Menasse, by contrast, does not situate himself in Austrian cultural life as a Jewish writer. Explicitly Jewish themes are continually submerged in his work. Yet he does share with Rabinovici a sense of
being an outsider, of not belonging. "Österreich," he writes, "ist eine
Nation, aber keine Heimat."[13] Unlike Rabinovici, Menasse does not tie
this sense of homelessness to his Jewish identity, but rather universalizes
it. In the constellation of the Second Republic, a deeper sense of identification and belonging has not been cultivated; the concept of nationality
has dominated Austrian consciousness, but for Menasse the concept is
too abstract and lacking in content to elicit a deep sense of identification.
This sense of homelessness is for him constitutive not of the Austrian-
Jewish experience, but of the *Austrian* experience. Additionally, it is a
feeling that is intensified in the peculiar cultural space of Vienna.

In a recent essay, Menasse describes the physical space where he does
his writing. He rents a writers' studio in a building at Girardigasse 10 in
Vienna's 6th district. The building, which is a few steps from the Theater
an der Wien and the Naschmarkt and a short walk from the Staatsoper
and the Hofburg, formerly served as a bordello, the first structure in
Vienna that was constructed explicitly for that purpose. The building has
a nondescript facade, which conceals a far more striking interior. A
grand, winding staircase snakes up the walls, providing numerous vantage points from which to survey the entire scene, with landings opening
onto many tiny rooms. The building is mainly inhabited by writers, since
each of the too-small rooms, designed after all for brief encounters between two people, are unsuitable as living spaces. Menasse describes the
theatrical quality of the building, immediately apparent to visitors seeing
the space for the first time. Most visitors conclude that the building must

have formerly housed a theater, but noting the lack of space for a stage, the second line of speculation often suggests a prison. For Menasse, the bordello is, in a sense, both of these things: "Theater oder Gefängnis und verdrängte oder vergessene Geschichte. Schöner Schein, unklares Sein."[14]

In this house, built with conscious concern for outward appearances, Menasse sees a reflection of the city of Vienna. Just as the plain and respectable exterior of the building conceals the original purpose of the structure, Vienna is deeply marked by a discrepancy between its appearance and its deeper reality. "Wien," notes Menasse,

> ist nicht die Stadt, als die sie errichtet scheint. Das Imperiale gehört keinem Imperium mehr, das Barocke keinem Phäakentum, das Biedermeier keinen sanften Idyllen, die Moderne keinen Modernisierern. Sowie an den Galerien dieses Freudenhauses keine Lust wandelt.[15]

Menasse's analogy suggests a questioning of reality in a city of appearances. What does it mean for the artist to live and work in an environment that is all "schöner Schein, unklares Sein?" Menasse seems at first to imply the impossibility of a productive existence in this unreal space. "Wien ist eine Stadt der Kulissen. Man kann nicht hinter alle blicken, aber vor fast allen kann oder muß man denken: Hier ist etwas gewesen. Was ist dahinter? Nichts. Vorne ist der Schein ohne Sein, dahinter das Sein ohne Schein."[16] Here the vitality of the city is located squarely in the past — in the *gewesene*. Vienna, he suggests, is like a cell, too small and isolated, cut off from life. Yet Menasse's image does not ultimately suggest an empty or dead space. The vitality of the city is not extinguished; it is merely different from that which it projects. In the *Sein ohne Schein,* tucked away in the former bordello with the misleading exterior, is a colony of artists at work. Menasse closes the essay with a reference to his writing, which serves as a reminder that his Vienna, in all of its complexity, is in fact a productive environment: "Dann schreibe ich weiter an meinem Roman, in dieser Zelle, in der man sich weggesperrt fühlt vom Leben, wie es scheint, und sich auf diesen wenigen Quadratmetern doch in der Welt fühlen kann, wie sie ist, zumindest in dieser seltsamen Stadt, in Wien."[17]

In his penetrating essay "Das Land ohne Eigenschaften," Menasse reflects at length on the problematic concept of Austrian identity. He laments Austria's stubborn reluctance to engage in serious self-evaluation: "Kein Land der Welt hat sich selbst öffentlich so wenig problematisiert und grundsätzlich reflektiert wie die Zweite österreichische Republik."[18] In Menasse's view, Austrians long ignored the question of national identity just as they suspended the difficult work of coming to terms with recent history. This work has occurred in Austria only in response to challenges from without, as when the election of Kurt Waldheim to president in 1986 drew international criticism and finally sparked a national debate and process of self-reflection. He characterizes this process as forced and superficial and sees Austria's relationship to history as highly selective, based on a model of forgetting rather than remembering. The Austrian model of relating to the past is not, he suggests, the Freudian therapeutic model of "Erinnern, wiederholen, durcharbeiten," but rather: "Vergessen, wiederholen, dem Ausland erklären."[19]

Though Rabinovici and Menasse occupy different positions concerning the "Jewish" component of their identities and their works, they both seek to challenge this amnesiac model, stemming against the erasure of Jewish history and memory by constructing new narratives of the Jewish experience of the past and present. We now turn to fictional works by Menasse and Rabinovici, as well as Robert Schindel (b. 1944), to examine the relationship between narrative and identity in contemporary Austrian-Jewish writing. All of these writers seek to turn a position outside of the cultural mainstream into a productive position from which to write.

In Menasse's novel *Selige Zeiten, brüchige Welt* the character Judith reflects, "Das Exil der Eltern bedeutet auch Exil für die nächste Generation, und die ist im Exil, egal wo sie ist. Da oder dort, das ist doch ganz egal. Die Frage ist: kann im Exil etwas entstehen? Und die Antwort wurde doch schon längst vielfach gegeben."[20] Judith has grown up in Brazil, the site of her parents' exile from Vienna. When she goes to Vienna to study and experience the place of her parents' past, she does not feel at home but accepts this position of foreignness and unfamiliarity as the inevitable condition of her existence. The important issue for her is simply whether this position can be productive. Judith's comments could apply to the whole generation of writers who are children of survivors. For these writers, the difficult project of negotiating a Jewish identity is approached through writing and cultural memory is mediated through the telling of stories. Further, these stories are intricately bound up with the stories of their parents — which the official Austrian version of history refuses to tell.

Robert Schindel has characterized the process of writing his novel *Gebürtig* (1992, translated as *Born-Where*) in terms of working through his traumatic personal history:

Es war schon ein bißchen Kaddisch auf meine Familie, die mit Aus-
nahme von zwei Leuten umgekommen ist. Ich habe mir nicht wirklich
etwas von der Seele geschrieben, sondern würde es eher eine "Angst-
bannung" nennen. In dem Moment, in dem ich die Angst in Worte
fasse, geht sie in mir weg.[21]

The Jewish characters in Schindel's novel exhibit a variety of ways of
relating to their Jewish background, but they seem to share Schindel's
sense of a compulsion to write. The narrative structure of the text reflects
both the importance and problematic nature of writing, as the narration
shifts back and forth between Alexander Demant (who is also referred to
as Sascha Graffito) and his twin brother Danny, who together occupy the
twin roles of actor and observer. It is never firmly established whether
the main narrator of the novel, Alexander, actually exists as a character;
his is a paper, note-taking existence that does not yield a coherent narrative but merely shields him from the need to participate actively in life.
At the same time, his other half, Danny, is able to live unproblematically
by avoiding the obsessive writing that consumes Alexander. Nearly every
other important character in the novel is somehow engaged in the process of writing. Emanuel Katz, the son of survivors, takes up a number of
writing projects and "leert seine Seele indem er Manuskriptseiten füllt."[22]
The Jewish playwright Hermann Gebirtig, a survivor whose parents died
at Auschwitz, pointedly writes comedies from his New York home and
avoids the subject of the war, as well as the German language and the
German publishing industry. While many of the characters in the novel
engage in writing as identity-formation, it is striking that only the non-
Jewish Konrad Sachs seems to have an unproblematic relationship to
writing. Indeed, Sachs "comes out" as the son of the Nazi former gover-
nor general of Poland by writing his memoirs, freeing himself of the guilt
unleashed by the return of repressed memories from his childhood. His
book — while not universally well received — is the only one that has
any evidence of reaching the public in this novel.

Writing and language are in Schindel's novel the means by which
identity is established and expressed, but such projects are continually
fraught with problems. Whether one tries to write one's story as an
Austrian Jew or to write oneself out of such an identity, the task appears
to be impossible. The latter attempt is represented in the novel by the
Austrian-Jewish poet Paul Hirschfeld, who refuses to emphasize his
Jewish identity —"Ausserdem lass' ich mir nicht von Hitler vorschreiben,
wer ich bin"[23] — and fears disappearing into a "ghetto" of Jewish writers.[24] The editor Danny Demant tells him, however, that his "Verhältnis

zur Sprache hat was Jüdisches."[25] When he protests that he writes "ein tadelloses Deutsch," Demant responds that it is precisely this endless attempt to prove that he can write as an Austrian and not a Jew that sets him apart from non-Jewish writers.[26] There is thus no way out of the double-bind of a need to tell one's story and an inability to tell that story effectively.

Like Schindel's *Gebürtig,* Rabinovici's novel *Suche nach M.* (1997, translated as *The Search for M*) can be seen as something of a ghost story, in which the post-Shoah generation is haunted by the victims of the Shoah and the unresolved questions of guilt and responsibility that they pose.[27] Though Rabinovici's novel does not explicitly deal with the process of writing, it does seem to connect the trauma experienced by the main characters — Arieh Arthur Bein and Dani Morgenthau — to their parents' unwillingness and inability to tell their own stories. Arieh's father has continually changed his name and identity throughout his life, recreating himself and his life story several times, and seems to bequeath this instability of identity to his son, who has the talent of being able to profile criminals by putting himself in their place. Dani Morgenthau demands from his parents "eine richtige Geschichte"[28] yet he gets only the repeated and aborted opening line: "Es war einmal ein kleiner Junge, und der hieß Dani."[29] The attempts at a continuation of the story repeatedly confuse Dani with victims of the Shoah, leading to Dani's curse/talent of experiencing the guilt of those around him. Neither Rabinovici's novel, nor Schindel's novel, ends on a particularly hopeful note that a satisfying story can ever be told. In fact, *Gebürtig* ends with a highly-ironic scene of the Austrian-Jewish characters in the novel serving as extras on a location shot of an American film about the Holocaust set in a concentration camp. Unable to tell their own stories, they end up as characters in an American version of their story — a narrative only possible because of the spatial and temporal distance that Americans have to the Holocaust, a distance that is impossible for Austrian Jews.

This difference between Austrian and American Jews is comically portrayed in Rabinovici's short-story, "Der richtige Riecher" (1994, The Right Nose). At the opening of the story the protagonist, a young Austrian Jew named Amos, comes upon a demonstration and counter-demonstration over past and present racism in Austria. The demonstration turns violent, blows are exchanged, and one of the participants shouts to Amos: "Wenn es euch hier nicht paßt, dann geht doch nach Israel — oder nach New York."[30] "New York is more fun," an American Jewish professor at Columbia University tells Amos a couple of weeks later.[31] The professor continually repeats this statement, explaining that in New York Jews come out on top because, as he puts it, "alle rassisti-schen, spießigen Juden aus Brooklyn" are free "die Schwarze[n] zu hassen."[32] Not in spite of this fact of America's being more fun, but precisely because of it, Amos announces that he would choose Israel over New York. However, this is not the real choice presented in this story. For, as Professor Rubenstein quickly adds, Israel too has its attractions to Jews, especially American Jews who travel to Israel, "um dort mit noch besseren Gründen Araber hassen zu können."[33] Jews in both America and Israel have it good: they exist in large numbers and are able to hate another minority group. Jews in Austria, in contrast, do not have it so good, as Rabinovici details in the continual encounters with both overt and latent anti-Semitism in this story. But precisely this difficult existence, the argument runs, makes Austrian Jews stronger, tougher: the climactic act of the story comes at its conclusion, when Amos is con-fronted with the confused anti-Semitic comments of a non-Jewish friend and responds by punching him in the face and breaking his nose. This parallels the physical attack on a foreign counter-demonstrator at the opening of the story and makes Amos "zum Helden der Familie."[34]

The argument of the story is clear, as Sander Gilman has recently noted: Jews in America may indeed have more fun, but precisely because of this, they have become weak, and indeed less "Jewish." When Amos' family invites the family of the Columbia Professor to a Passover seder, the Americans are described as enjoying the ceremony without really understanding it:

> Rubensteins waren weder traditionell noch sentimental, ließen sich je-doch Chale, Kreplachsuppe, gefilten Fisch und den Rest des Menüs gut schmecken. Sie verstanden zwar keines der Gebete des alten Getreider, waren aber von den hebräischen Liedern und sonstiger Folklore hellauf begeistert.[35]

The Rubenstein family's relationship to Judaism is primarily culinary: Pesach is fun. In this fantasy about American Jews, they do have more fun, but they are "inauthentic." Austrian Jews, on the other hand, are continually confronted with racism and must negotiate on a daily basis a territory with a terrifying past. As a result, they are seen as tougher and thus more "authentic" Jews. Contemporary Austrian-Jewish writers, such as Rabinovici, Menasse, and Schindel thus continually emphasize the importance of both halves of their identities — as Austrians and as Jews, and crucially also as writers — and simultaneously demonstrate both the pressures and the productive possibilities of living in what Rabinovici has termed the "Widerhall vieler Kulturen."

Notes

[1] Doron Rabinovici, "Literatur und Republik oder Ganz Baden liest die Krone," in *"Was wird das Ausland dazu sagen?": Literatur und Republik in Österreich nach 1945* (Vienna: Picus Verlag, 1995), 128.

[2] Robert Menasse, *Selige Zeiten, brüchige Welt* (Salzburg: Residenz, 1991), 16.

[3] Marsha Rozenblit, "Jewish Ethnicity in a New Nation-State: The Crisis of Identity in the Austrian Republic," in *In Search of Jewish Community: Jewish Identities in Germany and Austria 1918–1933*, edited by Derek J. Penslar and Michael Brenner (Bloomington: Indiana UP, 1998), 136.

[4] Harriet Pass Freidenreich, *Jewish Politics in Vienna, 1918–1938* (Bloomington: Indiana UP, 1991).

[5] Arthur Schnitzler, "Autobiographische Notizen," [1912] in A. S., *Jugend in Wien* (Frankfurt am Main: S. Fischer, 1981), 322.

[6] Doron Rabinovici, "Der nationale Doppler," *Der Standard* (18 October 1999), available on the website of the organization SOS-Mitmensch (http://www.sos-mitmensch.at/schwerpunkte/kk_k_rabinovici.htm).

[7] Rabinovici, "Der nationale Doppler."

[8] Rabinovici, "Der nationale Doppler."

[9] Rabinovici, "Der nationale Doppler."

[10] Rabinovici, "Literatur und Republik," 129.

[11] Rabinovici, "Literatur und Republik," 138.

[12] For a discussion of the politics of dissent in contemporary Austria, see Matthias Konzett, *The Rhetoric of National Dissent* (Rochester, NY: Camden House, 2000). On the Austrian-Jewish context, see especially 131–50.

[13] Menasse, *Das Land ohne Eigenschaften* (Frankfurt am Main: Suhrkamp, 1992), 103.

[14] Menasse, *Dummheit ist machbar* (Vienna: Sonderzahl, 1999), 85.

[15] Menasse, *Dummheit ist machbar*, 89.

[16] Menasse, *Dummheit ist machbar*, 89.

[17] Menasse, *Dummheit ist machbar*, 89.

[18] Menasse, *Das Land ohne Eigenschaften*, 12.

[19] Menasse, *Das Land ohne Eigenschaften*, 71.

[20] Menasse, *Selige Zeiten, Brüchige Welt*, 140.

[21] "Ich war kein schlechter Ping-Pong-Spieler," available at http://www.hainholz.de/wortlaut/schindel.htm.

[22] Robert Schindel, *Gebürtig* (Frankfurt: Suhrkamp, 1994), 162.

[23] Schindel, *Gebürtig*, 264.

[24] Schindel, *Gebürtig*, 275.

[25] Schindel, *Gebürtig*, 275.

[26] Schindel, *Gebürtig,* 275.

[27] Michael Roloff refers to *Gebürtig* as a ghost story in the afterword to his English translation of the novel. See Robert Schindel, *Born-Where,* trans. Michael Roloff (Riverside, CA: Ariadne Press, 1995), 287–94.

[28] Doron Rabinovici, *Suche nach M.* (Frankfurt am Main: Suhrkamp, 1997), 27.

[29] Rabinovici, *Suche nach M.,* 27.

[30] Doron Rabinovici, "Der richtige Riecher," in D. R., *Papirnik* (Frankfurt am Main: Suhrkamp, 1994), 60–73. Here: 61.

[31] Rabinovici, "Der richtige Riecher," 62.

[32] Rabinovici, "Der richtige Riecher," 63.

[33] Rabinovici, "Der richtige Riecher," 63.

[34] Rabinovici, "Der richtige Riecher," 73.

[35] Rabinovici, "Der richtige Riecher," 62.

Works Cited

Freidenreich, Harriet Pass. *Jewish Politics in Vienna, 1918–1938.* Bloomington: Indiana UP, 1991.

Freud, Sigmund. *Der Mann Moses und die monotheistische Religion.* Frankfurt am Main: Fischer Taschenbuch Verlag, 1975.

"'Ich war kein schlechter Ping-Pong Spieler': Interview mit Robert Schindel." *Göttinger Zeitschrift für neue Literatur.* Available at: http://www.hainholz. de/wortlaut/schindel.htm.

Konzett, Matthias. *The Rhetoric of National Dissent.* Rochester, NY: Camden House, 2000.

Menasse, Robert. *Dummheit ist machbar.* Vienna: Sonderzahl, 1999.

———. *Das Land ohne Eigenschaften.* Frankfurt am Main: Suhrkamp, 1992.

———. *Selige Zeiten, brüchige Welt.* Salzburg: Residenz, 1991.

Rabinovici, Doron. "Literatur und Republik oder Ganz Baden liest die Krone." In *"Was wird das Ausland dazu sagen?": Literatur und Republik in Österreich nach 1945.* Vienna: Picus Verlag, 1995.

———. "Der nationale Doppler." *Der Standard* (18 October 1999). Available on the website of the organization SOS-Mitmensch (http://www.sos-mitmensch.at/schwerpunkte/kk_k_rabinovici.htm).

———. "Der richtige Riecher." In *Papirnik.* Frankfurt am Main: Suhrkamp, 1994.

———. *Suche nach M.* Frankfurt am Main: Suhrkamp, 1997.

Rozenblit, Marsha. "Jewish Ethnicity in a New Nation-State: The Crisis of Identity in the Austrian Republic." In *In Search of Jewish Community: Jewish Identities in Germany and Austria 1918–1933,* edited by Derek J. Penslar and Michael Brenner. Bloomington: Indiana UP, 1998.

Schindel, Robert. *Born-Where.* Trans. Michael Roloff. Riverside, CA: Ariadne Press, 1995.

———. *Gebürtig.* Frankfurt: Suhrkamp, 1994.

Schnitzler, Arthur. "Autobiographische Notizen." In *Jugend in Wien.* Frankfurt am Main: S. Fischer, 1981.

Contributors

THOMAS PAUL BONFIGLIO is Associate Professor of German at the University of Richmond. He has published on Romanticism, romantic science, and, most recently, on the dynamics of gender and sexuality in Foucault, Kant, and Winckelmann. He is also the author of *Race and the Rise of Standard American* (2002), a study of the role of race-consciousness in the standardization of the pronunciation of American English.

DOUGLAS CROW is Professor of German and Sculptor-in-Residence at Baylor University. Among his publications are a video documentary on Viennese sculpture in the twentieth century, entitled *Three Artists,* and contributions in language pedagogy. His sculptural works have appeared in numerous exhibitions, including La Fédération Internationale de la Médaille and The American Artists Professional League and are included in the collections of over 50 institutions, corporations and private individuals.

RÜDIGER GÖRNER is Professor of German at Aston University in Birmingham and Director of the Institute of Germanic Studies, University of London. Recent books include *Nietzsches Kunst. Annäherungen an einen Denkartisten* (2000), *Literarische Betrachtungen zur Musik. Essays* (2001), and *Grenzen, Schwellen, Übergänge. Zur Poetik des Transitorischen* (2001).

ERNST GRABOVSZKI is Lecturer at the Department of Comparative Literature (University of Vienna) and is an assistant editor of the *Internationales Archiv für Sozialgeschichte der deutschen Literatur.* He is the author of *Methoden und Modelle der deutschen, französischen und amerikanischen Sozialgeschichte als Herausforderung für die Vergleichende Literaturwissenschaft* (2002).

HILLARY HOPE HERZOG received her doctorate from the University of Chicago. She has taught at the University of Illinois at Chicago and DePauw University. She has written articles on Arthur Schnitzler and Irmgard Keun, and is currently at work on a book about masculinity and medical culture that centers on Austria-Hungary at the turn of the twentieth century.

TODD HERZOG is Assistant Professor of German at the University of Cincinnati. He is the author of several articles on contemporary German Jewish and Austrian Jewish culture and is co-editor of *A New Germany in a New Europe* (2001).

GEOFFREY C. HOWES is Associate Professor of German at Bowling Green State University in Ohio, and co-editor of *Modern Austrian Literature*. He has published on Peter Rosei, Ingeborg Bachmann, Peter Turrini, Thomas Bernhard, Elfriede Czurda, Lilian Faschinger, Robert Musil, Joseph Roth, Michael Scharang, and Bertolt Brecht, and translated Rosei, Faschinger, and Gerhard Kofler into English.

DAGMAR C. G. LORENZ is Professor of German at the University of Illinois-Chicago, and focuses in her research on Austrian and German Jewish literary and cultural issues and Holocaust Studies. Recent book publications include *Keepers of the Motherland: German Texts by Jewish Women Writers* (1997), and *Verfolgung bis zum Massenmord. Diskurse zum Holocaust in deutscher Sprache* (1992). Edited volumes include *Contemporary Jewish Writing in Austria* (1999), and *Insiders and Outsiders: Jewish and Gentile Culture in Germany and Austria* (1994).

JOHN PIZER is Professor of German and Comparative Literature at Louisiana State University. Among his publications are works on Austrian writers such as Franz Grillparzer, Karl Kraus, Peter Handke, Paul Celan, and Joseph Roth. He is on the editorial board of *Modern Austrian Literature*. His most recent books are: *Toward a Theory of Radical Origin: Essays on Modern German Thought* (1995) and *Ego-Alter Ego: Double and/as Other in the Age of German Poetic Realism* (1998).

WILLY RIEMER is Associate Professor of German Literature and Film Studies at the University of Delaware. He has published on Austrian literature and film, including Thomas Bernhard, Marlene Streeruwitz, Hermann Broch, Peter Stephan Jungk, Evelyn Schlag, Heimito von Doderer, and Michael Haneke. He edited *After Postmodernism: Austrian Literature and Film in Transition* (2000).

JANET STEWART is Lecturer in German at the University of Aberdeen and Co-Director of the Centre for Austrian Studies at the Universities of Aberdeen and Edinburgh. She is the author of *Fashioning Vienna: Adolf Loos's Cultural Criticism* (2000).

Index